Living
Underground

Living
Underground

A History of Cave and Cliff Dwelling

David Kempe

The Herbert Press

First published in Great Britain 1988 by
The Herbert Press Ltd, 46 Northchurch Road, London N1 4EJ

Designed by Pauline Harrison
Printed and bound in Great Britain by
Butler & Tanner Ltd, Frome and London

British Library Cataloguing in Publication Data:

Kempe, David
    Living underground.
    1.Cave-dwellers——History
    I. Title
    307.7'7   GN414.C3
    ISBN 0–906969–86–7

Half-title illustration: Garibaldi Cave, Ventimiglia, Italy.
(Italian State Tourist Office)
Frontispiece: Montezuma Castle, Arizona, USA.
(Werner Forman Archive)

Contents

For my dear wife, Crustie, who I think enjoyed most of it and certainly put up valiantly with the rest!

Acknowledgements

The following have provided assistance in a variety of ways and to them go my grateful thanks: Michael Barnet of Shiel & Morrison, Berwick-upon-Tweed; Dr A.W.R. Bevan; David M. Bills; the BBC; Alan J. Criddle; Dr C. Dortch; Dr Paul Henderson; Julia MacKenzie; Helen Mulligan; David G. Noble; Roy Paulson, librarian of the British Cave Research Association; Dorothy Ritchie and others at the Local Studies Library, Nottingham; Professor A. Ronen; I.B. Smith, the Photo Centre, Berwick-upon-Tweed; Dr Jack E. Smith; Professor Ralph S. Solecki; Dr J.W. VanStone; Professor Stephen Williams; Professor R.B. Woodbury; and many other friends and colleagues. The staffs of the British Museum (Natural History) General and Palaeontology, Anthropology & Mineralogy Libraries, London; the Institute of Archaeology Library, University of London; the Royal Anthropological Institute Library, Museum of Mankind, the British Museum, London; and the Royal Geographical Society Library, London, provided invaluable help. Without these libraries, this book could not have been written.

Finally, the National Tourist Organizations of the following countries provided photographs, acknowledged individually in the text, for which I am sincerely grateful: Australia, Egypt, France, Greece, Israel, Italy, Jordan, South Africa, Spain, Tunisia, Turkey, USA and Yugoslavia.

Introduction

Who would want to live in a cave? For the first cave men, in the Stone Age, there was little option, unless one preferred to live in the open. Once the secret of fire had made cave dwelling so much safer and easier, it must indeed have been the first choice. But what is so surprising is the number of people who continued to opt for the troglodytic life, not only throughout the Dark and Middle Ages but right up to the present: J. G. D. Clark places the peak of troglodytism at between 200 and 300 AD. In France there are an estimated 25,000 people still living in caves and rock dwellings. In Spain, Turkey and Tunisia there are considerable groups or communities living by choice in caves, apart from a few who for various reasons still have little option. The last cave dweller in Britain is thought to have vacated his stone house only in 1974. This book attempts to explore the history of cave dwelling and the other uses man has made of caves and underground chambers.

Treating the subject as a whole, remarkably little has been written about people who live underground. On the other hand, a great deal has been written about Stone-Age cave men. There are a large number of books and monographs about notable and scientifically important individual caves; they always include a section on the remains of their Palaeolithic or later occupants, as well as their artefacts and the other traces they left behind. The very many books on prehistory, either in general or on specific areas, also include sections on caves and their occupants.

Herodotus, the first anthropologist, wrote in 450 BC that the Ligurians slept in the open, and rarely in huts, but usually they inhabited caverns; he may well have been thinking of the caves that riddle the rocks of San Chamas, overlooking the Etang de Berre. And Tacitus, rather more improbably, thought that the ancient Germans lived in underground cabins heaped with dung to keep them warm in winter. Nevertheless, in 1977 J. S. Kopper wrote a paper which he called 'Troglodytism', for the 6th International Spelaeological Conference in Prague. Before going on to give an account of three contemporary groups of Stone-Age cave dwellers, mentioned later in this chapter, he included a very brief review of the subject and concluded with this statement: 'No specific treatment of troglodytism, *per se*, exists in the literature beyond that of Fewkes (1910).' That has only changed marginally. The following year, 1911, the Reverend S. Baring-Gould, author of 'Onward, Christian Soldiers' and 'Now the Day is Over', published a lengthy treatise: *Cliff castles and cave-dwellings of Europe*. Thus, J. Walter Fewkes' Presidential Address, delivered to the Anthropological Society of Washington in April 1910, and Baring-Gould's volume, together with William Boyd Dawkins' famous book *Cave Hunting* published in 1874, remain the last general reviews of people who live underground. Although Fewkes called his account 'The cave dwellings of the old and new worlds', he extended his coverage, as did Baring-Gould, to the cliff and cone dwellers; this book follows the same pattern and Fewkes' worldwide review and Baring-Gould's European volume have been sources for what follows.

People who live in natural caves are certainly cave dwellers; further they live underground. Freud may have said that they were seeking a return to their mother's womb, an escape from real life. Carleton Coon thinks a contemporary interest in caves may indicate a subconscious wish to return to the first days of man: the happy cave-dwelling hunter gatherer who will feature largely in this book. Some people would call them troglodytes, but in practice this term has generally been used only for the more recent cave dwellers: say from the time of Christ. One hardly ever hears of Neanderthal or Cro-Magnon Man – or even Neolithic or Bronze Age people – referred to as troglodytes! But living underground in this book will also include, as well as all of these, those who live in cliff dwellings and in cone dwellings. It will include the priests and other holy men who occupied rock-cut temples, some of them built out to a considerable extent from the original rock face. Tunnels are different. People do live in them but, usually, only for a very specific reason and, again usually, not for long, although there are exceptions. The reasons people live in tunnels, which are always man-made, are varied. Sometimes, it is for temporary shelter or sanctuary, including defence or fortification, although all these reasons can also apply to caves. Far more commonly, tunnels are designed and used specifically for military reasons or for mining, communication, water flowage or irrigation or for supply purposes. Here, the new journal *Subterranea Britannica* has been most helpful. The organ of the Federation of Subterranea Britannica, founded in 1974, the journal covers tunnels, mines, quarries and similar practical underground structures. However, it also spans man-made caves, souterrains and fogous, earth houses and hermitages, built for burial purposes, storage and sometimes for occupation, as well as the quite extensive range of man-made underground cavities whose function and uses is still a major subject of discussion and investigation. A modern descendent of the 'man-made underground structure' is 'earth sheltered housing', a new field of architectural design in which much attention is paid to natural caves, led perhaps by the Underground Space Center at the University of Minnesota and their publishers, Van Nostrand Reinhold, and directed towards energy conservation and nuclear shelters.

The bone caves, rock shelters, hollows, overhangs and *kopjes*, occupied by 'cave men' and associated with the evolution of true man from the first hominids and his early life, are numerous and some are well known: almost household words in a few cases. For them, of course, the availability of caves was vital. In Great Britain, some ten caves or groups of caves are known to have been occupied from the early Stone Age; the first human remains in England came from an open-air site, at Swanscombe, Kent. The best-known British caves are perhaps Goat's Hole at Paviland, in Glamorgan; Kent's Cavern at Torquay, Devon; Creswell Crags, Derbyshire; and, of course, Wookey Hole and Gough's Cave, Cheddar, in the Mendip Hills of Somerset. In Europe, although there are many caves, surprisingly few are well known. Certainly, the most famous are the Lascaux and other painted caves around Les Eyzies, in the French Dordogne, and the other Franco-Cantabrian Cro-Magnon caves in northern Spain, especially Altamira in Asturias. In the Middle East, there are the Mount Carmel rock shelters and the Belt and Shanidar Caves; in southern India, the Dravidian caves. In China, Choukoutien and in Australia Devil's Lair and Kenniff Cave are well known. Africa – the home of one of the first bone caves, Sterkfontein – also has the Cango Valley Caves, the Olduvai Gorge rock shelters and Haua Fteah, the 'extraordinary cave' in Cyrenaica, Libya. Man arrived relatively late in the Americas. When he did, the Desert cultures left their traces in many well-known caves, including Danger, Utah; Ventana, Arizona; and Bat and Sandia Caves, New Mexico.

Especially well known of the cliff dwellings are those of Mesa Verde, Colorado, and Matmata, Tunisia. Cone dwellings can only mean Cappadocia, in Anatolia, Turkey, and gypsy cave dwellings those of Guadix, in Granada, Spain. Lastly, rock-cut temples conjure up Abu Simbel, in Egypt, Elephanta Island, near Bombay, and Ellora – two of many in western and southern India – and perhaps Meteora, in Thessaly, Greece. The final mention, however, must be of recent and present-day cave dwellers. These are surely less well known: in fact usually almost entirely unnoticed. In France, especially, and even in sandstone caves in the English Midlands, they were not uncommon until very recently. Stone-Age cave dwellers still exist in Sri Lanka, Sulawesi and the Philippines, and alongside Cappadocia and Guadix, a small but not insignificant new group of cave-dwellers has grown up around the world: the hippy squatters and the bourgeois week-enders.

Caves in which people have lived provide very valuable anthropological and archaeological information about their occupants; many have 'living floors', with *in situ* hearths and abundant associated traces such as ashes, food remains and of course bones and artefacts. Often they are more interesting and informative than the so-called 'open-air' sites. Documentation on modern examples of cave living and using is therefore also extremely welcome and to be encouraged wherever possible.

The early occupied caves were all natural, but by 3000 BC the first man-made cave was excavated at Gezer in Palestine. Many more followed, especially in western Europe. Most occupied caves had vertical, 'walk-in' entrances, but some required climbing down a 'well' or ascending a cliff, using a ladder. Some were left 'open' but some – the 'closed' caves – had walls built round their entrances, others were closed by a 'door' which might consist only of a large, more or less spherical stone which was rolled into position. From the cave dwellers evolved stone builders. At first, beginning with the hide-and-pole shelters erected by Palaeolothic Man, people started to construct simple buildings within their caves, especially in southern France. There is interesting evidence of an extension of this from Russia. Possible tent-like structures of Gravettian age, known as 'tectiforms', are known from the banks of the Don and Desna Rivers in the Ukraine and the Angara River in Siberia. These 'buildings' appear to have been oval, built in depressions in the loess, with low walls made of the excavated soil to eliminate draughts, and post-holes as part of their structure. These were the semi-subterranean pit-houses, most common in areas where limestone and other rock caves were absent. There are belts of these, from northeast and southern Europe through North Africa to Siberia to central Asia and China, and also down the northwest coast of North America. There were also pockets in South America and East Africa. Hearths have been found, and also an abundance of mammoth as well as rhinoceros and other mammal bones. The strongest evidence of tectiforms is perhaps the depiction of these 'tent-like' structures on cave walls. The development of the technique of building with stone outwards in front of a cave, both as temples and as extensions of living areas, to provide extra space, soon and easily followed; it was then a simple and obvious next step to progress to the building of free-standing structures.

The word troglodyte, literally 'people who go or get into, or live in, a hole', from the Greek *troglodytes*, derived from *trogle*, hole, and *dyein*, to get into, has a chequered history. *Troglodytes* is also the genus for birds of the wren family. Troglodyte, however, has in addition been misapplied to mean an anthropoid ape and also, equally erroneously, a sect of Jewish heretics and idolaters. Ezekiel refers to seventy old men who, with their censers in their hands, secretly adored all kinds of animals and reptiles painted on the wall.

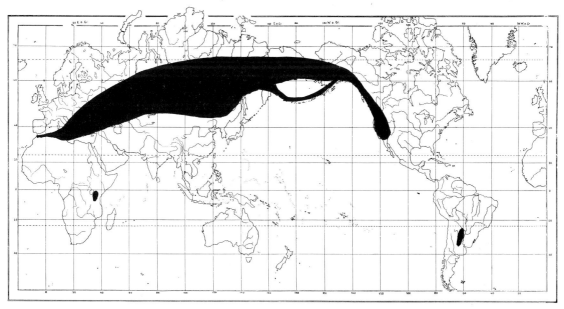

World map showing the approximate extent of the tent-like or 'tectiform' pit-houses.

But as the prophet showed, it was in secret parts of their houses, and not in subterraneous caverns, that the seventy Israelites idolatrised; thus the term troglodyte had no true application.

Even more confusing is the ancient classical interpretation, followed in the writings of Herodotus, Aristotle, Artemidorus, Diodorus and – especially – Agatharchides, writing in about 250 BC, and later of Strabo and Pliny, resulting from the chance inclusion of the letter 'l' which converts into troglodytes a group of primitive people living in Trogodytica, the Red Sea coast of 'Ethiopia' and particularly northern Sudan, from Suez to the Straits of Bab el Mandab, near Aden, and possibly down the Nile, although Cluverius and Strabo placed them in Arabia and Syria, and Aristotle had them as pygmies. They may have extended to the Caucasus, northwest Africa and possibly the east coast of the Red Sea. Known as *Trogodytae*, they were ruled from Meroë and lived in caves which were either natural caverns or mountains excavated by their own labours.

They mostly went naked, apart from shell necklaces and possibly a loin cloth, and were armed, lightly with bows and arrows and spears, heavily with raw ox-hide shields and clubs decorated with iron-plated knobs. They lived a nomadic life, subsisting off their flocks and fighting for pasturage: when the going got really rough, the old women, who were greatly respected, intervened and restored peace. They ate a sort of haggis, made of the minced flesh and bones of their cattle – only the sick and aged – which was then wrapped in the raw hides and roasted. When the torrential rains came, they drank a mixture of milk and blood, separately seethed and then mixed. (In this last respect, it might be noted, a similar practice is followed still by the Masai of East Africa.) The *Trogodytae* did not regard human beings as their ancestors, according their parentage to the cattle and sheep which provided them with food; again, a comparison with the Masai, who revere their cattle, is suggested. They decocted a drink from the thornbush and for the sheikhs made a mean kind of must from a certain flower. Pomponius Mela is quoted as saying that they lived on serpents and lizards and occupied caves in the ground. They squeaked like bats, screeched like owls or hissed. They talked gibberish; as Mela put it, they did not 'properly speak' but rather 'shrieked'. The *Trogodytae* were very swift of foot, kept women in common without marriage, practised circumcision and were governed by tyrants, one to each group. They buried their dead by binding their necks, knees and heels together, pelting them with stones until covered over and, amidst communal laughter, placing a goat's horn upon the corpse. The old and infirm, however, were killed off and the old men would often commit suicide by tying a bull's tail round their neck and being dragged to death. There were no over-sixties.

This, basically, is the splendid version of events which found its way into Rees' Encyclopaedia in 1817. In well over a page, they are treated to a lavish history. William Jones conjectured that they were the first people of Africa, in due course to become the builders of magnificent cities, founders of seminaries for the advancement of science and philosophy, and the inventors of symbolical characters. Jones concluded that these Ethiops of Meroë were the same people as the first Egyptians, and possibly, likewise, the original Hindus. The learned Bryant and the much travelled Bruce traced them back to the Cushites or Cuthites – the gypsies of Cush, from the Red Sea area of Arabia – and their migration to Abyssinia. The descendents of these so-called 'troglodytes' then migrated south again, to embark upon careers of outstanding achievement. Advancing on the homes of their ancestors, from Meroë to Thebes, they set about improving the architecture and building towns, which they began to substitute for the caves their Cushite ancestors had originally occupied. They became traders and farmers, astronomers and artificers; and meanwhile, remember, their brethren in the mountains were confined to their caves by six months of gales and continual rain; further, they were frequently persecuted by swarms of flies.

The trading – not to mention the scientific – activities of the southern, newly migratory Cushites in their new and highly successful lives required them to remain more or less permanently at home. To distribute their goods, and generally to act as messengers and carriers, a new occupational group sprang up, to be designated Berbers or Shepherds. These carriers employed the camel – the ship of the desert, unknown to the *Trogodytae* – to disperse African and Arabian goods throughout the continent.

Most of the other encyclopaedias are less generous – the current 15th edition of Britannica omits the word troglodyte altogether. However, earlier editions, down to the 11th (1911) and some other encyclopaedias, especially the Penny Cyclopaedia of 1843, give it paragraphs of varying length. This might perhaps be because it would be difficult to follow Rees.

Not altogether so, however. In recent accounts (1942 and 1967) travellers have reminded us that while the Trogodytica was ruled by Meroë, Philadelphus – Ptolemy II, in around 250 BC – coveted the elephants to be found in that distant land; his own, Egypt, had none. Elephants, incidentally, were also highly desirable to the Greek adventurers. Philadelphus sent Satyrus to discover how the *Trogodytae* captured them. In fact, they slew them by hamstringing, but Satyrus' report was lost. Nevertheless, Ptolemy sent successful expeditions to catch some elephants young and send them back in special ships to Egypt. This report continues with an account of the people of the Trogodytica. There were eight groups, including the Therothoae (the original swift-footed troglodytes of Herodotus), who ran down gazelles by endurance rather than speed, and the Ichthyophagi, who ate the much despised fish, frizzed out their hair and carried no spears, being expert archers. Their sick and maimed were 'helped out of life' and their aged committed suicide; consequently, there were no over-sixties.

The other traveller, exploring the land of the Tibu people around Tibesti, in southern Libya and northern Chad, to the west of northern Sudan, found some of them living in stone shelters, which reminded him of Herodotus' troglodytes. They have been identified with the Tibboos of Fezzan. *Tu-bu* means 'rock people' and there are many stone circles around. He tells us that Tilho recorded 'troglodyte villages' in the Emi Koussi crater area of Tibesti, while several hundred mountain Koussados were 'living miserably in caves'; the other Tibu group, the Garamantes, chased the despised troglodytes . . .

Little remains, then, by way of a definition of troglodytes beyond: people who live in caves or holes in the ground; den-dwellers, spelaean people, hermits or even anchorites, perhaps.

So the book that follows attempts to recount the history of as many as possible of the diverse types of dweller in caves and underground chambers, with a suggestion of why and some ideas as to how they lived in this way. As we have said, odd it may seem to most people, to elect to live underground, but for some there was no choice whilst for others it seemed eminently sensible. As Isaiah prophesied: 'They shall go into the holes of the rocks, and into the caves of the earth, for fear of the Lord, and for the glory of His majesty.'

CHAPTER I

On caves

M ost people, at some time in their lives, have found themselves peering into a cave. Some will have ventured in, others will have decided that it was far too like a dark and damp cellar: not for them. But a tremendous number have found themselves fascinated. How far in did it go; were there other rooms around the corner and perhaps a stream? It would probably be too much to expect stalactites and stalagmites; if it were that sort of cave, somebody would have put a fence round it and charged for admission. The majority probably decided that it was rather fun to have found a cave at all; one could sit in it, out of the rain, and perhaps have a picnic. There is a chance, too, that some sort of story or legend exists about the cave; if not, it presents too good an opportunity to miss to make one up; that makes it more exciting. The very first people to encounter caves would also have been frightened. With some justification, for in their day the cave would probably have been inhabited, not by people but by animals – hyenas, bears or wolves. These people, between one and two million years ago, would also have been curious but their curiosity would have had a more serious edge: could they find a use for this new discovery. Indeed they could and caves became the first habitation of man. True, most early cave dwellers lived in what we now think of as rock shelters; these are far more common, available as we will see throughout the world and not only in the limestone areas where most of the major true caves are found.

It is these true caves that have captured the imagination of modern man and led to the development of an interest that is partly sport and partly hobby and is allied to a scientific discipline: spelaeology or the study of caves.

Spelaeology has a vast literature of its own. The word derives from the Greek *spelaion* and the Latin *spelunca*, meaning cave, and the Greek *logos*, meaning study. Hence, spelaeologist, for the person who practices the study of caves. For the less scientific, there is the term 'caver' in great Britain, or 'pot-holer' – this is usually confined to the English caver who explores caves in Yorkshire, Derbyshire or the Mendips. The North American equivalent is 'spelunker'.

OPPOSITE: Mammoth Cave, Kentucky, USA. (United States Travel and Tourism Administration)   15

Probably few activities manage to combine science with hobby and sport to the extent that caving does. Think of a cave. Here is a large – possibly vast – cavern or system of caverns within natural rock: the possibilities are endless. Firstly, it has to be explored. This may have been done years ago but there are a surprising number of caves newly explored each year, or at least with newly discovered areas and extensions. These need to be surveyed, a very technical skill that requires the follow-up of the draftsman. The rock needs describing in detail, and this is the province of the geologist. Many caves have the spectacular formations of calcite or aragonite known as stalactites, if they grow downwards, and stalagmites if they grow upwards. Here the mineralogist comes into his own, especially if there is anything of unusual mineralogical interest in this particular cave. Next, the biologist, for here is a huge new arena, full of strange and unusual animals and primitive plants. For the chemist there is interest aplenty, for conditions here need explaining; likewise with the physicist, for particular temperatures obtain, and humidities, found nowhere above ground and leading to a new physical environment. If the cave has been lived in, of course, the floor – which is probably layered with a succession of strata of different deposits – will be minutely and meticulously examined by the anthropologist and the archaeologist. The word 'cave' covers most rock spaces in the English-speaking world; cavern really means the same thing but in practice, and especially in America, tends to be applied to the larger, multi-chambered caves. Grotto also means cave but perhaps sounds more attractive to the tourist; it is sometimes restricted to imitation caves or to those formed by the dissolution of limestone. In French, a cave is a *grotte*, and a *gouffre* is a gorge or chasm; sometimes, however, it becomes confused with cavern. A *cave*, of course, is a cellar, usually used for wine. In German a cave is *Höhle*, from the same root as *Hölle*, meaning hell. The Italians suffice with *grotta*, and the Spanish with *cueva*; this last, however, also does for megaliths, such as dolmens, which can again be confusing.

Most caves occur in limestone. This is a consequence of the composition of the rock, calcium carbonate ($CaCO_3$), which is easily dissolved in acid. In the laboratory, any of the common acids – hydrochloric, sulphuric, nitric – will dissolve calcite or (more rarely) aragonite, the minerals which form limestone; in the kitchen, vinegar, which is acetic acid, will do it – albeit rather slowly. In nature, limestone is dissolved by carbonic acid (H_2CO_3). The ensuing process is rather surprising; an underground river or stream, rich in calcium bicarbonate, is in effect dilute carbonic acid. Having dissolved away some of the limestone it becomes supersaturated in calcium carbonate and, assisted by evaporation encouraged by any breath of air current that may be present, it proceeds to precipitate some of it, in that form of calcite known as travertine, to produce stalactites and stalagmites. In scientific terms, the

OPPOSITE: Geological timetable showing the sedimentary strata in which some of the more important caves occur.

ERA	PERIOD		AGE	
		EPOCH	(MILLION YEARS)	
CENOZOIC	QUATERNARY	HOLOCENE		lava caves, Hawaii
		PLEISTOCENE		Guadix Glacial clay
	TERTIARY	PLIOCENE		
		MIOCENE		Cappadocian tuff
		OLIGOCENE		Nummulitic Limestone: Haua Fteah; Amud
		EOCENE		Doura limestone
		PALAEOCENE		
MESOZOIC	CRETACEOUS		66.4	Mesa Verde Sandstone / Chalk and *tuffeau* / Qamchuga Dolomitic Limestone: Shanidar / Franco-Cantabrian caves limestone
	JURASSIC		144	Great Oolite / Matmata, Tunisia
	TRIASSIC		208	Keuper Sandstone / Bunter Sandstone
			245	
PALAEOZOIC	PERMIAN			Magnesian Limestone: Creswell Crags / Carlsbad Cave, New Mexico
	USA PENNSYLVANIAN		286	
	MISSISSIPPIAN		320	
	DEVONIAN		360	Kent's Cavern limestone
	SILURIAN		408	
	ORDOVICIAN		438	Tassili n'Ajjer Sandstone
	CAMBRIAN		505	Durness Limestone
	PRECAMBRIAN		570	Dolomite Cave Formation, Transvaal, South Africa

NEW RED SAND- STONE

UK

COAL MEASURES
MILLSTONE GRIT

LOWER CARBONIFEROUS
LIMESTONE

UK Mendip, Derbyshire and Yorkshire caves

USA Mammoth Cave, Kentucky

water which is mainly responsible for the formation of caves is termed *phreatic*; this is the groundwater which lies below the water table in the saturated zone and produces the delicate formations in the rock. The upper water, known as *vadose* or wandering, is transient; it enlarges the caves and produces ripple-like structures such as flutes and scallops. The process is greatly assisted by temperature – and other – factors because, as with one's kettle or hot water pipes if you have hard water, calcium carbonate is best dissolved at low temperatures and precipitated or redeposited at high temperatures. This is why there is very little, if any, 'fur' in your cold water pipes, and none at all if you have soft water. The solution process which produces caves is, of course, very slow, involving thousands if not millions of years. The 'type' area, to use a biological term, is the *Karst* region of northwestern Yugoslavia, bordering the eastern Adriatic, where large areas of limestone with an extensive underground drainage system have developed a network of caves and underground channels. Limestone solution cavern systems occur all over the world, with their elaborate complexes of passages, chambers, underground streams and lakes. When a passage contains a deep stream, a low bar from the roof sometimes results in a 'sump': to continue it is necessary to dive into the stream, under the bar, and up the other side. The huge cathedral-like chambers are well known, especially those in the United States. In the Mendip Hills of southwest England a particularly spectacular chamber known as the 'Throne Room' contains a stalagmitic statue of 'Queen Victoria'.

Perhaps the best-known cave areas are those in England, southern France and northern Spain, and the United States. However, good examples are also found in Belgium, Majorca, and all through the Alps to Yugoslavia. Further examples occur in the Levant, southern China and southeast Asia, as well as Australia and New Zealand and the larger islands of the southwest Pacific. In the Americas, they extend from the Canadian Rockies to the Andes in the south.

In England, the three main natural cave areas of the Mendip Hills in Somerset, Derbyshire and Yorkshire all occur in Lower Carboniferous Limestone, formed about 325 million years ago. Similar ages apply to the Mammoth Caves, Kentucky (Mississippian, 325 million years) and the huge Carlsbad Caverns system, New Mexico (Permian, 250 million years), in the USA. Younger than all of these are the Cretaceous limestones of the Franco-Cantabrian caves and the even younger Eocene Nummulitic limestone which houses some of the major Middle Eastern caves.

The Mammoth Caves contain the longest known cave system: some 330 miles have so far been surveyed. The temperature in the Mammoth Caves remains nearly constant at about 12°C or 54°F, with a humidity of about 87%; this is typical of many cave systems and explains their popularity as a

Carlsbad Caverns, New Mexico, USA. (The J. Allan Cash Photolibrary)

refuge or even as a dwelling. Although humidity tends to be uncomfortably high, and can reach 100%, caves rarely become too hot or too cold, except that altitude results in a drop in temperature to around 5° C at 1000 feet. The record for the largest known underground cavern is held by the Lubang Nasib Bagus or Sarawak Chamber in the Gunung Mulu National Park, Sarawak. It is 2300 feet long, an average of 980 feet wide and a minimum of 230 feet high. It is even bigger than the Carlista Cavern of the northern Spanish coast. The largest chamber here measures some 20 acres, exceeding the Big Room at Carlsbad and the Pierre Saint Martin Cavern in southwest France. This last is the deepest known cave, with a depth of 4838 feet.

Speleothems – from the Greek *spelaion*, cave, and *thema*, deposit – are the secondary calcite or aragonite mineral growths found in caves, in the carbonate form known as travertine, which provide the caving fraternity with a large part of their interest. The best known, stalactites, form from the roof of a cave downwards, by dripping water, saturated in calcium carbonate, which very, very slowly precipitates new carbonate at the end of the pendant stalactite. On the ground below, the dripping water precipitates more carbonate, to form an upward-building column or stalagmite. Various measurements suggest that stalactities and stalagmites grow at rates very approximately between 0.05 and 2 mm per year. The Grotte de Grand Roc at Les Eyzies, in the Dordogne region of France, is one of the few caves to have eccentrically growing speleothems of calcite and, rarely, aragonite, sometimes named helictites. These are attributed to seeping water, impure water or wind action, but the final minerals are exceptionally pure. The mechanism is not understood, but the resultant mineral growths are very beautiful and the French are understandably proud of them. Cave pearls are spherical speleothems ranging from pinhead size up to six inches in diameter, usually formed around a nucleus. First named by Norbert Casteret, the famous French cave explorer, they are regarded as a rare prize by speleologists.

Calcite is by far the most common of the minerals occurring in caves, but there are more than eighty different mineral species to be found. After calcite come gypsum, ice, aragonite, the hydrated iron oxide goethite and the manganese mineral birnessite. The others include a number which contain phosphorus, the origin of which derives of course from the bat – and occasionally swift – populations of a large number of caves.

The study of the zoology and botany of caves is a huge and fascinating branch of biology. The total darkness which prevails means that for plants the common method of obtaining energy from the sun, which is then used with its chlorophyll to synthesise food, cannot operate; instead different groups, including algae, use organic and inorganic material in the cave to provide nutrients. Troglobitic animals – from *trogle*, hole, and *bios*, life – which live in caves, mainly flatworms, snails and slugs, crustacea, millipedes and centipedes, insects and spiders, and fish and amphibia, also have to adapt to a unique environment without sunlight; many of them are colourless and some lack sight. In addition, the visiting population of insects, bats, birds and some mammals are legion. The birds include swallows and the swiftlets of the larger southeast Asian islands, amongst whose numbers are the species providing 'birds' nest soup'. The bats are even more important for their guano is often quarried as a valuable fertiliser.

In these days of conservation, when many groups are campaigning on behalf of bats, their supporters are nevertheless likely to find themselves opposed by a number of lobbies. In Poland a tunnel said to house 20,000 hibernating bats of eleven species is required for the disposal of nuclear waste. In Holland a lengthy tunnel-cave in limestone beloved of bats is threatened whilst in Malta protests from school children have saved a cave much frequented by bats. The destruction, for obvious reasons, of fruit bats in Israel has also killed insectivorous species – a distinctly unwelcome side effect – and in Thailand the habit of eating fruit bats as a delicacy by the local population and its spreading to restaurant menus has led to a search for more bats on a scale that has resulted in the pillaging of caves used by the local human population as a source of income – the sale of the bat guano. Caves also occur in dolomite – the magnesium-rich form of carbonate rock – and marble – the form limestone adopts after being strongly altered by metamorphism caused by heat and/or pressure, as in the Alps. Both, being carbonates, will dissolve in acid but not so quickly as limestone and, since they are less common rock types, the chances of their forming caves is further reduced. Perhaps the most famous dolomite cave system is the South African Precambrian Dolomite Cave Formation in the Transvaal, which includes the Taung and Sterkfontein Caves. The development of these caves, through the widening of joints known as *avens*, or sometimes as pot-holes, to produce openings from the original caverns to the surface has been extensively studied.

Sandstone caves are also found; these are usually restricted to the type of sandstone that has its quartz grains bound together by a calcite matrix, a kind of sandy limestone. They respond to acidic water in the same way, though to a lesser extent, as does limestone; sandstones with a siliciceous matrix, on the other hand, cannot be dissolved by acid water. In some cases, the sandstone simply becomes friable, regardless of its matrix, and erosion to form caves occurs in this way. In fact, many of the English caves, especially those that were man-made or man-enlarged within historic times, such as those of Nottingham and other areas of the Midlands, are found in Triassic sandstones. Some of the other best examples of sandstone caves are the Mesa Verde cliff dwelling complexes of Colorado, and of Matmata in southern Tunisia, and many of the rock-cut temples. Gypsum and salt are rare as rock types, but they do occur and occasional caves are formed, especially in Bulgaria and the USSR; more commonly, caves or tunnels are dug in these materials, as shall be seen. Caves that can be easily extended into dwellings are very localized in their distribution. When they do occur, however, in tuff – consolidated volcanic ash and dust – as in Cappadocia, Turkey; loess, in China; and glacial clay, in Granada, Spain, they are very extensively exploited.

Earlier on, rock shelters were mentioned. These are not true caves but merely formations of rock formed by normal erosion and leading to overhangs, hollows or miniature caves that can be used effectively as shelters. These, of course, can be formed in any type of rock. Some of the most common examples occur in granite in Africa where uncounted rock shelters – known as *kopjes* – can be found; many of them were used as shelters by early man. Obviously, a climate where warmth is less of a problem than in the northern hemisphere greatly encouraged such use. The islands of Hawaii, Iceland, and Lanzarote in the Canaries have some spectacular lava caves but these do not encourage occupation, although some in Hawaii have been lived in, and do not feature here. Nor do igloos, which could perhaps be regarded as ice caves.

Without this variety of cave materials, the study of their landscapes would be greatly impoverished. Contrast the majestic gorges and canyons of the limestone caves in France, Spain, the USA and England with the *kopjes* of the southern African veldt. Or the moonscape loess cavelands of China and the clay patches of Spain with the gentle sea caves in sandstone fissures to be found in Scotland. Whether the Neanderthal and Cro-Magnon people who were the first cave inhabitants gave much thought to the quality of their environment must be in doubt. But one wonders about some of the Bronze-Age folk, the early Christians, the monks and the gypsies, all of whom came along later. The Palaeo-Indians who founded the Pueblo cliff-dwelling tradition may not have noticed anything striking about their choice of abode, but the Cappadocian Turks, in their tuff cones, must surely have had a strong sense of humour!

Finally, what use are caves now, after having provided homes for cave men and troglodytes for more than a million years, since *Australopithecus* right up to the present, and keeping spelaeologists and – equally important – spelunkers happy and out of trouble? There are, it seems, an incredible range of answers; for these I am indebted mainly to G. W. Moore and G. N. Sullivan and Franklin Folsom.

Tourism apart, the French use caves, predictably and as already stated, for storing wine; they use man-made *grottes* for the same purpose, as at Les Baux, in the Chaîne des Alpilles in Provence. They have also extended the tourist side of things here to include a newly created *Cathedral d'Images*, a

Cathedral d'Images, Les Baux-de-Provence, Chaîne des Alpilles, France.

cave complex carved out of the soft limestone to represent many of the ancient Egyptian wonders such as the Pyramids, the Sphinx and some of the early temples. In Hungary, the cave system of Buda Castle, Budapest, is partially used as a waxworks museum. The famous Postojna Cave of Yugoslavia, with graffiti dating back to 1213 on its walls, large enough for the 'Concert Hall' chamber to seat ten thousand people, also has a small castle built within it. In World War I Russian prisoners of war built a bridge across a deep chasm inside, which is still used by tourists. In the more recent World War II, it contained a German ammunition dump which was blown up by Partisans.

Caves across the world have been used for many more mundane things. Guano quarrying (or mining) comes easily to mind, as at Frio Cave, Texas, and Bat Cave, Nevada. But caves can also be used to grow things such as mushrooms and rhubarb, and for ageing cheese or beer; they are natural refrigerators, can provide cool, fresh – albeit damp – air for air-conditioning, and must be the world's best nuclear shelters. The Americans mined nitre (or saltpetre), used for the manufacture of explosives, from the Mammoth Cave, Nevada, and also from Texas, as well as celestine. Spanish gold and other treasure was hidden in American caves, which were also used as counterfeiters' studios and as a retreat for guerrilla fighters in the Civil War. The US Southern Railway ran the Natural Tunnel through the mountains in southwest Virginia.

But this chapter must end on the story, recounted by Folsom, of how

Postojna Cave, Yugoslavia. (Yugoslav National Tourist Office)

Interior of Postojna Cave, Yugoslavia. (Yugoslav National Tourist Office)

in World War II the Americans planned the 'big bat-bomb campaign', proposed by a doctor-inventor, to finish off Japan. Texan bat caves were to be stripped of their Mexican Free-tailed Bat inhabitants, each weighing some third of an ounce, by fitting wire enclosures, equipped with doors, across their cave entrances. The bats would then be kept in cool damp surroundings, resembling their hibernation environment, to induce the dormant state. Each would be individually fitted with a one ounce, timed fire-bomb; then, loaded 1000 to 5000 at a time into bat-bombs, they would be dropped by parachute at 1000 feet over Japan. The bats would be released automatically and would be able to fly, carrying a load equal to three times their own body weight, for 10 to 20 miles. Searching for a roosting site, they would find no caves and select instead the eaves of houses – wood and paper, mark you – until in due course the houses would all go up in flames, all over Japan. The plan would undoubtedly have worked; as it was – for better or worse – the preoccupation with, and eventual dropping of, the A-bombs put a stop to it.

24

CHAPTER 2

The first cave dwellers

Man is thought to have originated near Lake Turkana, in northern Kenya. Here he may have dropped from the trees and, for the first time, staggered upright – on two legs. He wasn't to maintain this posture for long, however – that followed perhaps a million years later – but, instead, he roamed the ground on all fours, rather as the great apes do today.

West of the lake, the remains have been found of *Australopithecus boisei*, a very early fossil man, dated at 2.5 million years, and first found at its type locality, the Olduvai Gorge, further south in the rift valley of northern Tanzania; in both regions, the slow and painstaking working out of man's early history owes a very great deal to the Leakey family. These earliest of men of the Upper Pliocene have left only the flimsiest of traces; a few skull fragments, the occasional bone, are all that remain. Probably partly because of the climate, the earliest men, emerging in Africa, had relatively little need of shelter. Nonetheless, they almost certainly made use, right from the start, of any primitive rock shelters, little more than overhanging cliffs, that happened to be available. They probably treated such shelters as temporary camps, as they migrated with the seasons, from winter to summer, in search of food: the herds of game animals which also migrated with the seasons. The geology of Africa lent itself to these shelters and the granite overhangs were certainly exploited in southern Africa. Throughout the uppermost Pliocene and Lower Pleistocene, *Australopithecus* slowly developed humanoid characteristics in east and southern Africa, and also in Indonesia. *Australopithecus robustus,* or Robust Man, was the larger of two species of the genus and possibly a vegetarian; *Australopithecus africanus* was smaller, more slender, and probably because he was partly carnivorous, was the first tool maker. Apart from a few rock shelters, most of the sites in which hominid and early humanoid remains have been found have been open-air sites or layers in recent volcano-sedimentary deposits, such as Olduvai Gorge. The tools or industries left behind by early man have always been used first to identify the type of people living at the cave or site. Radio-isotope ages can then be

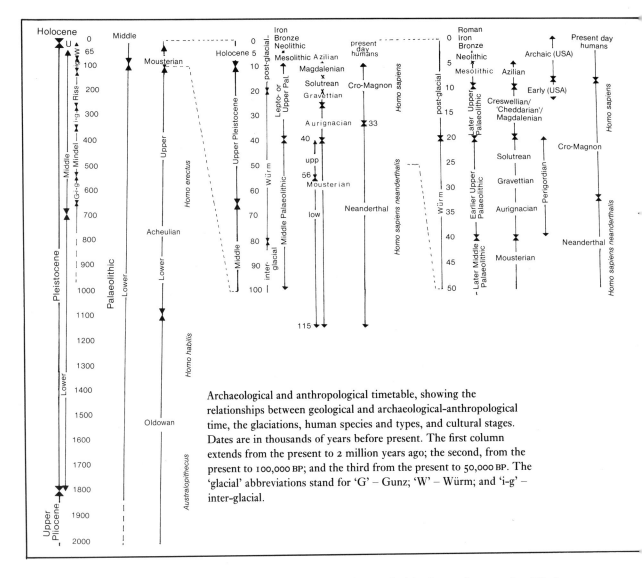

Archaeological and anthropological timetable, showing the relationships between geological and archaeological-anthropological time, the glaciations, human species and types, and cultural stages. Dates are in thousands of years before present. The first column extends from the present to 2 million years ago; the second, from the present to 100,000 BP; and the third from the present to 50,000 BP. The 'glacial' abbreviations stand for 'G' – Gunz; 'W' – Würm; and 'i-g' – inter-glacial.

employed to date the associated deposits and this dates the people. Their industry type, or culture, is thus also dated and can be used at future sites to date people who use similar tools, before isotope ages are available. The two types of date are then used reiteratively, to refine each other. Remember that this was the Pleistocene period, the Middle and Upper Pleistocene being the time of the Ice Age. During the four glacial periods, separated by the warm inter-glacials, even Africa was affected by the cold and man no doubt reacted to the need for shelter then as now.

The earliest South African men were one-million-year-old *Australopithecus africanus* who lived in caves in the Precambrian Dolomite Cave Formation in the Krugersdorp area of western Transvaal: Taung, Sterkfontein, the Makapan Valley, Swartkrans and Kromdraai. The first two are the oldest. The human remains, with their simple bone and pebble tools, occur in the debris which fell through *avens*. These are joints in the rock which become widened by surface water and permit openings to develop between the original caves, formed in the usual way, and the surface. As time went on, more people lived in these widening funnels or cave entrances and more debris and remains developed. All these, with the calcareous travertine being precipitated from the water, forms a breccia. If the entrance floor collapses an even larger cave space is made accessible. Taung, across the border in Botswana, had a different origin: it formed in the travertine in a cliff or scarp of the Precambrian dolomite which was subject to seasonal springs and rapids, which eroded it rapidly. It was then quarried extensively before being recognized as a fossil cave, called at first Hrdlička's Cave after the anthropologist. The remains of *Australopithecus robustus* have also been found in the Transvaal, in shelter caves near the Makapan limeworks. Although often thought to have been vegetarian, many animal bones are associated with his remains here, including shattered leg bones possibly cracked open to obtain their marrow.

By the Middle Pleistocene, or the upper Lower Palaeolithic, *Australopithecus* had given way to *Homo habilis* or 'able man', with his Oldowyan culture, and *Homo erectus*, with the Acheulian culture. Human remains had become far more common by now and *Homo erectus* left his in China, where they were found just west of Peking, at Choukoutien. Others were found in Java, in Heidelberg in Germany, in Budapest in Hungary and possibly in the Petralona Cave in Greece, as well as Africa. Man now really did walk erect; this was the last stage before *Homo sapiens*. Choukoutien, now spelt Zhoukoudian, is a famous group of deep caves in a cliff on north Longgushan or Dragon Bone Hill, near Peking or Beijing, which incidentally has also provided new evidence on climatic changes. The earliest traces of man were of Middle Pleistocene age, around 500,000 BP or before the present, found at Locality 13; they were patinated chert chipping tools found in red clays (*terra rossa*) in a shallow fissure. The original cave, opening to the northeast, seems to have suffered a series of collapses during Middle Pleistocene times, after each of which man appears to have reoccupied it. When excavated it was 575 feet deep by 165 feet across, with many tens of feet of earth, clay, sand and stone deposits, formed in two main stages of filling. It is probable that the game animals brought in were elephant, rhinoceros, camel, buffalo, horse, boar, sheep and musk-ox; probably some predators – lion, tiger, leopard, cave bear and hyena – were also killed by man, and did not die in the cave naturally.

However, it was in the great cave, Locality 1, that Peking Man, *Sinanthropus*, now known as *Homo erectus*, was found, with his pebble and flake

Map of Africa showing the approximate locations of caves and places mentioned in the text.

tools. Although not the oldest – Yunnan Province had yielded remains 1,700,000 years BP and Xi'an some that were 700,000 years old – he is certainly one of the most famous. As we shall see, he possessed fire.

Probably of similar age were men from Guanyindong Cave, Qianxi, Guizhou Province; Yun Xian Man, from Longgudong Cave; and Yunxi Man from White Dragon or Bailongdong Cave, the last two both from Hubei Province. Early Palaeolithic Man also came from Shilongtou Cave, Daye County, in the same province. A later group of Middle Pleistocene people came from Locality 15 at Zhoukoudian, only 230 feet away from Locality 1, with similarly aged remains from other provinces, some resembling Java's Solo Man. The deposits are in a fissure and have yielded many stone artefacts and animal bones, but no human remains. The stones used included quartz, sandstone, chert, flint, slate, limestone and volcanic rock.

Locality 4 had a later type and, finally, the Upper Cave at Zhoukoudian, exposed by erosion, contained the Late Pleistocene remains of the most developed of China's early men. The elderly male and two adult females all seem to have met death by violence. They were all of *Homo sapiens*, Neanderthal type but said to possess 'differing racial characteristics'. The Upper Cave contained modern animal species but also the extinct cave bear. Blades, some of them steeply retouched, such as choppers, burins, scrapers and knives were found there. Among the antler and bone artefacts were eyed longbine needles, implying clothing made of skin, and many personal ornaments including beads made from stone, shell, perforated red deer and badger teeth, tubular bird bones and, interestingly, fish vertebrae. All these find a parallel in the Upper Pleistocene of Eurasia. The stone beads, with hour-glass perforation, were painted red. Also, there was evidence of the deliberate burial of the dead in the cave with the use of ochre in the burial rites; it is thought that the cave men imported oolitic hematite for ochre from 95 miles to the north, marine shells from 125 miles to the southeast and freshwater pearl mussel shells from 220 miles to the south. Caves from several other provinces contained similar remains but those left by the occupiers of caves from Szechwan to Kwangsi and Taiwan showed that in the southern provinces people continued in the Upper Pleistocene to make tools from pebbles in Middle Pleistocene style.

The discovery of fire

Although *Australopithecus* may have had fire, Peking Man – *Homo erectus* – and his immediate predecessors at Locality 13 at Zhoukoudian definitely had fire. Its arrival was a truly momentous moment in man's story. Not only did it keep wild animals, like the great cave bear, at bay, provide warmth and – more importantly – a little light in a dark cave, it introduced cooking, almost certainly by accident. The process made meat and other food more palatable and easier and quicker to eat, by rendering it more tender and improving the taste. Also, man prefers to eat warm food, apart from the fact of its being cooked. It made it more nutritious, by killing the dangerous parasites and increasing the food value, releasing the valuable sugars and amino acids. Cooking made it possible to suck the marrow from a broken bone, instead of having to crush or split it. There are examples of this in the Neanderthal Mousterian Sirgenstein Cave in Württemberg, with its many broken marrow bones, and the Krapina Rock Shelter used by Neanderthal bone marrow-eating cannibals. So the use of caves – invaluable for cooking and eating – may well have increased as a result; the cave floors were littered with the charred bones of sheep, large horse, pig, buffalo and – especially – deer. Kenneth Oakley does not think that man really took to living in caves until he possessed fire; he then discovered that the protection of having 'your back to the wall' and a wind break for the fire were reassuring and helpful, reducing the chances of your food being stolen or at least having to be eaten raw.

Fire also burned off the inedible hairy skin from game. It probably helped in the 'preparation' of clothes, perhaps in lieu of 'tanning'. It widened the choice of material for tools and weapons: heating tempered and hardened wood and bone so that they could be used more successfully. And soon, of course, it was found that it also helped in hardening flint and other types of stone: the forerunner of burnt flint in the knapping process of tool making. In the Palaeolithic period fire was occasionally used as an alternative to the saw and axe for cutting down trees, while from the Neolithic onwards it was useful for clearing woodland.

Fire first appeared by chance as a result of volcanic activity, lightning, the focusing of the sun's rays or spontaneous combustion. The latter could have resulted from oil or gas seepages or the ignition of coal or oil-shale in a damp environment by the rapid oxidation of pyrite nodules. Another form of spontaneous combustion that could have yielded fire is produced by the bacterial decay of refuse or dung or fodder heaps. At first fire was probably lost and found again and again; at all costs it had to be kept alight until the Neanderthal and Cro-Magnon people who were definitely able to make fire deliberately. It probably began during tool-making by the percussion produced by striking siliceous stone on sulphurous stone, such as pyrites, producing sparks. Or by sustained friction between pieces of wood being rubbed together, perhaps when sharpening one stick with another. This last process led to the method of igniting tinder consisting of dried grass and leaves by rubbing two sticks together. The method remains good even today and is still used by Boy Scouts; not until the Iron Age was the flint and iron method discovered. However, percussion is thought to be an older method than friction. Flint struck on flint or quartz on quartz, by the way, only produces the non-incendiary *triboluminescence*.

Zhoukoudian had fire from 500,000 BP but there are traces in Africa dating back to 1,500,000 and from Yuanmou in China from 1,250,000. In Europe France had fire at L'Escale 700,000 years ago, and from 400 or 300,000 BP it was known at Terra Amata and Pêche de l'Azé; also at Dolni Vestonice in Czechoslovakia and Vertesszöllös in Hungary. It appeared in Spain and in Suffolk in England at 200,000 and in west Asia at 50,000 years

Sterkfontein, South Africa. (South African Embassy)

BP. Interestingly, the first certain African occurrence was at the Cave of Hearths in the Makapan Valley, also 50,000 years ago.

The oldest known fire-making device was an iron pyrites nodule with a deep groove from much striking found in the Magdalenian layer in the Trou de Chaleux bone cave in Belgium; pyrite nodules were also possibly used in the Cave of the Hyena at Arcy-sur-Cure in northeast France. In the case of friction, Lucretius thought that the accidental rubbing together of two tree branches in a gale of wind might have produced fire. However, this is unlikely, and even more so is it that man would have appreciated its potential as a method of fire-making if it had. The Mesolithic red deer hunters at Star Carr,

 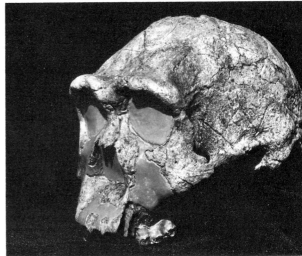

LEFT: Model of *Homo erectus* in Africa. (National Museums of Kenya). RIGHT: Skull '3733' of *Homo erectus*, dated 1.5–0.5 million years ago, East Africa. (National Museums of Kenya)

east Yorkshire, collected the flammable loose bracket fungus, *Amadou*, for use as tinder. The fire-twirl and fire-plough that appeared in the very late Palaeolithic were followed in the Neolithic by the bow-operated fire-drill; the oldest known certain fire-drill was Ancient Egyptian, some 5000 years old.

After the arrival of *Homo sapiens*, in the Upper Pleistocene or Middle Palaeolithic, there was a small explosion of cave dwelling to mark the arrival of that highly sophisticated sub-species, *Homo sapiens neanderthalis*. Neanderthal Man is thought to occupy a special position, somewhat tangential to the main line of evolution, between *Homo erectus* and modern man, *Homo sapiens sapiens*.

There are several varieties of Neanderthal physique. The so-called 'classic' type, based on the European group first found in a cave in the type area, the Neander Valley near Düsseldorf in Germany, was short and stocky, with a large head, overhanging brow and receding chin. The 'generalised' type had less pronounced features. It was the heavy, ape-like features that led to Neanderthal Man being regarded as markedly sub-human. This was a gross misjustice, as the study of the best-known culture associated with the group, the Mousterian, will show. The way of life of these earliest of men, whether they lived in caves, rock shelters or in open-air sites or encampments, varied geographically. Western and southern Europe were probably ideal for Neanderthal Man, providing him with superb ready-made cave and rock-shelter homes. Further, these areas had better conditions for preservation than the northern countries such as Germany, Poland and Russia, still in the throes of the last, Würm, glaciation. In Africa the climate even in the glacial intervals was warm, hence the almost casual use of rock shelters. The vegetarian gatherers would have had relatively few problems; their carnivorous cousins meanwhile were developing primitive tools, made out of siliceous rock chips, to assist them in their search for small mammals, lizards and snakes, and crabs and other crustaceans. Their middens, or piles of refuse, leave evidence to testify to this. The early cave dwellers were hunters, gatherers and foragers. The hunters, the men, were more necessary than the gatherers, the women, so female babies were killed by infanticide, resulting in a predominance of men over women in the communities. In winter, at least, they lived in caves with their entrances facing south, away from the Arctic. They had hide-and-branch 'doors' over the entrance, and a single fire. There must have been an appalling smell of unwashed bodies, excrement and decaying food but a pine-branch fire would usually prevail. They kept meat in a 'refrigerator' storage pit, covered with a stone slab to keep off plundering animals, and cooked it by throwing it on to hot stones and eating it half raw. They probably worked round their domain seasonally returning to winter in their caves as do the present-day Kurds at Shanidar (see pp. 166–70).

However, it is the little village of Le Moustier, in the Dordogne, that gave its name to the first major advanced human culture, because of the remains found in the rock shelters there. The Mousterian period lasted roughly throughout the Middle Palaeolithic, from about 115,000 to 40,000 BP and Mousterian Man may be traced through his culture from western Europe and North Africa to Uzbekistan and central Asia, in a rough ellipse encircling the Mediterranean, Black, Caspian and Aral Seas. He was present at Zhoukoudian in China, and Rhodesian Man and Javanese Solo Man are similar, although they did not have the true Mousterian culture; in the east this is found only at Shanidar in Iraq. Neanderthal Man had three principal cultural communities: Europe, the Levant centred on Mount Carmel, and the Zagros Mountain region, spanning Iraq and Iran. The first two were closer to each other than the last two. They all shared a limited stone technology, with no bone industry or art, and they all showed the first signs of concern for their dead, from western France to Uzbekistan. An excellent example of this occurs in Israel, where in the Tabun rock shelter at Mount Carmel a Neanderthal cemetery of ten graves was found. Altogether, the remains of some 155 Neanderthal people have been recovered from sixty-eight sites, most of them in Europe. Forty-five have been found in western Asia or the Middle East, including the ten from Mount Carmel. In the following chapter Neanderthal Man and his near neighbours in time will be examined in this geographical setting.

CHAPTER 3

Neanderthal Man

Although he probably originated in East Africa, man in due course migrated northwards into Europe. The oldest cave site in Europe is the Acheulian Le Vallonet, just on the French side of the Italian border, occupied 700,000 or more years ago. In southwest France, Le Lazaret Cave, with its low rubble walls, dates back to 500,000 BP. One suggestion divided Palaeolithic caves into four age groups: the ages of the cave bear; the mammoth and the woolly rhinoceros; the reindeer; and the bison.

Rather later, Neanderthal Man took his name from the discovery in 1857 of a skull cap in a cave in the Neander Valley by some workmen looking for limestone. The cave is small, set in a gorge near Düsseldorf, in Germany. A Neanderthal skull had in fact been discovered in 1848 in Gibraltar, in Saint Michael's Cave. The skull was of a female and there is now a waxworks display depicting her and her family.

Gibraltar has a magnificent system of caves which it owes to the arrangement of whitish limestone and duller shale of which it is built. The limestone faces north and east, the shale south and west. First 'vertical', then 'horizontal' caves were formed by folding and erosion, including sea wave action, to give tunnels, halls, passages, rooms, cells and amphitheatres, all inside the rock. The floors of the caves are covered with a strange dark brown powder like snuff, composed of travertine, vegetable mould and bat guano. With the rise and fall of the ice ages, like Mindel and Riss, lasting some 40,000 years or more, and the longer interglacials of, say, 200,000 years, the water level rose and fell and the temperature did likewise. Gibraltar varied from very cold to equatorial. All this led to beaches, cliffs and sea caves, at different levels during the different glacials and interglacials.

The history of occupation of *The Rock* has been chronicled in the book of that name by John Masters, giving historical and fictional accounts in tandem for each period. He describes how Gorham's, the large cave, and the Devil's Tower Rock Shelter, were first occupied by Neanderthal Man, who hunted deer, ibex, rabbits and water birds, and gathered fruit, nuts and shellfish. They drank both animal and human blood. The people lived in the

Map of England showing the approximate locations of caves and places mentioned in the text.

Holy Island
Inner Farne
St Cuthbert's Cave
Cuddy's Cove
Warkworth
Kielder
Rob Roy's Cave
Kirkhead
Kirkdale
Scarborough
Stump Cross
Victoria
Old Mother Shipton's
St Gile's
Pontefract
Dale Abbey
Dove Holes
Poole's Cavern
East Retford
Creswell
Crags
Mansfield
Flynnon Bueno
Pontnewydd
Thor's
Cotton's
Dream
Reynard's 'Robin Hood's Stable'
NOTTINGHAM
Hawkstone
Sneinton
Repton
Pendrill's
Ironbridge
Tong
Beckbury
Higford
Bridgnorth
Kinver
Southstone Rock
Blackstone
Redstone
Grimes
Graves
Royston
Buntingford
Evesham
Ware
Ogof-yr-Esgyrn
King
Arthur's
Clearwell
West
Wycombe
LONDON
Greenwich
Blackheath
Chislehurst
Greenhithe
Chatham
Margate
Ramsgate
Eastry
Goldney
West Kennet
Paviland
Bacon's
Hole
Aveline's Hole
Monkton
Basingstoke
Cheddar
MENDIPS
Farleigh
Guildford
Westerham
'The Garth'
Dover
Castle
Wookey Hole
Godstone
Brighton
St Clements
Hastings
Bo-Peep
Lydford
Exeter
Beer,
Seaton
Dunterton
Hennock
Durlston
Sheep's
Tor
Kent's
Cavern
Roche
Tornewton
Windmill
Kitley
Seaton
(Cornwall)
arn
uny
Halligye

35

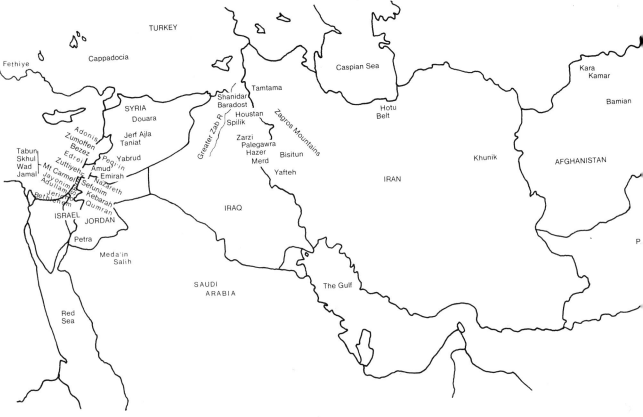

Map of the Middle East showing the approximate locations of caves and places mentioned in the text.

caves and also buried their dead in them, but by conducting ceremonies and leaving artefacts, they recognised that death needed special recognition.

The earliest remains in Europe were found in Le Vallonet Cave, in a limestone cliff near Roquebrune-Cap-Martin, Alpes-Maritimes, where a chamber 16 feet in diameter is reached by a 16-foot entrance passage. Other early remains are scattered across France, showing how widely dispersed was this early form of man and his animal contemporaries. In the Jura the Baume Cave has yielded the bones of cave bear, sabre-toothed tiger, horse, ox, wild boar, elephant, rhinoceros and spotted hyena. On the banks of the River Vézère in the Dordogne region are the two rock shelters at Le Moustier, about six miles from Les Eyzies, which gave their name to the main Middle Palaeolithic stage, the Mousterian (115,000–40,000 BP). The upper shelter is 43 feet above the lower and more important one. Both were full of Middle and early Upper Palaeolithic deposits, with a Mousterian sequence in the lower shelter. The Dordogne area is particularly rich in evidence of early man, both Neanderthal and Cro–Magnon, who came on the scene in about 33,000 BP. There are several shelters at La Micoque and La Ferrassie, and Combe Grenal Cave, all near Les Eyzies, with Mousterian sequences in two

36

ghao

INDIA

at La Ferrassie. Early remains, including some of Mousterian and Aurignacian age, have been found as far west as Charente, in the Fontechevade Cave on the River Tardoire. The oldest occupied caves in Spain include Torralba and Ambrona, with Acheulian Lower Palaeolithic remains.

Largely because of the Würm Glacial with its Full Last Gacial and Late Last Glacial episodes, Britain had a relatively small Neanderthal population when compared with southern Europe, Africa and western Asia. If La Cotte de St Brelade in Jersey is disregarded, since it then formed part of France, the earliest British caves to be occupied appear to have been Pontnewydd, Creswell Crags, the Mendips and Kent's Cavern, Torquay. Pontnewydd, probably the oldest, is in a Carboniferous Limestone scarp above the River Elwy, near Cefn Clwyd, North Wales, and was found in 1874. It may have been occupied before 225,000 BP or even earlier, certainly by 125,000 BP. It was a hunter's camp, full of debris, horizontal inside and with a very small entrance. A human molar, Mousterian artefacts and the remains of a curious collection of animals including hyena, hippopotamus, rhinoceros, bear, reindeer and badger were discovered. Igneous and pyroclastic pebbles used for the manufacture of tools were found and were of local derivation, but the flint had had to be imported from seven miles away. During World War II the cave was fitted with a brick guard chamber and wall and used as a store for land mines and depth charges.

Kent's Cavern (or Hole), in a low cliff of Devonian Limestone on Lincoln Hill, near Torquay, in Devon, and Pin Hole, Robin Hood's Cave, Church Hole and Mother Grundy's Parlour, all at Creswell Crags caves in Derbyshire, date at least to the Middle and earlier Upper Palaeolithic Mousterian stage. Kent's Cavern was occupied from about 100,000 BP but most of the radiocarbon dates are of 28,000 BP with another cluster at 18,000 BP when the Last Glacial reached its maximum severity. Most of the tools in the Cavern came from the Black Band in the Vestibule and date from about 13,000 BP. At Pin Hole 15,000 pieces of bone were recovered including thousands belonging to birds and fish and it is thought that this cave was occupied from about 70,000 BP. The Creswell Crags caves, set in the sides of two Magnesian Limestone cliffs facing each other across the river gorge, produced engraved bone fragments, Britain's earliest examples of Palaeolithic art. After the Full Last Glacial there was a great increase in activity in the Mendips in Somerset, with two major base camps at Gough's Cave and Aveline's Hole, with the Hyena Den and more than ten smaller surrounding camps. Britain's only two *bâtons de commandement* or chief's rods of authority, were among the more than 7000 artefacts yielded up by Gough's Cave and there were good finds of bone here and at Aveline's Hole. Eleven hundred bones including those of the mammoth, reindeer, woolly rhinoceros and lion, and the cave, brown and

The Cavern End, Kent's Cavern, Devon, England. (By courtesy of Kent's Cavern)

grizzly bears, indicating long occupation, were found in Windmill Cave, Brixham, Devon, together with thirty-six very primitive flint implements.

The evidence suggests that the caves were mostly visited by people from further south during Interglacials and during the summers. They would have been hunting parties, following the seasonal migration of deer and other animals. The country was almost treeless at this time but after the Last Glacial, with some fluctuations, trees and shrubs mushroomed and began to spread rapidly. It has been difficult to establish much of our prehistory for certain for it is a story of possible occupations, reoccupations, migrations and conflicting dates. The ebb and flow of the glacial and interglacial episodes had much to do with it, as hunting parties came and went, camping for long periods and then disappearing again.

One of the more unusual insights into this period is provided by the bear cult revealed in the high-level limestone caves of Switzerland, Bavaria, Les Furtins in eastern France and Croatia in Yugoslavia. There is obviously some significance in the way in which bear skulls and bones have been arranged but its exact nature can only be a matter of conjecture. A chamber in the Drachenloch in Switzerland had a stone cist that had been built to house stacked bear skulls, while long bones had been piled on slabs along the walls of the cave. Another heap contained the skull of a bear through which a leg bone had been forced, the skull resting upon two more long bones, each from a different bear. In a cave in the Bavarian Petershöhle, ten bear skulls had been laid out on a platform. Again, we can only speculate on the meaning of this. A similar ritual may have taken place in the cave at San Felice de Circeo, Monte Circeo, Italy, where a human skull, with a mandible from another individual, was found at the centre of a circle of stones while many animal bones were heaped around the cave. The skull had holes cut in it, perhaps to allow the brain to be extracted.

On the border of Italy and France, at Grimaldi, near Menton which was then in Italy and Ventimiglia, is La Grotte du Prince – Italy's most famous cave and one of several excavated by Prince Albert I of Monaco. The deposits here go back to the Lower Palaeolithic Acheulian, more than 100,000 BP, but the caves are best known for their much decorated ochre-smeared Cro-Magnon burials and early steatite Venus figurines.

Cavillon Cave nearby yielded human bones, charcoal, flint flakes and decorative perforated sea shells, together with the teeth and bones of hyena, lion, woolly rhinoceros, mammoth and other animals. Elsewhere in Italy there is evidence of Mousterian occupation of caves, as in the well-known Grotta Romanelli at Castro in Puglia where deposits of *terra rossa* are overlain by a *terra bruna* containing remains from the Mousterian period to about 12,000 BP. Other early inhabited caves were in the Dolomites, in the Friuli region and in the Veneto, near Venice, where there are ten or so Mousterian caves and rock shelters. In Hungary the Mousterian type site is Szeleta Cave.

Moving further east it is clear that there were roving groups of late Mousterian people in Greece in about 40,000 BP, occupying the Asprochaliko Rock Shelter in the Louros Valley in Epirus. Further proof of the widespread existence of man in Mousterian times is provided by artefacts found in a cave at Vychvatincy in the Dniestr basin in the USSR, where the bones of mammoth, woolly rhinoceros, bison, horse, deer, reindeer, bear and wolf were also found. Further south in the Crimea important Mousterian artefacts were found in the Starosel'e Rock Shelter in a ravine of a tributary of the Churuk-su River and in the upper level of a shelter at nearby Kiik-Koba.

Outside Europe there is a whole series of caves proving the presence of Neanderthal or near-Neanderthal people, mostly of the Middle Palaeolithic Mousterian period, running across North Africa from Tangier through the Middle East to Afghanistan. They usually had different names assigned to their stages and cultures but to avoid confusion their European equivalents are sometimes used in order to relate them to the European framework. An added complication is that the Upper Palaeolithic may have arrived earlier in western Asia than in Europe.

Flake tools, human bones and bones from forty-two animal species have been found in the High Cave at Tangier, Morocco. The animals include elephant, lion, wild buffalo, hippopotamus, giraffe, hartebeest, gnu and rhinoceros. It is interesting that the mammoth and bear remains found in European caves were absent here, proving how much warmer the area was, avoiding the severity of the ice age, and yet man still occupied caves. The disposition of the tools and game animal remains found here suggests that people ate all but the head and four quarters – that is, the trunk and entrails – outside the cave, after which they carried the quarters and the heads inside, where they cracked open the skulls to get at the brains and smashed the long bones for their marrow. It seems that this was a common habit amongst Mousterian people.

Further east is Haua Fteah – the 'extraordinary cave' – on the Cyrenaican coast of northeast Libya, the largest prehistoric cave of its kind known to us. It was discovered in 1951 by a group of Cambridge archaeologists and lies at the foot of an escarpment of Tertiary Nummulitic Limestone. It has a semicircular roofed area with a diameter of about 260 feet. The vaulted roof rises 65 feet above a level floor composed of fine-grained deposits which are 45 feet thick, derived from falls from the roof and side and also from material which had been washed in. The cave was occupied by man perhaps from 70,000 BP and at least from 47,000 to 43,500 years ago. The bones of sheep, goat, gazelle, gnu, horse and rhinoceros can be tied in with five warm and five cold geological stages and seven cultural phases, for which there is also evidence from the flake-blades and large angle-burins used for cutting limestone tablets.

Flake flint tools also occur at Tabun at Mount Carmel, where the remains of ten humans, of two different types of Neanderthal or near-Neanderthal Man, were found at Et-Tabun and Mugharet es-Skhul. Tabun Man was very close to the 'classic' Mousterian Neanderthal while Skhul produced a possibly transitional, progressive stage between Neanderthal and early *Homo sapiens* such as Cro-Magnon. The other important caves in the Wadi-el-Mughara at Mount Carmel, near Haifa, are Mugharet el-Wad and Mugharet ej-Jamal, with Sefunim and Kebarah nearby. In the same region, at Zuttiyeh Cave near Lake Tiberias (Sea of Galilee), the first more or less Neanderthal Man to be found in Asia was discovered. The four important Yabrud (or Jabrud) shelters in Syria are also near here. In the same area is the Amud Cave in Eocene limestone on the northern shore of the lake, first found in 1960, where Upper Palaeolithic end-scrapers and angle-burins were discovered together with Middle Palaeolithic retouched points and scrapers. Mammal remains include those of the horse, deer and fox. Very early remains were also discovered in the Mugharet el Bezez Cave and the Abri Zumoffen, both near Adlun on the coast between Sidon and Tyre.

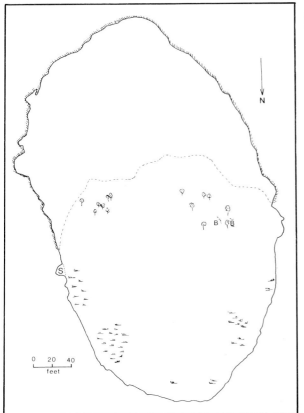

LEFT: Plan of Haua Fteah Cave, Libya. The dashed line represents the 'dripline', which is also the present extent of the roof of the cave, which faces, and was entered from, the north. Trees and shrub areas are shown. Recent burials are indicated by 'B' and shelters by 'S'. (After C.B.M. McBurney) RIGHT: Excavations at Tabun, Mount Carmel, Israel. (A. Ronen)

Further evidence for the presence of early man in this area came from the discoveries by Japanese anthropologists at Mugharet ed Douara I, in the Palmyra Basin 125 miles northeast of Damascus. This cave is in the Eocene limestone of the Jebel ed Douara and contains Middle Palaeolithic Levallois flint flakes, blades, points, side-scrapers and denticulates, as well as blanks, and there is also a big hearth. Taniat al-Baidha – the White Pass – and Jerf Ajla – the Heifer's Outwash – which are also in the Palmyra area both yielded Middle Palaeolithic flint tools.

One of the most important sources of information about Neanderthal Man came from the series of digs conducted by Ralph S. Solecki between 1951 and 1960 on the Big Cave at Shanidar, above the village of Mergasur

41

Shanidar Cave, Iraq. (Ralph S. Solecki)

on the east side of Baradost Mountain, above the Greater Zab River, in Kurdistan in northern Iraq. Solecki not only deciphered the cave's prehistory from about 100,000 to 12,000 BP, from Mousterian to Baradostian to Zarzian, but he also chronicled the present-day Kurds who winter there. The cave is in Cretaceous Qamchuga dolomitic limestone, reached by a steep valley path, and faces south. It has an earthen floor, a mouth 26 feet high and a width of 82 feet. In 1953 the first skeleton was unearthed, a Middle Palaeolithic Neanderthal infant at a depth of nearly 26 feet in the lowest layer. This layer 'D' was Mousterian in character and spanned the whole early period from 100,000 to around 45,000 BP. The skeleton was named the Shanidar child and was the first Palaeolithic skeleton from Iraq. By the 1956–7 season the richness and value of this cave were becoming apparent with the unearthing of three male Neanderthal skeletons. One had been pitifully crippled before being crushed by a rock fall and had also been plagued by arthritis, apparently a common ailment amongst Neanderthals. The man, known as Shanidar I, had been about forty, equivalent to an age now of about eighty, and had been born with only a stump of a right arm, as well as probably being blind in the left eye. The signs of wear on his teeth suggested that he used them for grasping, in lieu of a second hand, and he may have been a sort of early 'kitchen hand', since his body was found near two of the hearths. He may in fact have undergone a 'mercy killing'. Shanidar II was also horribly crushed by the rock fall, as was Shanidar III; like I, he was also incapacitated, this time by a stab wound in the ribs which seemed to have been in the process of healing. Solecki believes that the survivors of the cave's inhabitants returned to find the dead after the rock fall. They placed mounds of loose stones over Shanidar I and II, who possibly had a fire lit over his as a form of burial, and left mammal bones there, perhaps the remains of the funeral feast. From this evidence, Solecki thinks that Shanidar I may have been regarded with at least some esteem by people who, in the past, had been thought to be thoroughly brutish.

Helped by the disposition of rodent burrows, which sometimes point to the position of a skeleton, the final season in 1960 produced five more skeletons, IV, V, VI and VII and an infant who was number VIII. The major significance of these finds was the recognition of a 'family' grave group in which baby VIII had been interred first, followed by the two females whose bones are confused and might have been involved in secondary interment. The male was buried last and was the central focus of the ceremony. These were the first 'Flower People'. Palaeobotanical study of the pollen found in the grave showed that the male member of the group had been buried with a cluster of at least eight species of mainly small, brightly coloured, wild flowers, including grape hyacinth, bachelor's button, hollyhock and a yellow-flowered groundsel. The flowers may have been woven into the branches of a pine-like shrub. The pollen distribution analysis showed that they could not have got there by accident or by any agency of bird or animal; they were not dispersed individually or randomly but bunched, in groups, and must have been collected from further afield than just the vicinity of the cave. Someone must have ranged the hills looking for them, with a definite purpose, probably in or near the month of June. Some of the plants have a herbal, medicinal value; whether the Neanderthals knew this is beyond our current knowledge but it is reasonably safe to say that they probably sampled them all at some time or other. Reflecting on all this, Solecki notes the total lack of flowers in cave art, despite the frequent depiction of food animals, which doesn't help, but he also notes the 'growing wealth of information on the economic uses of plants in prehistory'.

The rock fall ended the occupation of Shanidar by Neanderthal people and shows how dangerous earthquake-generated rock falls could be then, as now: Solecki's group experienced earth tremors. But in Mousterian times, re-occupation seems to have taken place soon after each rock fall.

The Zagros Mountain people, in which area Shanidar falls, had fewer game animals than those on the Levant coast; they included goats, sheep, wild cattle, pigs and land tortoises. Other bones found in their caves are the rarer bear, deer, foxes, martens and gerbils. They probably hunted communally, perhaps driving herds of animals off cliffs or into *cul de sac* gorges set with traps. Mousterian tools varied considerably, and may have been related to the different game animals, which required different types of butchering. The Zagros people did not hunt large game animals and so did not need large cutting and hacking instruments. Types of tool were also related to the climate. They certainly cared for their sick and so lived to some extent a communal life, although there may have been the individual stalker-hunter as well. Various anthropologists have given their ideas of a hunting scene: perhaps twenty-five men working an area of anything from 1000 to 14,000 square miles. For living, a prehistoric cave man is supposed to have needed about 108 square feet. The present Shanidar floor space is some 13,800 square feet, allowing for a hundred and twenty-eight persons, but the present 'complement', as we shall see, is only a little over forty. However, Solecki thinks that there were far fewer occupants in the Palaeolithic, less than the present forty, in fact, despite the available space. Although the Shanidar area has several other habitable caves, including the 'valley of caves', the main factor controlling the limit was probably the potential of the hunting area.

Other important Mousterian caves in the Iraqi–Iranian border area are the Cave of Houstan, at Barzan, recently used as an animal pen; Spilik; Tamtama; Zarzi; and the Dark Cave, one of six at Hazer Merd. In Iraq the Great Cave of the Baradost, in Cretaceous dolomitic limestone, gave its name to the stage which followed the Mousterian in western Asia as the Aurignacian did in Europe. Just inside Iran are Yafteh and, near Kermanshah, Bisitun Cave where the remains of a Neanderthal man and his flake tools were found. This lies above the famous cliff of Behistun – the ancient form – where Sir Henry Rawlinson, dangling on a rope, deciphered the trilingual cuneiform inscription of 500 BC in which the Assyrian Emperor Darius I the Great commemorated his military successes. On the south coast of the Caspian Sea is Belt Cave – Ghar-i-Kamarband – in white Jurassic limestone. Here was found a Neanderthaloid girl of about twelve; she had been buried after her flesh had either been stripped off or decayed away, her bones then being painted red with ochre. The body was buried with the head, upside down, cradled between her thighs. Nearby is the associated Hotu Cave.

Further east is Khunik Cave and in Afghanistan, near Mazar-i-Sharif, is Kara Kamar – Black Belly – of 34,000 BP or more. The most famous Afghan caves, however, are at Bamian, where the 'twelve thousand galleries' and their associated cliffs run for eight miles.

There were Soan Valley people of Acheulian age who lived in caves and rock shelters in India and Pakistan, perhaps near Kurnool in Andhra Pradesh.

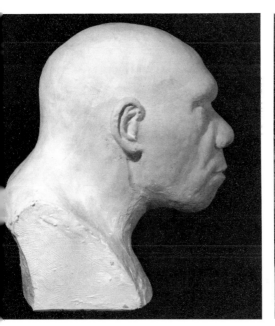

ABOVE LEFT:
Reconstruction of the
head of Neanderthal
Man. (By courtesy of
the British Museum
(Natural History))

ABOVE RIGHT:
Reconstruction of
*Pithecanthropus
pekinensis* at
Zhoukoudian
c. 350,000 years ago.
Compare these figures
with Neanderthal
Man. (Drawing by
Maurice Wilson. By
courtesy of the British
Museum (Natural
History))

LEFT: Reconstruction of
near-Neanderthal Man
found at Mugharet es-
Skhul, Mount Carmel,
Israel. (Maurice
Wilson)

45

Cliffs at Bamian, Afghanistan. (Edgar Knobloch)

In northern Pakistan Sanghao Cave, 22 miles northeast of Mardan, discovered in 1963, was occupied from 45,000 to 20,000 BP. The many other sites in the subcontinent include Attirampakkam or Gudiyam Cave, just southwest of Madras, and the Dravidian caves of the south. In the east, the most famous is the Great Cave of Niah in Sarawak, occupied by 40,000 BP or earlier. This vast cave is 800 feet wide at its mouth and 200 feet high in places, enclosing some 26 acres.

46

As well as moving north and east, man migrated south from East Africa where he originated. Mousterian people of Neanderthal type lived in Bambata and other caves in the Matopo Hills, Matabeleland, Zimbabwe, the type area for the Still Bay culture; some of these caves are painted. Still Bay tools are also found in the Port Epic Cave, just south of Dire Dawa, in the Danakil Rift of Ethiopia. In South Africa there is evidence of caves and rock shelters being occupied from about 120,000 BP in the Cave of Hearths and other caves at Makapan, and at Sterkfontein, 20 miles northwest of Johannesburg, as well as at the mouth of the Klasies River, about 60 miles west of Port Elizabeth in Cape Province. More than a quarter of a million stone artefacts have been found here and it is clear that it was a stable and successful community, living mainly off the sea and consuming a great deal of shellfish. These people fashioned stone balls, found singly or in threes. It is possible that they were *bolas*, employed then as now on the end of a length of string or cord to bring down moving animals or birds by wrapping them around their legs or wings. They are still used in Patagonia and by the Arctic Eskimo, whilst in Tanzania they form part of the bolas-and-hoop game.

Mousterian Man was also present in this part of the world, living some 80,000 years ago in caves and rock shelters like Boomplaas in the Cango Valley, southern Cape Province, some of which were decorated with paintings and engravings. Hunter gatherers used them as hunting camps, stockpens and stores for oil-rich fruit.

Neanderthal Man was at first thought – by a Frenchman – to have been brutish or near-bestial in appearance, with his overhanging brow and ape-like face, massive jaw, thick neck, stooping shoulders and shuffling gait. He certainly had massive limbs, bulging, prominent eyebrows and a heavy, coarse-featured face but this is no longer held against him so much, as a French woman has pointed out! A new concept involving a gradational sequence of Neanderthal Man has evolved, the later folk being the people who showed us the first stirrings of social and religious sense and feeling; they buried their dead under flowers, as do the modern flower-loving Kurds, and were certainly not an ancestor to worry about.

Altogether, the remains of some 155 Neanderthal people may have been recovered from sixty-eight sites, most of them from Europe. Western Asia or the Middle East follows, with forty-five; of these, Skhul, at Mount Carmel, produced ten and Shanidar nine. Solecki presents a very interesting theory on the ages of early man. In the 31 to 60-year age group, which represented old age in those days, there were 35.8% of all Neanderthals found; 26.7% of all Upper Palaeolithic Eurasians; and 12.7% of all Mesolithic people. Clearly, advancing technology did not help with longevity.

CHAPTER 4

Cro-Magnon Man
and after

The Neanderthals were followed in France by the Aurignacians, named after the cave near Aurignac in the French Pyrenees where their remains were first recognized, and in western Asia by the Baradostians, named after the Great Cave of the Baradost in Iraq. These were the first of the Lepto- or Upper Palaeolithic people, dating from 40,000 BP, possessed of new stone tools and a wood-working technology lacked by their predecessors. They seem to have been very good at this, adept at making the wooden traps which they constructed with their wood-cutting tools. This in turn helped them to adapt to a new lowland forest environment, well stocked with game, after they probably had to leave the mountain forests to escape the cold. The Aurignacians had mobiliary or 'home' art, often consisting of sexually exaggerated female figures such as that found at Sireuil, in the Dordogne. This was engraved on calcite but limestone, ivory and bone were also used. The Aurignacians were the first people to have musical instruments: deer phalange whistles, with a hole on one surface, and hollow bone pipes or flutes. The former was merely a decoy whistle, possibly also used for signalling during hunting. The pipes, on the other hand, had a number of holes which just might have produced a very simple form of 'music', involving variation in pitch but no tonal system. The music may have been enjoyed for its own sake or the flutes may have been used for some sort of ceremonial purpose, or both. The Aurignacians practised burials, including group burials. Their artefacts have been found in Provence in southern France, Gibraltar, western Italy and Britain, as at Ffynnon Bueno, Vale of Clwyd, in North Wales, with dates of about 34,000 to 29,000 BP.

The first true *Homo sapiens sapiens*, the first modern man, was Cro-Magnon Man. He appeared in about 33,000 BP, overlapping with the Neanderthal Mousterians and the Aurignacians, the latter's culture spanning both human types. He would have fought with the Neanderthals, over shelter, game and other sources of food, until the latter became extinct in about 32,500 BP. Cro-Magnon Man was a hunter gatherer who lived in various parts of the world in the drier climate which followed the Würm Glacial and he survived until the beginning of the Mesolithic, in about 9 or 10,000 BP. He was named after a corruption of Magnou, a hermit who lived in a limestone rock shelter in the Gorge d'Enfer near Les Eyzies, in the Vézère valley in the Dordogne: the capital of prehistoric France. The discovery of the remains of five Cro-Magnon people was made in 1868 by workmen cutting through the cliffs behind the shelter whilst constructing a new railway line. Their skulls had the high-domed cranium and small jaw characteristic of modern humans. Hearths, charcoal, flints and an elephant tusk were also found in the shelter.

The change between the way of life of Neanderthal and Cro-Magnon Man probably came about as a result of improved communication through the development of language, a simple method of counting, social organization and the appreciation of symbolism. Speech must surely have been the most important single factor, enabling Cro-Magnon Man to discuss his problems, work out strategies and tactics, and instruct his children. He was a very skilled hunter, who invented the spearthrower, a rod about a foot long with a hook at one end to engage the butt of the spear, enabling him to hurl it far faster than before, from a far greater range and thus far more safely. He also had more advanced and sophisticated stone, bone, antler and wood tools than his Neanderthal relative. They included scrapers, cutters and sewing needles, enabling him to make better jewelry and to remove, scrape and dress animal skins to make clothing and tent-like houses – the latter usually erected over birch poles within his rock shelter, their entrances facing inwards and the skin coverings anchored down with stones. Cro-Magnon Man also had pointed burins, perhaps encouraging his growing interest in working bone and antler, and then in engraving on stone. These, it must be remembered, were the people responsible for the famous cave paintings in France and Spain.

Cro-Magnon art, especially cave or parietal art, is thought to provide evidence of their indulgence in magic and ritual, led by the *shamans* or sorcerers, dressed in the skin and head of, say, a bison and playing a bone flute. It was they who, for example, performed the initiation rites introducing young boys who had arrived at puberty into adulthood. Parallel lines apparently scored by finger tips on the soft, or by flint chips on the hard, sandstone forming the walls of the Koonalda Cave in southern Australia in about 20,000 BP are thought to be evidence of rites conducted by the early occupants of that continent. The most famous example of this in France, with its renowned shaman, was found at Les Trois Frères, in Ariège in the Pyrenees, the second most famous of the decorated caves. A detailed account of the Lord of the Beasts is given in the next chapter. Early Cro-Magnon Man's interest in decoration is illustrated by the perforated teeth and shells they used for their bodies, their perforated antler batons and other tools, and their engraved plaques, pebbles and ivory Venuses.

In France, the Laugerie Haute shelter, also on the Vézère River, had Cro-Magnon remains up to the Magdalenian period, for which the La Madeleine Rock Shelter, on a loop of the Vézère, is the type site. Flint blades and burins, harpoons and numerous engravings and bas-reliefs on bone, antler and stone were found here, including some finely sculpted animal figures on ivory and antler spearthrowers. This area is extraordinarily rich in the remains of our ancestors and other well-known caves and rock shelters include Les Combarelles and Font de Gaume, once halfway up a cliff, and the Laugerie Basse, Cap Blanc and Solutré Shelters, the latter giving its name to the Solutrean stage, which was characterized by leaf-shaped flint blades. These shelters contained innumerable flakes, rude stone-cutters, awls, arrow and lance heads, hammers, flint and chert saws, together with bone needles, sculpted reindeer antlers, engraved stones, harpoons and pointed bones. The broken bones of food animals included reindeer, bison, horse, ibex, saiga antelope and musk sheep. The presence of cave bear, lion, Irish elk and hyena were found in one cave each while the mammoth was found in five.

Although the Dordogne is rich in traces of Cro-Magnon Man, there are other important rock shelters and caves of the period elsewhere in France.

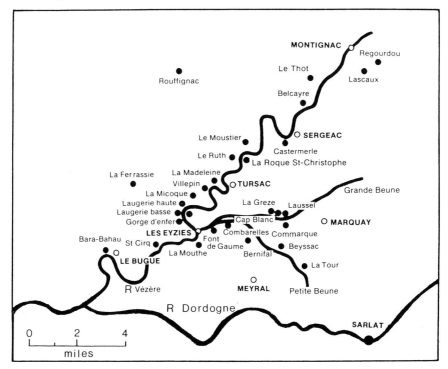

Les Eyzies area of the Dordogne showing the location of the important caves. (After Aubarbier and Binet)

La Madeleine Rock Shelter, France. (The J. Allan Cash Photolibrary)

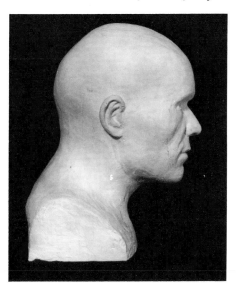

Reconstruction of the head of Cro-Magnon Man. (By courtesy of the British Museum (Natural History))

Reconstruction of a family group of Magdalenian hunters in S.W. France c. 10,000 BC. (Drawing by Maurice Wilson. By courtesy of the British Museum (Natural History))

Neander

BELGIUM
Maastricht
Grotto of Han
Les troux

GERMANY

Kent's Cavern

Artois

Picardy

Orrouy

● PARIS

Marne

La Cotte de St Brelade ○

Caen

R Seine

Brittany

R Loir
Trôo
Orléans

R Loire
Blois
Châtres-sur-Cher

Saumur
Chinon
Tours
Dénéze-sous-Doué
TOURAINE

Besançon

Arcy-sur-Cure

Chauvigny
Poitiers
Chaffaud
R Creuse
R Vienne
R Charente
Sireuil

Puy
Mt Dore

Haute-
Savoie
La Colombière

Charente
Brantôme
R Dronne
Aubterre
Auvergne
Haute-
Loire
St Emilion
R Vézère
Lot
Cantal
R Dordogne
Brive
Pech-Merle
Lascaux
Cabrerets
Gironde
Perigord
La Mouthe
R Lot
Lozère
Les Eyzies
Rouergue
Cevennes

Grima

Campi delle Alte
& Mont Agel
Le Vallon

Montauban
R Garonne
Bruniquel
Gard
Les Baux
Moustier-Ste-
Marie
Le Lazaret
Montespan
BR
Tarn
Nîmes
Fontbrégoua's
Carcassonne
Var

Cangas-de-Ones

ASTURIAS
Santander
El Castillo
Carlista
Peña de Candamo
Altamira
La Pasiega
La Clotilde
Pindal
Covalanas

Pierre St Martin
Urdos

Mas d'Azil
Ariege
Gargas
Niaux

Faron

Tuc d'Audoubert
Les Trois Frères
Rs Volp

Montserrat

PORTUGAL

MADRID
La Guardia

LEVANT
VALENCIA

Minorca

rock-cut tombs

Cordova

Sacro Monte
Woman's
Ardales
Granada
Guadix
De Los Murcielagos
De La Pileta
Palomas

GIBRALTAR

High Cave,
Tangier

These include the Montespan, near Nîmes; Tourasse; and La Colombière Rock Shelters near Poncin, forty miles northeast of Lyon. Poncin is a large shelter in Jurassic limestone of Kimmeridgian age with a width of 150 feet and a height of 40 feet at the maximum projection of the overhang. Remains found here date from 20,000 to 12,000 BP or older. Bruniquel, towards the Pyrenees, in a Jurassic limestone cliff 40 feet above the River Aveyron, has a sheet of stalagmite over the floor on top of earth, stone blocks and breccia, all blackened with charcoal particles. Below this *limon noir* was *limon rouge*, red earth, with many remains of wolf, rhinoceros, horse, reindeer, stag, Irish elk and bison, as well as human bones and flint and bone implements, some of the latter decorated with carved horse and reindeer heads. In the Pyrenees themselves, in Ariège, the Lombrive Cave yielded two skulls, the bones of humans and also those of brown bear, auroch – or wild ox, the ancestor of modern cattle, small ox, reindeer, stag, horse and dog. In Spain the northern caves of Altamira, El Castillo and Covalanas, all in Asturias, are typical of the Magdalenian or late Cro-Magnon period, with living floors and *in situ* hearths. They were occupied in about 14,000 BP and were rich in food remains, manufacturing debris, stone burins and end-scrapers, and antler bladelets. As well as the wall paintings, similar in style to those of southwest France, they contained many items of mobiliary art. There are similar caves in Andalusia, including the Cueva De La Pileta, the southernmost outpost of the Franco-Cantabrian province, discussed in the next chapter. The Valencian caves are typified by Parpallo, six miles west of Gandia. Here were found the bones of ibex, rabbit, horse, cattle and roe and fallow deer, together with Cro-Magnon backed blades, burins, end-scrapers and blade cores. On Gibraltar Sewell's Cave (Cave S) was occupied by Cro-Magnon Man from around 40 to 30,000 BP; it was re-examined in 1966 and found to contain engravings of men, fish, boars and other animals.

The evidence for the presence of Cro-Magnon Man in Britain is more widespread than for his Neanderthal predecessor. In the late Upper Palaeolithic he occupied Goat's Hole, Paviland, set in a steep 100-foot limestone cliff overlooking the Severn Estuary in Glamorgan, as well as nearby Cat Hole. Goat's Hole was dry, well lit, with a natural chimney to carry off the smoke from the fire and a rocky platform in front equipped with natural rock seats. A 'highly desirable hunting lodge', in fact, borne out by the large midden on its red loam floor containing the bones of horse, bison, woolly rhinoceros, hyena, mammoth and cave bear. The occupants buried their dead here on occasion, leaving a skeleton and implements including flints, sea shells, small ivory rods and an ivory ring. The Lower Carboniferous Limestone King Arthur's Cave near Whitchurch, Hereford and Worcester, overlooking the Wye Valley, was explored in 1871 and found to be a hyena den, containing

OPPOSITE: Map of France, Spain and neighbouring countries showing the approximate locations of caves, places and regions mentioned in the text.

53

King Arthur's Cave, near Whitchurch, Hereford and Worcester, England.

the gnawed remains of lion, Irish elk, mammoth, woolly rhinoceros and reindeer, together with flint flakes. The Mendip caves were occupied and there is now a suggestion that around 12,000 BP the dwellers in some of the Cheddar caves practised cannibalism. Both in Yorkshire, Victoria Cave, Settle, and Kirkdale Cave, in the Vale of Pickering, first found in 1821, were other hyena dens, containing the bones of two to three hundred individual hyenas as well as those of lion, cave bear, wild boar, hippopotamus, rhinoceros, bison and horse. The bones had all been gnawed by animal teeth and the marrow licked out. In contrast, the Dream Cave, near Wirksworth, Derbyshire, discovered in 1822 by lead miners following a mineral vein, contained animal bones in perfect condition. An untouched rhinoceros skeleton was found on the red earth floor of the cave together with the bones of horse, reindeer and auroch. Human remains of Upper Palaeolithic age have been found in Kirkhead Cave, on the north side of Morecombe Bay in Cumbria, Thor's Cave in the Manifold Valley of Staffordshire and the Tornewton Cave, near Torquay. Elsewhere in Europe there are scattered remains from the Upper Palaeolithic era. In a limestone cliff above the River Lesse near Liège in Belgium there are several *troux* or holes – the Trou du Frontal, the Trou des Nutons and the Trou Rosette – all found to contain human skeletons, flint flakes and animal bones. The large Trou de Naulette had human bones as well as those of rhinoceros, mammoth, reindeer, chamois and marmot.

54

Map of the British Isles showing the approximate location of caves and places in Scotland and Ireland mentioned in the text.

There are occupied caves of this period in Switzerland and Germany, as at Vogelherd Cave, and open-air sites such as the Dolni Vestonice locality in Moravia, Czechoslovakia, home of famous clay Venuses. Caves in Russia have yielded burials involving great use of ochre, which was thought to have symbolized blood. The Potočka Zijalka Cave in Yugoslavia, 6600 feet high, provided evidence of early Cro-Magnon cave bear hunters. Also in Yugoslavia is the cave at Grabak, on the island of Hvar off the Dalmatian coast. In neighbouring Greece the cave at Kastritsa was occupied from about 22,000 to 11,000 BP.

Cro-Magnon Man was widespread in Europe but he was also present in Asia, for example at Shanidar, and in Africa. Cro-Magnon hunters occupied the large Nelson Bay Cave in a 200-foot sandstone cliff 300 miles east of Cape Town; it is now 65 feet above the beach. They ate nuts, seeds and berries as well as hunting ostrich, baboon, antelope, hartebeest and the huge giant buffalo until the herds migrated; they then adapted to a diet of fish, caught by the men, and limpets and abalone, gathered by the women. Other Cro-Magnon caves are known from Cameroon, Nigeria and Sudan.

Palaeolithic life involved knapping stone tools, breaking and polishing bone, tracking animals, using the spearthrower, collecting aquatic food, scraping hides, sewing clothes, making fires, cooking meat, boiling water without pottery, playing the flute, and decorating the cave walls. It was quite a diverse life, with open-air encampments as well as caves and rock shelters. People exploited the seasons and resources, settled when necessary, and did not just wander erratically from meal to meal. Cro-Magnon life, however, was distinguished from that of its predecessors by its sophistication. This is most apparent from its art, discussed in the next chapter, but is also clear from its artefacts, the style of its burials and in other ways.

Mesolithic and later man

In the Mesolithic period, Cro-Magnon Man merged almost imperceptibly into present-day man, some of whom continued to live in caves. Mesolithic Man, however, was primarily a farmer who tended usually to build his house in the open. But from Neolithic times, into the Bronze and Iron Ages and the Roman and historic eras, cave use increased again. It is not over yet. As Grahame Clark said: 'Prehistory is not something human beings lived through long ago. It is with us still.'

In Britain, Wookey Hole in the Mendips was certainly occupied by Neolithic people, who left behind beautifully polished weapons. They were followed by others in the Bronze Age and also by Christians, who left behind coins such as the monogrammed *labarum*. Victoria Cave near Settle, Creswell Crags and Derbyshire caves such as Bat House and Thirst House were reoccupied in Mesolithic and Neolithic times. Kent's Cavern at Torquay was used in the Neolithic, Bronze and Iron Ages and Neolithic Man may have lived in the entrance of Poole's Cavern, Buxton, as did the outlaw who followed much later and gave the cave its name. Bronze-Age and Roman people occupied Victoria, Thor's and Kirkhead Caves, and followed the cave bear, sabre-toothed cat and other animals to dwell in the Ogof-yr-Esgyrn or Bone Cave, part of the Dan-yr-Ogof complex in the Brecon Beacons of South Wales. In Scotland Mesolithic and Neolithic Man lived in the limestone Reindeer Cave, two miles up the burn in Inchnadamph Nature Reserve, in caves in Argyll, and in the New Red Sandstone Sculptor's Cave, near Lossiemouth.

Neolithic Man followed Cro-Magnon in many French caves after a gap during the Mesolithic; remains of both were present in Fontbrégoua's Cave, Salernes, in Var, and Neolithic underground dwellings at Orrouy, Oise, included a sepulchral cave with the remains of fifty bodies. In Belgium Mesolithic and Neolithic Man followed Cro-Magnon in the *troux* and in the Bronze Age in the Grotto of Han. Similarly in Spain, Neolithic remains are found in the Cueva De Los Murcielagos in the Sierra Nevada of Andalusia, where a group of twelve skeletons was found. There were others in the Woman's Cave, near the Alhambra, Granada, and the remains of early Guanches, related to the North African Berbers, were found in the Canary Islands. On Gibraltar, Sewell's Cave was reoccupied in the Neolithic. Genista One cave was explored in 1865 by Captain Brome, the then 'chief explorer'. This cave is 200 feet deep, containing Neolithic human bones, charcoal, 'works of art' and pottery. Tools found there include flint flakes, polished greenstone celts, chisels, querns and rubbing stones, and a whetstone. There were bone needles, pins and spikes, and a bronze fish hook – the only metal object. It also contained the bones of rhinoceros, horse, pig, deer, auroch, leopard, hyena, birds and fish. Neolithic, Bronze and Iron-Age people were again present in nine caves around Ojcow, just north of Krakow in Poland, and in the Frauenmauer Cave – Wall of the Women – in Austria. Neolithic and Roman human bones and pottery were found in the Witch's Cave above Toirano, close to the coast near Albenga, Liguria. This limestone cave with two entrances was found in 1880 and has recently been re-examined, when human footprints of possible Neanderthal type were discovered. The Bronze Age occupants of the cave at Reggio, Modena, in the northern Apennines, were reputedly cannibalistic, like earlier dwellers in some Italian caves.

Several western Asian caves occupied by Neanderthal Man, as well as other caves, were reoccupied after a gap of some 15,000 years in the Mesolithic and Neolithic: the High Cave at Tangier, Tamtama, Bisitun, Belt and Khunik.

At Belt Cave, on the south coast of the Caspian Sea in Iran, lived Mesolithic people who compared with their Neanderthal predecessors appear to have had a casual – even cannibalistic – attitude towards their fellow humans. There were two groups: an older, who hunted the Caspian seal in about 11,500 BP and a younger, who hunted goitred gazelle in around 8500 BP.

Both had bows and arrows and St Bernard type dogs. The nearby Hotu Cave was used by the seal hunters and again by vole-eaters in 9200 BP. The Mesolithic people were followed by two groups in the Neolithic, by others during the Iron Age, and by Parthians in 250 BC. There was Mesolithic occupation of caves and rock shelters in Bihar in India, where the dead were buried in two forms: tightly flexed, with heads facing west, or extended, with one arm across the abdomen, facing east. In Thailand the late Palaeolithic to Mesolithic people who lived in Spirit Cave had a wood and bamboo culture for their hunting tools, instead of using bone. From 12 to 10,000 BP onwards others lived in caves and rock shelters along the Kwae Noi River, such as Sai-Yok, hunting and gathering along the river valley. They too sometimes buried their dead in the caves, in a flexed position, painted all over with red ochre which they obtained from hematite. Most of the caves were occupied later, by the Neolithic Quadrangular Adze people, so named from the cross-section of their adzes, who probably planted rice and millet and brewed beer from them. They raised pigs and buffaloes for sacrificial purposes, practised head hunting, built ritual megalithic monuments, and had bark cloth, pottery and outrigger canoes. Their successors in the Bronze Age possessed kettle drums. Neolithic to Bronze-Age caves included Spirit Cave in Burma and others in China, Cambodia, Malaysia and Indonesia. The Toala limestone caves of Patta and Leang Burung, east of Maros in southern Sulawesi (Celebes), are famous and date back to Cro-Magnon and Neolithic times. Of similar age is Tabon Cave, on the west shore of Pelawan, in the Philippines; like Niah in Sarawak it contained skulls of Tasmanian Negrito type.

In South Africa Mesolithic people lived in the Wilton Rock Shelter, Cape Province, and in caves in Kenya, where there was also a late Neolithic or Bronze-Age crematorium containing the remains of some eighty people. The Border Cave in the Lebombo Mountains of northern Natal is an Iron-Age grave and there is a famous Iron-Age cave, Leopard's Kopje, in Zimbabwe.

The stone and metal ages to some extent came and went at different times in different parts of the world; however, the Roman period which followed in Europe and subsequent historic occupations are considered, with their equivalents across the world, in the two chapters headed 'Recent'.

CHAPTER 5

Art and artefacts

Neanderthal Man may have placed flowers on the burial graves of their dead, but if there is one aspect of Palaeolithic Man which has changed our attitude towards our early ancestors, and aroused our interest in them, it is cave art. And who were the people responsible? Aurignacian Man, who came in at the beginning of the Upper Palaeolithic, 40,000 years ago, and, especially, Cro-Magnon Man who followed him seven thousand years later and persisted until the beginning of the Mesolithic in 9000 BP.

Cave art was the first human activity unconnected with man's immediate material needs. Why did the cave dwellers paint and sculpt? There have been – and still are – many and varied theories since cave art was first recognized in the 1830s, when a French notary named Brouillet first discovered a flat piece of bone on which were engraved two deer, while exploring the Chaffaud Cave, south of Poitiers. Could it have been 'art for art's sake', purely for decoration? Almost certainly not, although the result may well have pleased the artist and his companions. Was it a spare time activity, to be engaged in when game was abundant and people had time on their hands? Or was it the occupation of those who were past hunting, the 'old age pensioners' in retirement? Did people merely wish to depict themselves, and the animals associated with them, with no further reason unless, perhaps, to eulogise themselves and encourage their own fertility? 'Totemism', suggested by Salomon Reinach in about 1903, maintained that man was the protector, encouraging the multiplication of species and thus the maintenance of numbers of animals.

It was almost certainly linked to social and religious structure and culture; what else could explain the deep and hidden locations of many of the paintings. The most likely reason seems to be that the Cro-Magnon artists painted to invoke a 'sympathetic hunting magic', as first proposed by Burkitt; by painting animals you gained power and mastery over them and so could kill them – the game animals needed for food – more easily. If some 'fertility' magic was added, their replenishment and thus, again, the maintenance of numbers was encouraged. But basically it was a form of magical ensnarement; there are many pictures portraying arrows, darts, spears and slings, as well as nets, snares and traps, like the mammoth at Font-de-Gaume caught in a pitfall. Magic was also invoked by superimposing paintings one on top of the other; in one spot at Lascaux there are paintings four layers deep, although there is plenty of room. Some caves or areas seem to have been designated as 'lucky', imbued with good fortune, as at Les Combarelles where nearly 300 animals are crowded in. Overpainting one animal's head on another's body was also magic, and so was dot painting; the two chequered horses in the 'Sanctuary' of Pech-Merle are painted in red and black dots. The animals were painted singly, not in groups, and were always shown in splendid condition: bison with their humps full of fat, the females in calf with the males following.

Much of the symbolic hunting magic was directed by the *shaman*, who also led the ceremonies involving early 'religious' cults. He was the sorcerer, magician or doctor-priest, such as the Lord of the Beasts at Les Trois Frères. Certainly there was some fertility painting, and some of the geometrical designs are thought to have a sexual connotation, linked perhaps with symbols acting as seasonal markers. Much of this may have been made possible by the new Cro-Magnon facilities of speech and ability to count, already mentioned; the degree of similarity in the art from one cave to another suggests that there must have been extensive communication, at least through southern Europe.

Reconstruction of Cro-Magnon cave painters at work. (Maurice Wilson)

Dotted horses at Pech-Merle, Lot, France. Note how the artist has positioned the right-hand horse where the curve of the rock is in the shape of a horse's head.

The recognition of this has led to the abandonment of one earlier theory: that cave art came about by 'parallel development' in different places at the same time.

The refinements of cave art – in form, proportion and movement – suggest a strong artistic perception, imagination and ability, especially on the part of the artists who worked within the Franco-Cantabrian province of southwest France and northern Spain, with its outliers in southern Spain and Sicily, as well as southeast France and around Arcy-sur-Cure, the only place with cave art in France north of the Dordogne. One aspect of their work is very strange; there are notably few full human figures, while those that there are are stylized, usually masked, none of them to be regarded as a 'portrait'. Perhaps – especially if the hunting theory about the animal paintings is true – it was considered unlucky to portray humans; the same magical fate might overcome them. Primitive people still believe that to portray a person and then to mutilate the portrait or image can injure or even kill the subject.

This is all very frustrating for the anthropologist, who lacks a credible image of the cave dweller. The palaeontologists fare better, however; the animal images augment their bones and other remains, portraying the species living at any particular time, sometimes sharing the caves with people or at least living round them, and indicating when they became extinct. They provided information on what the Cro-Magnon people ate and how they obtained it.

Cave art tended to be concentrated in different parts of caves. Favourite sites were the entrances, the middles of the caves or their furthermost or terminal regions. These were late glacial times, when most of the caves and shelters were occupied, and the most common animals were bison and horse, followed by auroch, reindeer, red deer, mammoth, rhinoceros, ibex, chamois, boar, wolf, lion and bear. Some animals were never portrayed but there were also unidentified creatures, 'sub-humans', birds, fish, human hands and a great variety of signs and symbols. Scenes portraying events are very rare but Lascaux has in the shaft or 'crypt' an ithyphallic male human about to be trampled on by a partially disembowelled bison, together with a broken spear and a spearthrower.

The position of the art in a particular cave may lend credibility to one or other of the many theories. The 'sympathetic magic' theory is supported at Laussel, Pair-non-Pair and Teyjat, where the decoration was carried out during periods when the caves were more or less occupied. Some art – it may be called 'hidden art' – was placed far from the entrance, right at the back in the hidden parts of the cave, where nobody lived. Much of this was engraved, and must have required exceptional lighting. A small proportion of the animals have lines upon or approaching their bodies, holes in them, or circles on them. Some seem dead or wounded, with raised tongues and tails, exposed bellies, the nearside shorter than the offside legs and the toes pointing downwards, as if lying on the ground. All of these are generally found not at the cave entrances but a good way in. Other animals seem pregnant; it is possible that some species were worshipped, especially the 'noble' horse, bison, auroch and mammoth and the 'sacred' ibex and deer.

André Leroi-Gourhan in Paris studied more than two thousand animal pictures in sixty caves. He noted that 85% are of bison, aurochs or wild cattle and horses – all large animals and major food sources – which were placed in the middle of a panel or in the best site in the cave. Deer, ibex and mammoths are found in the less important positions, and rhinoceros, lions and bears were tucked away in the most remote parts. Reindeer, boar and fish were also depicted but did not seem to feature in the 'scheme'. More than 80% of the human females, both naturalistic and abstract, are in the central sites, while more than 70% of the males are not. This theory has been attacked because it presupposes a planned choice of caves to accommodate the sexual display, whereas all the evidence is of random decoration, sometimes spread over 30,000 years. This may provide the clue: over this period, all the symbols – hands, tectiforms, even some animals – may well have had different meanings at different times. It has been observed that sexual symbols were often displayed in daylight caves in the early art and in bas-relief in the later.

Noting the scarcity of pictures depicting human figures, Leroi-Gourhan conceived the use of sexual signs: for the female, there were triangles, rectangles and lattice-shaped, tectiform, oval and claviform signs, all found in the central parts of the cave. Male signs were barbed signs, short strokes and dots, found at the beginning and most remote parts of the sanctuary. There are also some paired signs, denoting dual forces. Grouping is based on pairing – not on coupling: there are no signs of human or animal copulation – of bison and horse; bison and mammoth; or auroch and horse. Thus is found a herbivore: a bison, less so an ox, rarely a hind, almost always associated with a horse, and with a third element: ibex, deer or, rarely, mammoth. This subordinate third element acts as a reminder of the pairings to be found at the entrances and the backs of caves. So, in summary, there are two types of pairing: bison and horse in the central areas, and horse with ibex and stag in the peripheral areas like the entrances and backs. The theory is based on the belief that the caves were decorated according to a systematic plan, an 'organised world' with an 'ideal' composition: a group of large herbivorous animals, one of which is nearly always the horse. A newer theory revises the old, reverting to the suggestion that each cave had a special artistic composition, with each animal occupying a special position and playing a particular part. Some animals, such as the horse, ibex or deer represented the 'male';

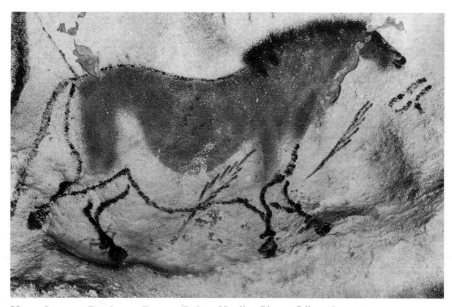

Horse, Lascaux, Dordogne, France. (Robert Harding Picture Library)

63

the 'female' was denoted by cattle, the bison or the mammoth. Each particular sign or symbol was also male or female. The male animals and symbols were placed in the cave entrances and depths, with the females in the central area, where a few males were also present. However, there are problems attached to this theory also.

Annette Laming-Emperaire, who worked on Lascaux and Pech-Merle, believed in open-air, daylight rock shelters, with bas-relief engravings, and in darkness caves, with paintings. She also attached importance to the preponderance of horse, bison and auroch.

Nevertheless, there are only about a hundred cave-art sites in Franco-Cantabria, including the outliers where the art is of a different character, with a total of several thousand representations carried out by a fair number of cultural groups. Trying to apply a single unilinear scheme of development to account for all of these, over the period of about 33,000 to 9000 BP, is an appallingly difficult task.

The Shaman

The most famous example of the shaman in France occurs in the famous cave called Les Trois Frères, linked with Le Tuc d'Audoubert Cave, in the little River Volp, in Ariège. It was named the Three Brothers by the Toulouse landowner and archaeologist, Count Henri Bégouèn, in honour of his three sons who helped him find it. The first cave he found, Le Tuc d'Audoubert, contained the Bridal Chamber, which led into the bison room. Here were two handsome bison, each about two feet long, modelled in dried clay. In a small inaccessible alcove were about fifty human heel prints, preserved in a crust of travertine, made apparently by five or six children. Then there were several clay 'sausages', presumed to be little phalli. It was thought to be a scene perhaps for fertility rites, where boys might have kept vigils.

Down a passage in the second, linked cave, Les Trois Frères, guarded by painted and engraved lions' heads, is a bell-shaped alcove containing a 'magic zoo': a network of animals engraved on the walls. A female reindeer has the front quarters of a heavy bison. Herding them all is a hybrid creature with human legs, a tail and a horned head – a jigging Pan or satyr dancing and playing a flute-like instrument. But the Lord of the Beasts is the partly painted, partly engraved figure at the top of the alcove: the shaman transcribed by the Abbé Breuil in 1902. Dressed in animal skins, with a head-dress of stag's antlers, owl-like eyes, wolf's ears, horse's tail, bear's front paws and the feet and sexual organs of a man, he is a hypnotic and terrifying masterpiece of Cro-Magnon magic art. There is, of course, no proof of sorcery or magic – it has been suggested that the Lord of the Beasts could have been a god or artist-magician rather than a sorcerer – but all the evidence suggests it. It was almost certainly connected both with 'willing' the success of hunting expeditions by conducting a ritual dance, perhaps, and placing a magic spell on the game animals by depicting them. But the inaccessibility of Les Trois Frères, involving a crawl of some 130 feet, has been frequently cited as strong evidence for the suggestion that ritual or ceremonial magic, perhaps concerning birth and death, fertility or puberty initiation rites, rather than just hunting magic, was involved here. Decorating these dark and secret corners must have required special lighting as well as considerable effort. Natural wall projections were probably used, as in Adelsberg Cave in Germany, to represent eyes, for example. The artists may have imagined they saw animal outlines on the walls, using their gifts of fantasy and imagination, and encouraged by their flickering torches. This theory is supported by the realistic nature of the drawings. It has been suggested that caves are cult places, like Ellora and Ajanta in India and Lung Men, Yun-Kang and Tun-hwang in China.

Another example of the shaman is the Bird-Man at Lascaux, a crudely painted bean pole of a man with a bird's head, matchstick limbs and only four fingers on each hand. His bird's beak is uplifted and he is surrounded, oddly, by a bird on a rod, which was possibly a spearthrower, a disembowelled bison with a huge pike leaning against it and an apparently disinterested rhinoceros. Breuil thought this was just a hunting scene; the man has killed the bison and has in turn been killed by the rhino. All this was found at the bottom of a 23 foot shaft, where Breuil thought the dead man's bones should be buried alongside, to confirm his interpretation. He dug for them but there was no sign of any bones. A later theory thinks that it might represent a symbolic clash between three clans using totemic symbols: birds, rhinoceros and bison. Others have suggested a sex clash between the male – the pike or spear – and the female – the bison with its looped intestines. A third, widely held theory maintains that the bird-man is a shaman, taking part in a ritual and toppled over in a trance. Support for this comes from the shamans in modern Siberia who are apparently often associated with a bird surmounting a stick or spearthrower. This link with Siberia is important: the modern shaman in the lives of Eskimo hunters plays a major role as diviner, healer and sorcerer. He extracts the illness from a patient's body and, going into a trance, predicts the future.

Certain caves have been designated 'sanctuaries'. Chief among these is the 'Grotte-Temple' of Pech-Merle in Cabrerets, near Cahors, while others include Le Cap Blanc, Niaux and Sautimamine. A cave supposed to have

Unicorn, Lascaux, Dordogne, France. (French Government Tourist Office)

been devoted to religious rites is Montespan, with its clay bear and other figures.

Other symbolic or magic drawings include the one hundred and fifty handprints at Gargas, one of more than twenty caves to have handprints or similar depictions, and the snaking barbed line at Marsoulas Cave, both in southern France; the cryptic dots and lines found elsewhere; and the geometric forms at Altamira thought by Breuil to be dwellings but by others to be traps, shields or coats-of-arms. The red and black dots covering the two chequered horses at Pech-Merle are certainly thought to be intended to ensure success in the ensuing horse hunt. At El Castillo, Spain, a cruciform sign with several hundred dots, in rows and paired with boxes, are thought to be sexual: the male represented by dots, the female by boxes, as religious fertility symbols. Here also are a male barbed sign and female bell-shaped signs, perhaps comparable with the Chinese yin and yang and the Roman Juno and Jupiter. There are also the painted pebbles of Mas d'Azil, decorated with spots, stripes, crosses and zigzags, as well as rude figures, thought to be linked with the painted pebbles from Scotland. There is an Aurignacian plaque of reindeer antler, three to four inches long, from the Gorge d'Enfer, in the Dordogne, on which are 167 cup-like markings arranged in a multi-looped line.

A. Marshack, of the Peabody Museum, Harvard, thinks these represent the phases of the moon: 25,000 years before the Sumerians invented cuneiform writing. The La Marche antler or *bâton de commandement* with its pregnant horse and eleven notches is taken to represent the length of the gestation period of the horse. Mobiliary 'touch' objects, such as the horse with twenty-seven darts in it, can symbolize killings. Compositions of dots, lines and signs are also found at Niaux, Altamira, Marsoulas, El Pindal and De La Pileta; they are thought variously to represent signposts, sexual symbols, calendars, lunar phases, counting aids, mnemonics, owners' or makers' marks, trees or fruit, to encourage a good harvest, and even early, pre-cuneiform writing. Some authors would like to see the subject reopened for investigation.

Technique

Some of the first cave art consisted of footprints and handprints, such as those found at Gargas. The Aurignacians, who preceded the Cro-Magnons by a few thousand years, used their fingers as brushes or palette knives. Those who followed were more sophisticated; for their cave art they needed lamps for illumination, especially in remote corners like Les Trois Frères, tools for 'pecking' their petroglyphs and pigments and brushes for paintings.

For lighting, they used skulls, sea-shells or grooved slabs of schistose sandstone for lamps, as at Les Trois Frères; or else cupel-shaped lamps, as at La Mouthe, some of which resembled simple Roman lamps. These often had a wick of hair, moss or grass and for 'oil' they used some sort of animal marrow, fat or grease, resin, pitch or bitumen. An alternative source of light was a charcoal torch. They must have had the problem of access, which they would have solved with ladders, ropes and possibly some sort of scaffold.

The Cro-Magnon sculptures were high-relief carvings made in the partially dry travertine of the cave walls using burins, sharp pointed flint tools. Natural irregularities in the surface of the walls were incorporated into the sculptures and detail could be achieved by chipping away at bits of the rock. In the early Magdalenian, towards the end of the Cro-Magnon period, enormous stone picks were also used, while a less permanent form of petroglyph could be obtained by drawing on soft clay with sticks or fingers.

The first stage of a painting might also involve the burin, used to trace or scratch the outline of the subject in the manner of present day charcoal pencils. For paint pots and palettes the artists used large flat bones or, as at Mas d'Azil, fan shells. In preparing their pigments they showed great ingenuity, employing a number of natural materials. Ochres were by far the most widely used substances. From the oxides and hydroxides of iron such as hematite, limonite and goethite they could obtain a range of yellow, orange, bright and dark red, chocolate and brown. It is possible, although thought unlikely, that they sometimes had blue and green, and even purple and mauve, from unoxidized iron ores or unstable vegetable dyes; violet is known only from Altamira. Black was common, from pyrolusite and other manganese oxides scraped from the walls of the caves, as well as burned bones, charcoal and other carbonaceous materials. White was a relative latecomer, obtained from kaolinite or bird guano, although both white and red chalk were used whenever they outcropped locally. The artists would end up with colours in liquid, paste or solid form, which they could spread with their fingers, apply from their palettes with brushes made of twigs, reeds, feathers, bristles or hair or with pads or 'sponges' of fur or moss, or blow dry, as a powdered pigment, onto the wet wall using a hollow tube, a method used by the Australian Aborigines. They even made primitive 'cut out' stencils and crayons, although these were rare, out of solid, usually red, ochre. To do this they probably powdered the pigment by grinding it with bone in a hollow stone and mixing it with fat, grease, fish or other oil, binding it with blood, urine, albumen, vegetable juices, honey, suet or bone marrow. The mixture would be dried and could then be 'sharpened' into a crayon. The same media would have been used in lesser quantities as an alternative to water to make a thick, adhesive paste pigment.

At Lascaux, the pigment was first dabbed as dots, the spaces then being filled in. The red and black horses at Pech-Merle are also painted in dots, filled in with brown paint. The German scholar E.R. Jaensch suggested in 1933 that some artists might have had an *eidetic* ability: they could 'project' a previously observed or even imagined object onto a blank wall or other surface and then trace its outline accurately.

The history of Franco-Cantabrian art

There were two sorts of art. Mobiliary art, or *art mobilier*, sometimes called home art, was drawn on pieces of bone and stone, found in the cave deposits along with dateable stone implements. It was this type of work – a piece of bone engraved with two deer – that marked the discovery of Palaeolithic art when it was found in the 1830s by the notary, Brouillet. The carvings feature horses, bison, reindeer, ibex, does, cattle, bucks and stags, humans, bear and fish, in that order. Far behind come lions, birds, mammoths and rhinoceroses. Females and males are in the proportion seven to one. Mobiliary art is much more widely distributed and largely beyond the scope of this book. As well as the carved bones and stones, it includes the painted pebbles and clay 'Venuses', among other items. There were, however, three sorts of specially ornamented reindeer antler artefact that should be mentioned. One is the spearthrower, previously known as the throwing stick or *propulseur*; this was a device for increasing the force behind a javelin and was similar to the North American atlatl. The pierced staff, previously the *bâton de commande-ment*, was a sort of chief's sceptre or rod of authority. Finally, there was the spear- or arrow-straightener, which was like the pierced staff only simpler and is still used today in conjunction with heat by Eskimo hunters to straighten and harden bone and antler missiles.

Parietal art – the cave murals – are the paintings or pictographs and engravings or petroglyphs that have captured the imagination of the world. The murals are nearly always on limestone, in caves and *abris* or overhanging rock shelters, where the deposit of calcareous travertine which is constantly forming helps to preserve them. Their great age, at first a subject of doubt and discussion, was testified to by the fact that the animals portrayed in them are extinct; their erosion by water; the depth of the calcareous deposits on top of them; and their colour changes. The first important cave to be found was Altamira, discovered in 1879 by a man hunting foxes. In 1901, H. Breuil and his colleagues found Les Combarelles, followed one week later by Font-de-Gaume. In 1906 El Castillo and Covalanas were discovered, but it was not until 1940 that a boy out rabbiting chanced upon Lascaux.

It began with the Aurignacians, living from about 40 to 26,000 BP, who in the west – but not in their Asian root zone – made the first simple animal drawings and human and other carvings in around 30,000 BP. These were primitive finger tracings of geometric designs or simple animal outlines, including cup marks and signs. Breuil had two periods, the first embracing the Aurignacians and the Gravettians or the first Cro-Magnons. This was the time when fingers were the first pallette knives, as at Gargas, followed by burins which could be used to cut lines on the hard rock, and then brush-like implements to paint in red and yellow ochre, and only rarely in black. The Gravettians were accomplished sculptors and produced the fertility 'Venuses', from the Pyrenees through Italy to Russia. The second period was that of the Solutreans and Magdalenians. No paintings are definitely Solutrean, but there were many petroglyphs in the middle of the period, for example at Roc de Sers, Cap Blanc, Les Trois Frères and Tuc d'Audoubert, and Montespan. The early Magdalenians had black line drawings, of which the best were at Altamira, El Castillo, Le Portel and Niaux, before the later explosion of colour. In many cases, the painting was in flat colour, in others the bodies of the animals were first coloured in with dots and then the spaces were filled in; this is specially well done at Pech-Merle, where black and red dots and brown paint were used.

Apart from cave painting, the Magdalenians excelled at mobiliary art. Their equipment was decorated, with parts of animals on bone points while weighted spearthrowers had whole animals. As well as horse, ibex and bison

Salle des bisons, Niaux, Ariège, France. (French Government Tourist Office)

on ivory, bone and antler, there were human figures on rods, for example. There were engravings on stone slabs and unworked pieces of bone, like the mammoth at La Madeleine and decorated shoulder blades at Mas d'Azil. Limestone slabs which were used as hearthstones were decorated with the usual animals and human figures such as obese females and hook-nosed males. One male is standing, shouting, gesticulating wildly with his arms, whilst surrounded by strange faces. The Magdalenians also used schematic art, employing chevrons and other linear designs to represent animals as pictograms.

To prove that most Franco-Cantabrian cave art was also Magdalenian is difficult and the proof is based mainly on analogies with mobiliary art. Paintings and engravings covered by datable Magdalenian deposits do occur. At Isturitz there are animal outlines cut into a stalagmitic cone; a remarkable sculpted frieze of animals and humans occurs at Angles-sur-l'Anglin; there is another frieze at the Reverdit Rock Shelter and engravings on stalagmitic flows at Teyjat; all these are examples. At Les Combarelles and Cap Blanc the caves contain Magdalenian occupation debris but this is not physically associated with the art. This was the highest point of prehistoric Cro-Magnon art, when thousands of animal figures were painted, realistic in pose and vivid in colour; after the Magdalenian, the standard of painting declined. A recent scheme has divided Franco-Cantabrian art into four styles or periods. Sufficient to say that they cover the period from about 30,000 BP to 9000 BP, from the Aurignacians to the beginning of the Mesolithic. Two are termed Primitive, one Archaic and one Classical.

The origins of cave art are obscure. Man imitated animals very early on; the 'painting' of hands may have been man copying the tracks left by animals. The life of reindeer-hunting man who also, we are told, enjoyed smoked salmon, was dominated by mammoths, rhinoceros, bisons, aurochs, wild horses, musk-oxen and reindeer, as well as cave-bears, tigers and lions. As well as aurochs, there were other now extinct animals, including the tarpan, hemione and megaceros deer. A new study of the number of animals depicted in Franco-Cantabrian cave art shows that reindeer form 1.5% of the animals represented in France and 10.5% in Spain; the horse 26% in France and 35.5% in Spain; bovids or cattle 32.5% and 39%; red deer 30.5% and 7.5%; and the ibex 9.5% and 7.5%. Outside the total, the mammoth is depicted 0.1% of times.

The caves

There is agreement that the six finest caves in the Franco-Cantabrian province are Altamira, near Santillana, nineteen miles from Santander, and Font-de-Gaume, Les Combarelles, Lascaux, Niaux and Les Trois Frères in France.

Others in France include Baume-Latrone; Chabot and Ebbou, both Ardèche; Le Portel, Varilhes; Tuc d'Audoubert; Montespan, near Nîmes; the huge Mas d'Azil; Gargas; Marsoulas, Haute-Garonne; and Bédeilhac, all in Ariège; Isturitz, the tunnel cave with its majestic horse; Pech-Merle and La Mouthe, both near Martel, Cabrerets, Lot; Sergeac, Vézère, near Montignac; Reverdit Rock Shelter; Laussel, with the Venuses and Archer, and Cap Blanc Rock Shelter, Les Eyzies; La Grèze, Dordogne; the Gorge d'Enfer Rock Shelter with the Abri du Poisson; Laugerie Haute, with its mammoths; the Grotte du Trilobite, with the woolly rhinoceros; La Colombière Rock Shelter, Ain, with its engraved pebbles and mammoth bones; Angles-sur-l'Anglin; Barabao; Teyjat, near Varaignes; Rouffignac; Cougnac; Pair-non-Pair, lower Dordogne; Bernifal; La Calavie and Comarque; Tayac; and Javerlhac; Roc de Sers, near Angoulême; and La Magdelaine, near Montauban, Tarn. There are some Franco-Cantabrian caves in southeastern France and around Arcy-sur-Cure, the most northern example in western Europe.

In Spain there are Covalanas, with its frieze of 'dotted' hinds; Venta de la Perra, with its bear engraving; Santian, nine miles from Santander, with its frieze of human hands; El Pendo, with two bird engravings; El Castillo, fifteen and a half miles from Santander, rich in art and with twenty-five layers; La Pasiega, near El Castillo, with mainly Aurignacian engravings; Buxu, in the Libas valley, and Peña de Candamo, both with many bison, deer, ibex, horse, boar, chamois, stags and anthropomorphic figures and signs, all in Asturias; La Clotilde and Pindal, Bay of Biscay; Bolao Llanes, with nothing of beauty but a frieze of tectiforms on the arched roof overhanging an underground lake; this may have been made by older cave dwellers to indicate a spot to obtain cool water or for some 'water magic' reason; Los Casares; De La Pileta, Ardales and La Cala, all in Andalusia, near Malaga; Palomas, Cadiz; and Cave S in Gibraltar, depicting men, fish, boars and other animals. The geometric designs found in caves increase in number southwards. Thus there are very few in Perigord, more in the Pyrenees, yet more in Cantabria and most in Andalusia, as illustrated by the Cueva De La Pileta, near Ronda, on the top of the sierra where it overlooks a natural amphitheatre. Here there are four series of paintings. The first is yellow, comparable with the Aurig-

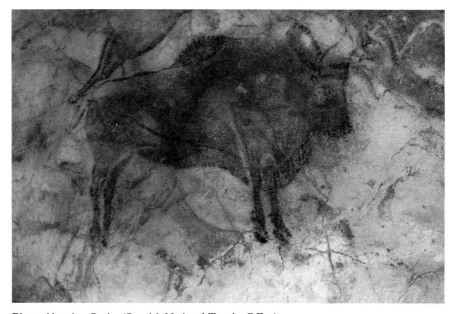

Bison, Altamira, Spain. (Spanish National Tourist Office)

nacian art of the north; the second red, comparable with La Pasiega; the third grey-black, like the early Magdalenian of the north; and finally the fourth, coal black, very like the Neolithic conventionalized drawings from the Spanish Levant. Examples of these four have been over-painted, which enabled Breuil to establish their relative ages.

There are a few Franco-Cantabrian caves in Italy, such as Levanzo Island, in the Aegadian Islands, west of Sicily; Romanelli, in Puglia, southeast Italy, with some rather poor engraved horses; Addaura, west of Palermo; and Niscemie.

Of the caves open to the public, the best are considered to be Altamira, radiocarbon dated at 15,500 BP, with its Painted Hall where the ceiling has many animals crowded into a space of sixty by thirty feet, as well as other rich galleries; Lascaux II; Pech-Merle, famous for its two chequered and dotted horses, one with a vague fish on its back, and the associated human hands; Cap Blanc Rock Shelter, containing large sculpture; Cougnac; Font-de-Gaume, with paintings and engravings; Les Combarelles, with engravings only; the late Cro-Magnon Azilian cave at Rouffignac, with its great mammoth frieze and serpents' dome, six miles long and with an electric railway, but thought by Glyn Daniel, in his book *Some Small Harvest*, as well as others to be a fake; La Mouthe; Gargas; Niaux; and Mas d'Azil. Specialists only, with permission, are allowed into Lascaux I; Montespan; Le Portel; the two Volp stream caves in Ariège, Les Trois Frères and Le Tuc d'Audoubert, with the famous clay bisons; Peña de Candamo; El Castillo; La Pasiega; and Pindal. Montespan was discovered in 1923 by Norbert Casteret. Here was the Aurignacian headless clay bear, once given a real bear's head and embellished later by the Magdalenians. With it were thirty other clay statues and fifty engravings, including the bison wall. Casteret was also involved in Labastide, and in Gargas, with more Aurignacian art including the mutilated hand-points: depictions of the human hand with the finger joints cut off, and the panel of complex engravings including horses, an elephant – probably a mammoth – and a bird, very rare in Palaeolithic art.

The Spanish Levant

The Levant of eastern Spain has rock shelters associated with post-glacial groups of hunter gatherers who may have ranged beyond the areas in which they left their cave art. This is found in the hilly areas from the Pyrenees to the Sierra Nevada, near the eastern coast around Valencia but not in the coastal areas. It was never painted deep in caves but under overhangs, in niches and shelters often at the base of cliffs above scree slopes.

It was very vigorous work, which although known about earlier was only properly noted in about 1903. The main examples are at Els Secans; Val del Charco del Agua Amarga; Gasulla Gorge; Valltorta Gorge; Morella la Vella; Cuevas de la Araña; Alpera, in caves such as Minateda and Cueva Vieja; Cueva del Santo; and Cogul. There are only rare engravings and the paintings are nearly all monochrome, usually red, light to brownish, but with some black and white. The technique used to prepare a thin liquid paint was the same as that used by the Franco-Cantabrians; it was applied to the yellowish or greyish blue rock in stages with a simple brush. Again, the contours were drawn first, on a surface that had possibly first been prepared by painting over with a watery glaze. The subjects are human and animal, the figures isolated or grouped in scenes depicting activity, unlike Franco-Cantabrian art. Most of the figures are small, six to eight inches in length, although some animals measure up to thirty inches. The animals are naturalistic and the humans naturalistic or stylized: long-bodied, with stick-like legs, or short-bodied, with thick legs. There are some anthropomorphous figures. The groups often depict hunting scenes, such as tracking, chasing or 'shooting', while one shows a wounded animal turning on its attacker. Human groups are shown conducting feasts or ceremonial dances, or engaged in or marching to battle. Others show men honey collecting, warding off a swarm of bees, clapping or dancing women, while one depicts a mother with child. The hunters are mainly equipped with bow and arrow, the men usually naked but sometimes with loin cloths or 'breeches', and most have caps or feather head-dresses. They wear ornaments round their knees and sometimes round their arms; some have beards and moustaches. The females have naked top halves and wear long skirts.

The significance of these paintings is interesting. They could be pictorial narratives but why are they clustered in niches, apparently 'chosen' spots, with much superimposition, while other very suitable sites are totally ignored? Possibly these were places of worship or sanctuaries; some chosen niches are thought to have supernatural powers. In this sense the anthropomorphous figures should be thought of as the spirits of wild animals or bush spirits, rather than as masked men. They would then not be narrative but would deal with mythical incidents or conceptions.

Their dating is difficult. The caves have not been left intact and the animals depicted are early post-glacial species which could have lived in a warm or a cold climate and survived until relatively recently, such as deer, goat, boar and auroch. There is a possibility that some of the animals were domesticated but this is still uncertain; certainly all the activities shown depict hunter gathering. One stag-hunting scene includes a dog, and in these mountainous areas hunting may have survived undisturbed by the coastal agriculturists. The flint assemblages associated with this type of art include geometric microliths, possibly made by agriculturists from the coast who came up-country to hunt. Certainly the paintings were developed over a long period. Some people have regarded them as coeval with Franco-Cantabrian art, of Cro-Magnon times, but others think them Neolithic. In style they are certainly not related to the Franco-Cantabrian school, so one argument maintains that, since there are some Franco-Cantabrian offshoots in the Levant area as well as in Andalusia, it is most unlikely that two different schools would have developed so close together at the same time. They are not Upper Palaeolithic but are probably post-glacial; this suggests a possibly Mesolithic or even Bronze Age, but more probably a Neolithic age. Their links are not with Franco-Cantabria but might be with Africa: not with the north African Sahara and Maghreb but with Egypt, central Sahara, East Africa, Zimbabwe and, most likely, the Bushmen of South Africa.

Other European cave art

A good few caves in Belgium, Germany, Czechoslovakia, Hungary and Austria were lived in during the Palaeolithic, but although there are plenty of examples of mobiliary art, like the 'Venuses', there are no painted or engraved caves. However, one remarkable outpost of Franco-Cantabrian art,

Venus from Willendorf, Austria
c. 30,000 BC. (C.M. Dixon)

demonstrating the community of Upper Palaeolithic people over all of Europe, is found in Russia some 1900 miles east of the Dordogne, at Kapova (Kapovaya) Cave near Šulgan-Tăs, on the right bank near the south bend of the Belaia (Bielaya) River, in the south Ural Mountains. Here there is an impressive group of Gravettian wall paintings depicting stag, wild steppe-horse, mammoth, rhinoceros and cave bear, in yellows, reds, browns and black.

There is no definite cave painting or engraving in Britain but there are examples of bone and ivory fragments which seem to have deliberate designs scratched on them, associated with earlier Upper Palaeolithic artefacts. One example is the ivory point with a bevelled base from Pin Hole Cave, Creswell Crags, Derbyshire, with its fish design; another is the horse carved on a bone from Robin Hood's Cave, also at Creswell Crags, although this is more likely to be associated with later Upper Palaeolithic artefacts. A third example came from the Hyena Den, Wookey Hole, and in Scotland the painted pebbles can be compared with those from Mas d'Azil. The painted red bars at Bacon's Hole, Glamorgan, could be of any age.

Mesolithic people, unlike their predecessors and even when using the same caves, showed far less artistic complexity and ability. From 2000 BC Spain and Portugal have some Bronze-Age caves depicting demons and strangely shaped humans and spirits. On the Franco-Italian border there are some Bronze-Age caves: the Grotte du Prince, Grimaldi Caves, Ventimiglia, with more than fourteen hundred figures, Mont-Bégo and Tende. Italy also has Albenga and Voltri and Val Camonica, near Capodiponte, Lake Garda. Brittany and Ireland have Bronze-Age engravings in the megalithic passage graves and they also occur in cists in Germany. Anatolia, in Turkey, has some rock art.

There are Bronze-Age rock paintings in Scandinavia depicting men with ship burials, stylized vehicles, wheels, men with horses, daggers, fish and other animals at Bardal, Hammer, Balsford, Bogge, Romsdal and Rogaland. They nearly all occur on rock faces or crags where game was driven but there is one cave at Solsem, Nord-Tröndelag, with a grotto 120 feet long and 20 feet wide decorated with paintings. Men with huge phalli doing a cult dance are depicted, and many bones were found, with Neolithic harpoons and other objects. Similar aged engravings in Karelia, northwest Russia, western Siberia and the central Asian Arctic depict sorcerers and other subjects.

The Sahara and Maghreb

Most Saharan rock engravings and paintings and those of the Maghreb, of Morocco, Algeria and Tunisia, were found by officers of the French Foreign

Legion Camel Corps on patrol. They were first discovered in about 1850 but the earliest important find was by Lieutenant Brenans, in 1933. In the Tassili n'Ajjer – Plateau of the Rivers – near Djanet, eastern Algeria, Brenans saw on the walls of a dried-up river bed engravings of rhinoceros, elephants and giraffes.

The main areas for Saharan and Maghreb art are Tassili n'Ajjer and the Hoggar but examples are also found to the northwest, south and east-southeast of these. At first they were all line engravings; the oldest were made by cutting a deeply incised line, 'U' or 'V' in section, up to half an inch wide, which was then polished smooth. This technique was used for the contours but so too was 'pecking', also followed by polishing. However, no tools have been found that could do this. The best engravings are on sandstone but some are on granite and quartzite. The artists may have used a pointed stone chisel and a stone hammer, and polished their work with damp sand on stone or very hard wood. They have been dated by using the popular desert patina method. In hot arid conditions a patina of iron and manganese oxides forms on a rock surface, on top of the engravings, and its depth can be used to put them in chronological order. The types of animal portrayed can also be used; some are extinct but the camel was not introduced until the Christian era, while the elephant was Neolithic. There were also Cape buffalo, rhinoceros, oxen, wild asses, lions, panthers, leopard, cheetah, antelope, gazelle, mouflon (Barbary sheep), ostriches, rams and finally horses. These were naturalistic engravings of animals, and scenes depicting their being hunted, but also of humans, with Neolithic boomerangs and axes and, finally, swords, lances, javelins and armour, even down to firearms.

They have been dated into four periods. First the *bubalus*, 'round head' or hunter, up to about 7000 BP; then the pastoralist, showing herds of cattle, from about 7000 to 3000 BP; this was followed by the warriors, showing scenes of chariots, horsemen and their horses, from 3000 BP to 100 BC; and finally, from 100 BC to 1000 AD, very inferior paintings of camels, with modern offshoots down to about 1900. No skeletons have been found in the caves and rock shelters where these engravings and paintings occur, raising the question of whether they were local scenes or pictures of images people had seen elsewhere?

The paintings were only discovered between 1950 and 1957 and they are marvellous. Some are on the Hoggar granite but most – and the best – are on the Ordovician-Silurian Tassili n'Ajjer sandstone; there are more than 10,000. The Tassili cattle are superb; the Saharan *bubalus* school of painting probably led directly to Egyptian painting. The artists also painted a horned 'god' figure, animal magic, lions eating an ox, jackals, horses, sometimes with chariots, giraffe, antelope, camels, hippopotamus, an elephant dance, colossal

beasts, warriors, masked women and men, dancers and shepherds; they also left some sculpture. The 'extraordinary cave' of Haua Fteah, on the north Cyrenaican coast of northeast Libya, has naturalistic and geometric engravings on stone and also on ostrich eggs, coeval, perhaps, with the rock sculptures.

Central and East Africa

There is very little rock art in central Africa and what there is is divided into three provinces. In north Cameroon there are geometrical petroglyphs at Bidzar. The northern Central African Republic has three rock shelters with paintings; most are geometrical designs but Toulou has coloured humans and animals. The southern region and Zaïre have cups and petroglyphs of Stone Age and Iron Age dates, carved on indurated laterite and showing animals, tools, weapons and footprints. Other regions with paintings are the lower part of Zaïre, north to the Congo and south to Angola and including Mbafu Rock Shelter.

Rock art in East Africa is not found in deep caves but in rock shelters and overhangs. Commonly, as in Europe, there is no datable stratified material. Most of the earliest art was that of the Nachikufans of Zambia and Tanzania, dated by radiocarbon from 4500 BP onwards, but some of it was Wilton, from around 7000 BP, the same age as much of the South African art. As in Europe, the artists used iron oxides to produce their yellows, reds and browns, charcoal and manganese for black, and in later pictures, white obtained from kaolinite and bird guano. Again, there was very little blue and green; what there was would have been derived from vegetable dyes which would have faded until completely lost. Crayons were made by mixing red ochre with animal fat.

Once again the question of 'why' becomes perhaps the most interesting. It could have been mere chance, a form of 'doodling', but this is not considered likely. The two most likely motives seem to be 'wishful thinking' and 'sympathetic magic'. By depicting fat cattle and successful hunts, as well as beautiful girls, you may have hoped to improve your chances in those fields. And like the Franco-Cantabrians, but unlike the Bushmen, you hoped to make your prey or your enemy die or suffer, by depicting arrows in your prey and pins in an effigy of your enemy. Another possibility was to record major events such as hunts, rituals and battles such as were fought between Bushmen and Bantu. In Tanzania cave paintings were first found in 1908 near Bukoba, and then at Kundusi, Kolo and Kisese, north of Kondoa, in 1923. Bushmen living west of Lake Eyasi, at Kondoa, at Dodoma, at Tumbelo and at Cheke, north of Kolo, painted ostriches, giraffe, antelopes and dogs. Others lived on the Iramba Plateau, near Singida. The first art consisted of red line drawings,

OPPOSITE: Warrior, Tassili n'Ajjer, Algeria c. 3000 BC. (Robert Harding Picture Library)

followed by dark outline drawings which were coloured in afterwards, and finally by plain colour paintings, in that order. Many of the paintings are overlain, which of course helped to determine the sequence.

Among the subjects were very few small animals; although these were eaten, the large animals were regarded as the more important 'kill'. Carnivores were rare. There were elephant hunts; an elephant painted upside down might signify its being 'dead'. Antelopes were the most common animals, such as a herd of hartebeest, followed by giraffe and rhinoceros, including a courting pair. At Singida, an artist painting on boulders by a spring used the granite showing through the greyish overlying rock to help in portraying his elephant. Shelters at Bwanjai, Kiziba, show conventional human figures, mostly in red but some in black and white. In the Kondoa-Irangi area – the main centre – there are fourteen different styles. Many human figures are shown, including dancers and archers, flute- or pipe-playing musicians, a graceful procession, a tug-of-war fought by males over a female, a hunting blind or hide, and people frolicking by a river. The ancestral Sandawe and Hadza, who resemble the Hottentots and Bushmen, probably did some of these, portraying naturalistic animals in red and human figures.

Altogether there are nineteen superimposed styles, but as in Europe there are no true polychromes. Although thought at first to be Wilton in age, most are now known to be the later Nachikufan. Southern Tanzania and eastern Katanga have examples of early naturalistic art as well as geometric styles.

Other paintings are found in Dire Dawa and Sourre, in eastern Ethiopia; in the Horn of Africa; and in Sudan. Here, at Darfur, the hump-free cattle which are depicted are earlier than the Zebu cattle imported from Asia. There is only one painted cave known in Uganda and Kenya, near Kitale, on Mount Elgon, which shows cattle, although Uganda also has a few schematic or geometric paintings.

Southern Africa

Southern Africa has over three thousand sites containing cave paintings or rock engravings, dated from the Mesolithic down to about 1800 AD, which run in a huge sweep anticlockwise from the southwest up to the middle of the east coast. Little is known, however, about the artists' methods, nor has their work been correlated with specific skeletal remains. Giant handaxes and other chipped stone implements have been found in and around the caves but have received less study than their European equivalents.

Starting in Namibia, where at Twyfelfontein there are both pecked and burin engravings of giraffe, elephant, ostriches, antelope spoor and possibly a nest of eggs, the sites continue down to the Cape, where the Wilton Rock Shelter, dating from about 7000 BP, revealed impressive rock engravings and paintings, together with tools and personal ornaments such as perforated shale pendants and ostrich-shell disc beads. They run through the Drakensberg Mountains of Natal to the Transkei, where at Etheldale, Matatiela district, east Griqualand, there are dark red and bright red human hunting figures, some wearing masks. Then comes Botswana and the Transvaal.

The National Park in the Drakensberg Mountains has a sandstone gallery in which are illustrated red cow antelopes, elands and human beings. Examples of caves here include Xeni Shelter; Xmas Cave; Battle Cave; Eland Cave; Fulton's Rock; Sebaaini's Cave, with trackers and bichrome buck; The Cavern; Martens Shelter; Mushroom Hill Shelter; Game Pass Shelter; Poacher's Shelter in Ndidima Valley, with dark red and white Bushmen hunting antelope; Bellevue Shelter; Willcox's Shelter; Steel's Shelter; Barnes's Shelter; Willem's Cave; Main Caves; and Giant's Castle. Transvaal caves include Doornhoek, Magaliesberg, which is possibly Iron Age; Bosworth, near Doornhoek; and Haakdoorndraai, north Waterberg, a sandstone cave in the northwest Transvaal. There are engravings pecked for example on dolerite on exposed hill tops in open cave 'galleries', which often have sloping floors so that no datable stratified debris is present. These might depict an encircled rhinoceros or quagga.

Finally, the sweep continues up into Zimbabwe and Zambia, including the upper Zambezi River, to meet Tanzania. In Zimbabwe the granite Matopo Hills have painted sites, in Matabeleland usually showing hunting scenes but in Mashonaland depicting more complicated activities, some of which are mythological or ceremonial. In Zambia the Nachikufu group west of the Luangwa River has paintings in one of the shelters and in the only cave. The Chifubwa Shelter also contains engraved and painted schematic art, consisting of parallel lines and inverted 'U's with a central line; these are very like those in Franco-Cantabria and signify male and female.

There are thus three broad regions. In the north, from northern Namibia to Zimbabwe and the north Transvaal are the granite caves. The sandstone galleries, with their paintings, are found in a semi-circle round the coast of southern South Africa, as in the Drakensberg Mountains. Finally, there are the engravings found on smooth dolerite and similar exposed rocks in the interior.

Nearly all the paintings and engravings are naturalistic, apart from some geometric and curvilinear examples in Zambia. Most of the animals are modern species, such as cattle and fat-tailed sheep, and so are most of the humans: Bushmen, Bantu, Hottentot and a few Europeans. Some of the humans are small, carrying bows and arrows. All the best paintings were done by Bushmen, the hunters and gatherers who were driven out by the later Bantu pastoralists and agriculturists migrating from the north. The people were dwarfish, with tiny skulls, but also sturdy, graceful and powerful, with an amazing artistic sense; the Hottentots were related to them. The later Bantus left some paintings but these were very crude.

The Bushmens' *Weltanschauung* or mythology, like their painting, mainly concerns animals. They may have been on the lookout for manifestations of their mythological beliefs which could have been triggered off by vesicles in the rock or similarities of form and structure. The praying mantis was very important, representing both soothsayer and divine, miracle-working force. So was dualism: everything small, plump and weak is female, like the full moon, leading to a complicated mythology involving the moon but also the sun. One example is the rain legend: the mantis – portrayed as lightning – rents asunder the elephant – the cloud – to produce rain. The rain elephant is depicted in the Drakensberg Mountains and also in Philipp Cave, near Ameib in north Namibia: an elephant in white with a red springbok 'in its belly'. The elephant motif also appears in Franco-Cantabrian art in Baume-Latrone in Gard. The Bushmen never painted 'game' animals – sympathetic hunting art – but only animals involved in their mythology. Nor did they paint them as 'totems', as clan or tribal idols. On the other hand, the eland – the favourite animal of the sun, another manifestation of the mantis – is found everywhere.

Cosmic transcendentalism was also very important and the afterlife is frequently portrayed. It is shown as a paradise of animals in a beautiful landscape in huge granite caves in the Matopo Hills, south of Bulawayo in Zimbabwe, and in the Bambata and Nswatugi Caves, also in the Matopo, with their giraffe, zebra and scattered human beings.

India and the East

There are paintings in rock shelters in the low cliffs of Vindhyan sandstone in the central Indian Vindhya Plateau, such as Singanpur, Madhya Pradesh, once said to be late Palaeolithic but probably late Bronze or early Iron Age. In Morhana Pahar Rock Shelter there are figures with bows and arrows, and carts and animals; at Lekhania Rock Shelter there are Sambar and Chital deer; and at Roberts Ganj Rock Shelter there are more paintings of animals. The paintings are usually in dark red, with purple, green and white. Some are superimposed, representing different phases of central Indian rock art. Caves at Mirzapur, Adamgargh and Lekhahiya, Bihar, had rock

Three of the twenty-two damsels painted on the rock outcrop at Sigiriya, Sri Lanka. Dating from c. 484–495 AD, these are the only non-religious cave paintings in Sri Lanka.

paintings as well as microlithic industries. There were scenes of elephants and warriors on horseback which must be 'historic' but the underlying hunting scenes at Mirzapur could be prehistoric, possibly of the microlithic period. In the southern Deccan there are paintings mainly in the open on boulders or overhangs, and historic engravings of ibex and stupas are found near Chilas and northwards to Hunza along the Karakoram Highway in northern Pakistan. At Sigiriya, Sri Lanka, there are twenty-two paintings in a rock overhang.

Other cave-art sites are known throughout Asia, in Indonesia and in Sulawesi. Japan had seven pebbles of chlorite schist engraved with abstract human figures at the Kami-kuroiwa Rock Shelter, Shikoku island.

Australasia

It is not known when rock painting first began in Australia. There are two major groups: linear and geometric, and naturalistic; there are also some mixed zones. Cave art in the south and west may date back to 22,000 BP. Ochre is known to have been used 18,000 years ago by people occupying

83

LEFT: Aboriginal painting at Eidsvold, Queensland, Australia. RIGHT: Aboriginal painting from the Northern Territory, Australia. (Australian Tourist Commission)

Kenniff Cave, in southern Queensland, which has rock paintings depicting hafted axes; the Miriwun Rock Shelter, East Kimberley; and Clogg's Cave and Conic Range Rock Shelter, both in Victoria, but ochre was also used for ceremonial purposes. Paintings frequently overlook deposits of later Stone Age date, as at Kenniff Cave, but this does not prove them coeval. Paintings of apparently dancing figures resembling in style those at Jacky's Creek occur at Moonbi, New England. Koonalda Cave, on the Nullarbor Plain in South Australia, has rock art thought to date back 20,000 years or more. It includes meandering grooves made by bare fingers on soft rock surfaces, apparently in darkness and closely paralleled by Palaeolithic art in Europe, including Altamira. The best organized work is a grid formed by sets of more or less parallel lines engraved at right angles to one another.

However, by far the best known are the Aboriginal paintings of probably late Neolithic to Bronze Age right up to the present. These are the *wondjina* figures found under overhangs in the northwest. They are crude, anthropomorphous, recumbent figures with round heads, eyes and a nose but no mouth, executed in red and yellow ochre, and with a white body. They have to do with the origin of the earth: the wondjinas personified rain. In north Kimberley, as part of 'All-Mother' lore, Wallanganda, the Milky Way,

84

dreamed a spiritual force which was projected as red, black and white images on the walls of the caves of the Unumbal. Almost equally well known now is Ayers Rock, in central Australia, a focal point for Aborigines and since recently for tourists. Rock art here includes a head with beams and geometric *tjurungas*.

Rock picture-galleries, dated at some 5000 BP, with paintings in ochre, charcoal and kaolin, are found at Oenpelli, Unbalania, Arnhem Land, north Australia, together with skeletons. One famous gallery is Bala-Uru, where there are spiny anteaters, spiders, large fish, tortoise, black bream, wallabies and huntsmen. There are other galleries at Kolondjorluk Creek, with its figure; Cannon Hill, with a serpent-headed Namarakain woman; and Nour-langie Rock, depicting a 'thunder-man' who created fearsome storms in order to frighten people. The Djingaloo Aborigines of Wessel Island and Elcho Island decorate their caves with paintings of their dream life and of tribal dances.

Navajo paintings at Blue Bell Cave, Canyon del Muerte, Arizona, USA. (David Noble)

New Zealand has hundreds of shallow limestone rock shelters where the Maoris, like the Polynesians, painted human figures, dogs, seals, birds, fish and canoes. Similar paintings are found in the Melanesian and Microneasian islands.

The Americas

Central Washington State has petroglyphs on rock overhangs and cliffs engraved by American Indians of unknown age. But the best-known region for American cave painting is the Desert southwest. Here, Anasazi art of Basketmaker age depicts human figures at Atlatl Cave, Chaco Canyon, New Mexico, and Painted Cave, Canyon de Chelly, Arizona. Navajo art is found in Blue Bell Cave, Canyon del Muerte, also in Arizona. The Indians of the Pecos River, Texas, had shamans who invoked the spirits of the hunt in their thousand-year-old cave paintings.

Finally, in Naj Tunich, a remote Maya cavern in the Guatemalan lowlands near the Belize border, the Mopan Maya recorded about a hundred paintings as well as petroglyphs, inscriptions and hieroglyphics, some of them mathematical, in about 800 AD. They include many glyphs in the long Passage of Rites, some of them on stalactites.

Artefacts

The study of the tools and other artefacts left by Stone-Age Man is the subject of a very considerable literature and is far outside the scope of this book. However, it might be useful to take a brief look at some of the manufactured objects mentioned in the early chapters of this book.

The first tools were known as *eoliths* and were pebbles, cobbles and other pieces of stone taken out of stream beds or from the open ground and found by pure accident of nature to have a shape or form that could be put to practical use. Breaking them open might have increased the chances of obtaining a sharp edge. Pieces of the other materials used by early man – bone, antler and ivory, shell and wood – would also have been employed. These were the artefacts left behind by the Upper Pliocene and Lower Pleistocene or Lower Palaeolithic people, *Australopithecus* and early *Homo habilis*, employing the Oldowan and early Acheulian cultures.

Soon, however, man began to appreciate that some types of rock were far more useful than others and to experiment on how to improve their usefulness. Cracking pebbles obliquely produced longer and sharper edges. Chipping would produce points and useful flakes. Flint was at the top of the list, a nodular rock consisting of the microcrystalline form of silica which occurs in bands in the Chalk. Chalk occurs mainly in eastern and southern England, France and Belgium, but flint is only a form of chert and other forms of this, as well as massive quartz, occur all over the world. A similar rock is obsidian, a fairly rare volcanic lava. These rock types all possess the property of fracturing conchoidally, after the Greek word for shell. Glass, made largely from silica, has the same property. A sharp direct blow on a chunk or slab of these rocks produces a solid cone which resembles a limpet-shell, while an oblique blow on its edge yields a flake or chip resembling a mussel-shell. The edge on the flake could be improved by later chipping or dressing, known as retouching. If a pebble was flaked all round, in two directions, it developed two faces and was known as bifacial. The art of splitting or flaking flint, by direct percussion, indirect percussion perhaps using a bone punch or – most sophisticated method of all – pressure-flaking, is called 'knapping'; this art reached a high peak at the flint mines of Grimes Graves at Weeting, near Thetford, in Norfolk, where the necessary skills have been and are being rediscovered. Later Stone-Age Man discovered that heating the flint or chert improved its knapping qualities. In nature, large variations in temperature caused chert and flint to flake, as did frost which caused the water in joints and fissures to freeze and expand. These processes produced the flake-like eoliths. Other siliceous rocks which lack the conchoidal fracture but can be chipped into a desired shape are quartzite, sarsen stone and silcrete, a natural siliceous superficial concrete. Quartzite, especially, is widespread and was thus available for tools; other rocks, mainly volcanic lavas, would be used when nothing better presented itself.

Stone was needed for hammerstones, choppers, end- and side-scrapers, hand-axes, blades and microblades, knives, burins or pointed tools, spearheads and arrowheads, fishing weights and plummets, twist drills and 'celts'. This last term covers the hafted tools, such as axes, adzes or hoes, wielded by a shaft, and in their case toughness might be more important than mere hardness. These tools would be produced by rubbing, grinding and polishing rather than by flaking or chipping. The study of stone artefacts in England has revealed a number of interesting and surprising facts. Tools made of some rock types seem to have been traded mainly from centres far from their sources. Green rocks appear to have been particularly popular for battle axes and mace heads. Ceremonial axe-heads, such as a chief might carry, were made for preference from jadeite, a rare rock lacking from Britain and thought to have been imported – presumably at considerable effort – from the north Italian Alps.

Wood was used for spears, digging sticks, spearthrowers and needles, and later for bowls and shields. They would have been fashioned using stone blades and spoke-shaves; nearly all the Palaeolithic wooden implements have decayed and knowledge of them derives largely from the use present-day Aboriginals in Australia and some Pacific islands still make of wood.

Bone, antler and ivory were material for needles, awls, fish hooks, some with barbs, and harpoons, discs and beads, and a variety of other decorative objects. Shell was for beads and decoration but in some tropical islands, where rock was scarce or absent, hard shell has been used for making tools.

Only in the Desert region of the southwest United States was the arid and desiccated atmosphere in caves and at other sites capable of preserving from decay the other major type of artefact, made from fibrous materials and including textiles, a wide variety of basketry, cordage, matting, sandals, duck decoys and split-twig figures.

The Stone-Age cultures, referred to in the early chapters in this book, usually had associated industries, the name given to the assemblage or set of artefacts used by that group of people whose entire way of life made up the culture. As already mentioned, the oldest culture was the Oldowan, named after the German name for the Olduvai gorge in Tanzania. Their pebble industry included cobble hammerstones and anvil-stones which they used to trim other cobbles and flakes into scrapers. Their later tools were bifacial hand-axes. The succeeding Acheulian hand-axe culture was the oldest known from Europe, about half a million years ago, and was also widespread in Africa. The Acheulians merged into the Mousterians, who developed the first of the early blade cultures, that of Neanderthal Man. Soon after originating in Africa, man spread into Asia and developed along different lines, resulting for example in the chopper-tool culture found at Zhoukoudian. Early flake-tool cultures developed in Europe and are usually known as Clactonian; these were employed by the first inhabitants of Great Britain. Where the Clactonian flake-tool industry mingled with the Mousterian hand-axes, another culture named Levalloisian developed; they produced a type of tool known as the tortoise-core, after the resemblance between their flint cores used for producing flakes and inverted tortoise-shells. In this way flakes could be produced from flint nodules, as well as disks, that could be used directly as hunting implements without retouching. Following the Mousterian Neanderthal people, the Upper Palaeolithic cultures, starting with the Aurignacians and continuing with the Cro-Magnon, developed blade-tools of increasing sophistication, including improved blades, knives, saws, drills and the burins or gravers which they used for their bone and cave engravings. Along with bone and antler tools, a wide range of projectile points was developed in the late Palaeolithic. In Gravettian times came the proto-Solutrean point which developed into the Solutrean pressure-flaked 'willow-leaf' point and bifacial foliate 'laurel-leaf' blade. The Magdalenian culture produced beautiful barbed antler spears and harpoons; in Britain the Creswellian culture was of the same age. The Still Bay culture in southern Africa produced a point from a pointed flake with a faceted butt. And in North America the laurel-leaf point was followed by the Sandia, fluted Sandia, fluted Clovis or Llano, Folsom and Plano points.

In the Mesolithic, in cultures such as the Azilian, came microliths, some geometric in trapezoid or triangular shapes, some non-geometric. These were tiny blades, saw-knives and points of ever decreasing size. In western Asia microliths formed part of the Oranian and Capsian cultures. There were still hunters, using hafted stone axes for wood working, but the Mesolithic and finally the Neolithic were largely the times of the first serious agriculturists and fishermen. They required an entirely new style of tool, which they made largely from wood, bone and antler. There were antler sickles, with flint teeth; adzes incorporating stone blade, wooden handle and antler sleeve; digging sticks and saddle querns; as well as bone fish-spears, with microlith barbs; and red deer antler barbed points.

The most recent of artefacts include the wealth of ceramics – earthenware and other pottery – and the variety of articles preserved in the Desert region of the southwest United States. Notable among these are the textiles and fibrous items such as cordage, matting and sandals, duck decoys and split-twig figures. Lastly, there are five types of basketry known from prehistoric sites, including Big Bend and Goat Caves in southwest Texas, as well as modern Indian localities, and named after some of them. The Southwestern type is mostly coiled, made now by the Navajo, Ute, Apache, Havasupai, Pima and Papago. The ancient coiled basketry of the Zuñi, Sia, Hopi and Santa Ana resembles the Basketmaker-Cliff dweller type. The Ozark Bluff dweller had checker and twilling as well as coiled types, now made in the Basin and Plains areas. Lovelock basketry was coiled but there was some twining and wicker; it now comes from the north California-Puget Sound area and central California. Snake River produced coiled and twining, now practised in the Salish and Sahaptin area. Lastly, the California Cave coiled type is now made in southern California.

CHAPTER 6

The late comers

The cave dwellers of Japan, Australia and America are described in this chapter. To call them 'late comers' is probably true, certainly in the case of Japan and America, but new finds in Australia are continually putting the clock back, perhaps to as far as 100,000 years BP.

Japan and Australasia

There are some three hundred caves and rock shelters in Japan, in limestone and sandstone, as well as countless open-air sites. Most are in Honshu, although thirty-five are in Hokkaido. Four are Palaeolithic, with ages older than 12,000 BP, the oldest being 32,000 BP. The majority of caves are Jomon, with ages ranging from 9000 to 2300 years BP, or Yayoi, from 300 BC to 300 AD. The Palaeolithic caves contain obsidian microblades and microcores, more tools of andesite and other material, and pottery, together with bones and evidence of human and dog burials. At 12,000 BP, one earthenware shard from the south is the oldest known fragment of pottery. There are some petroglyphs; the limestone Kami-kuroiwa Rock Shelter, in Ehime Prefecture, Shikoku Island, contains various artefacts of around 12,200 BP, including seven incised pebbles of chlorite schist portraying abstract human figures.

Until recently, it was thought that man first arrived in the Northern Territory of Australia in around 22,000 BP, across a narrow land bridge from Asia. Now it seems possible that the ancestral Aborigines were established, and 'dreamtime' had begun, at least 60,000 years ago and perhaps as far back as 100,000 BP.

The best known of Australia's caves is Devil's Lair, three miles inland from the southwestern corner of Western Australia. It is a single chambered limestone cave of some 800 square feet, with deposits overlying its sandy floor, capped by a carbonate flowstone, up to a foot thick, spanning 20,000 years. It was first recognized as having been occupied by human beings in

the late 1960s, when Duncan Merrilees, palaeontologist in the Western
Australian Museum, found a human tooth. Subsequently, his colleague
Charles Dortch has made an extensive study of the cave. It was occupied by
Aborigines from about 30,000 until between 12,000 and 6000 BP, probably
used as a winter camp over the last 16,000 years. Artefacts found there include
scrapers, choppers and adzes, made of chert, calcrete, quartz and limestone,
but no grindstones. There was a perforated object made of marl, dated at
14,000 BP, and an incised limestone plaque dated at between 20 and 12,000 BP,
as well as bone points and bodkins, and beads. The people ate kangaroos and
wallabies, small mammals and reptiles, as well as emu eggs and freshwater
mussels. An unusual cave eight miles north of Devil's Lair is Mammoth Cave,
which contained extinct marsupial bones and charred bones dated at 37,000 BP.
Also in the southwest are Wilgie Mia and Koonalda Cave, a sink-hole used
as a flint quarry.

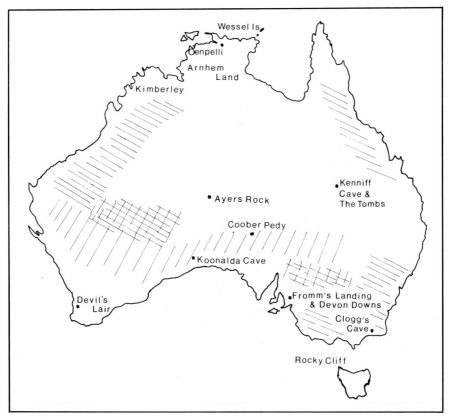

Map of Australia showing the approximate locations of some caves and places mentioned in
the text. Areas with naturalistic rock art are shown \\\; with linear and geometric art ///; and
with mixed art by crosshatching.

Next best known, perhaps, is Kenniff Cave, as well as The Tombs and many smaller caves, including the Cathedral Cave just to the southeast, on the Moffat Cattle Station, 150 miles northeast of Charleville in southern Queensland. Man may have lived in Kenniff around 13,000 BP, using ochre for decorating the walls. Frequently depicted are hafted stone axes. The commonest tools here are scrapers and various flakes, as well as bone pointed bodkins such as are known from Devil's Lair. Man then ceased to live there until 7000 BP, when the cave was reoccupied. The Tombs is a rock face with a cave and an adjacent rock shelter, occupied from about 9500 BP and also containing many decorations on the walls.

Malangangerr Rock Shelter, on the coastal plain of Arnhem Land, Northern Territory, has lenses of shell, bone, ash and charcoal, with a shell midden between one and three feet deep, as well as scrapers, flakes and edge-ground axes. These are dated at about 25 to 18,000 BP. The upper layers with points, rectangular scrapers and edge-ground axes range from about 6000 BP to 1900 AD. Other caves in the Northern Territory include Oenpelli, Kintore and Ingaladdi, and there are rock shelters at Burrill Lake, Miriwun, near East Kimberley.

Fromm's Landing Cave and, ten miles away, Devon Downs, both on the Lower Murray River near Adelaide, in South Australia, have a number of stratified hearths and layers showing various periods of occupation, the artefacts including pirri points; they are dated from 4850 to 3240 BP. Devon Downs Cave has more pirri points, dated at 4290 BP. There are Strong's Cave, and Mungo, Mount Burr, Clogg's Cave and Glen Aire in the southeast corner; and Seelands, on the coast of northern New South Wales.

Tasmania had a land bridge to the mainland in 8000 BP, the oldest date from the coastal cave of Rocky Cliff. Its occupants lived off the sea, on fish, shellfish and seals until about 4000 BP, when they turned away from seals towards marsupials and birds. Sisters' Creek is near Rocky Cliff, and there is

Ayers Rock, Australia. (Australian Tourist Commission)

Fraser Cave, in the southwest, dated at 20 to 15,000 BP and resembling Devil's Lair in the way of life of its occupants. Cave Bay Cave is on Hunter Island, off the north coast.

But whenever Stone-Age Man actually arrived in Australia, he survived until the arrival of the first Europeans – or perhaps until the present, as Ayers Rock, the Dead Centre of Australia, amply illustrates. There are many hundreds of shallow rock shelters in the limestone formations of New Zealand, and rock shelters at Kiowa, in the eastern highlands of New Guinea, dating back to about 10,500 BP, and Yuku, in the western highlands.

The Americas

A land bridge of the greatest importance linked Siberia and Alaska across the Bering Straits during the last glacial period. Some people believe that the earliest occupants, belonging to the pre-projectile industrial tradition of Asia, arrived between 40,000 and 20,000 years BP, probably post-37,000 BP. The land bridge was there, with no ice barrier, between 26 and 20,000, or between 12 and about 11,000 BP. But whenever man arrived in the western hemisphere, he certainly came from Asia, a conclusion supported by the great similarities between the Siberian and Alaskan cultures. It was not thought to be a major migration but more of a general 'coming and going'; there was plenty of game and a climate that was no worse and possibly better than it is now. Some of the best evidence comes from fire hearths found in Texas and dated at some 37,000 years ago.

A chronology has been developed based on the design of points, projectiles or spearheads, as they are variously called, which marked a major development in man's history in the west. The oldest and simplest of this type of artefact is the laurel leaf, dated at about 12,000 BP and matching those found in the Ust-Kanskaiya Cave in Siberia. The oldest chipped projectile point in America is thought to be the Sandia point, made with a barb or shoulder on one side only, and named after Sandia Cave, a 150-yard long tunnel in limestone, with an average width of ten feet, in Las Huertas Canyon, east of Albuquerque, New Mexico. Here the Sandia point represented the older of the two cultures found in the cave and is dated at between 20 and 10,000 BP. There were also the leaf-shaped Cascade point, from the northwest Pacific coast sites such as Cascade Mountain Cave, Oregon, and a refined or fluted Sandia point. Then came the Clovis fluted point, dated at about 11,000 BP, and the Llano point, to be followed by the beautifully regular spearhead called the Folsom point, with its smooth flutes on each face. They were found in a two-foot silt layer above the older band at Sandia, made by

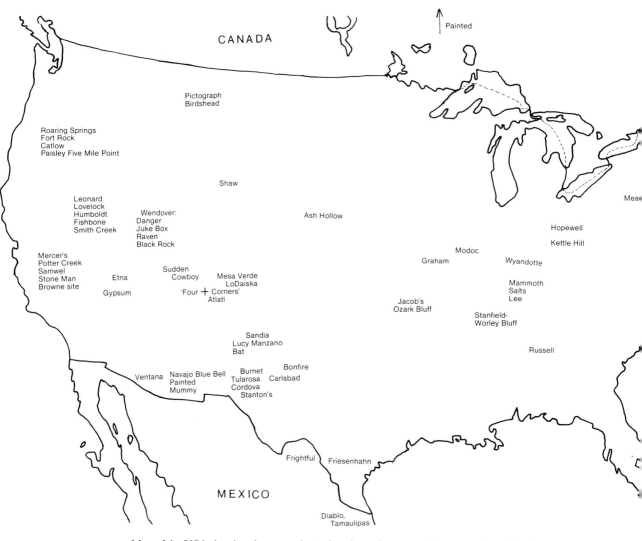

CANADA

Painted

Pictograph
Birdshead

Roaring Springs
Fort Rock
Catlow
Paisley Five Mile Point

Shaw

Meaс

Leonard
Lovelock
Humboldt
Fishbone
Smith Creek

Wendover:
Danger
Juke Box
Raven
Black Rock

Ash Hollow

Hopewell

Kettle Hill

Modoc

Graham

Wyandotte

Mercer's
Potter Creek
Samwel
Stone Man
Browne site

Etna

Gypsum

Sudden
Cowboy

Mesa Verde
LoDaiska

'Four + Corners'
Atlatl

Mammoth
Salts
Lee

Jacob's
Ozark Bluff

Stanfield-
Worley Bluff

Sandia
Lucy Manzano
Bat

Russell

Ventana

Navajo Blue Bell
Painted
Mummy

Burnet
Tularosa
Cordova
Stanton's

Bonfire
Carlsbad

Frightful

Friesenhahn

MEXICO

Diablo,
Tamaulipas

Map of the USA showing the approximate locations of caves and places mentioned in the text.

folk who lived about 11 to 9000 years ago, turning from hunting woolly mammoth to bison but also hunting camel and an extinct species of peccary. The final development was the Plano point. Other fluted points are found in northwest Canada, Mexico and central and south America, together with some unfluted types.

A simplified scheme refers only to three of these types. The Sandia point came first, overlapped by the Clovis which followed. The third, by far the most advanced culture, was Folsom.

Clearly, from 12,000 to 10,000 BP, man mushroomed in the Americas. The general term 'Early' period applies from the beginning to about 8000 BP; from then until 500 AD the term 'Archaic', which includes Woodland and Hopewell, is used. The Early people were range hunters, marked by the development of their projectile points. With the early Archaic, in the Neo-

94

thermal climate, came the beginnings of a way of life which continued until Colonial times. Remains found in the Russell Cave, Alabama, show how the people were adapting from hunting in the open to the forests; apart from the peccary, all their food animals still live there and comprise twenty-two mammals, nineteen amphibians and reptiles, thirteen birds, seventeen fish and fourteen molluscs. They mainly concentrated on whitetail deer, grey squirrel, turkey and box turtle, with freshwater mussels and snails. The middle Archaic brought in the domesticated dog – it was buried with people – and antler and bone tools, including barbed points and barbless fish hooks. They developed polished stone weights for the atlatl or throwing stick – a grooved board about two feet long used for throwing darts or lances; adze blades, both straight and hollow bladed; grooved axeheads; knife blades; and arrow heads made of ground slate. But they showed no evidence of any knowledge of metal working. Caves in Kentucky and Missouri show that around 4000 BP the sunflower had been domesticated, while the Jerusalem artichoke, marsh elder, goosefoot, pigweed and knot-grass were encouraged to grow. Numerous corn cobs are known from deposits at Hopewell.

In the Desert areas, there were very different conditions in the Great Basin between the Sierra Nevada and the Rockies, and to a lesser extent to the southwest and the Interior Plateau on the north. Conditions then were much as they are now. Needless to say, the inhabitants of these regions adapted their way of life accordingly, developing the Desert culture or tradition. Their story starts here and is continued in the next chapter.

The exceptionally arid conditions in some caves, such as Danger Cave, Utah; Roaring Springs and Fort Rock Caves, Oregon; Leonard Shelter, near Lovelock, and Gypsum Cave, both in Nevada; and Ventana Cave, Arizona, have led to the survival of many organic materials. As well as wooden objects and hair being preserved by desiccation, there were textiles, such as rabbit-fur cloth; baskets, which were first twined and then coiled; cordage, netting and matting; tumplines, which were used as a carrying device; sandals (from 9000 BP); and the atlatl. The people also left projectile points, darts, pointed shafts which were used without stone points, flat milling stones with cobble grinding stones, the digging stick, the fire drill and horn spoons. They were expert at flint work but also masters in the use of deer and antelope bones for tools and other artefacts. They chewed 'quid', obtained from the bullrush and other such fibres, which was the equivalent of chewing tobacco or gum. From about 10,000 BP they harvested, and then milled, small grains – some two thousand years earlier than in western Asia.

In northern Ontario there is the Painted Cave, home of the Ojibwa and early Algonkian Indians, decorated with bison and other animals, birds and humans. In the northwest of the United States, there are well-known caves in Montana, such as Pictograph and Birdshead; Wyoming, such as Shaw Cave, Platte County; and Nebraska, such as Ash Hollow Cave. Oregon has a series of caves and rock shelters in the pumice stone thrown out by Mount Mazama, where Crater Lake now fills the old crater, and Newberry Crater. They include Catlow Cave, Harney County, a large rock shelter; Paisley Five Mile Point Caves; Fort Rock and Roaring Springs Caves, where lanceolate points dated at before 13,000 BP have been found. They had woven sandals and fine twisted basketry in about 9000 BP. It is interesting that Mazama has been dated at about 6000 to 7500 BP but Newberry has a date of 2054 BP.

Fort Rock was one of the first of the Desert culture caves, leading to Danger Cave and the other two Wendover caves in Utah, Ventana Cave in Arizona, and Lake Texcoco, in Mexico. These were 'usufructian' caves, dating from about 11,000 or 10,500 BP, the term referring to the temporary possession of other people's property or land without harming it.

There are notable examples of Desert caves in Nevada. Fishbone Cave is one of seven in the Lake Winnemucca area of Nevada. It contained artefacts of perishable material, such as netting, matting and baskets, as well as a bone awl and stone tools. It is dated at around 11,000 BP. Smith Creek Cave has occupation floors dating from 12 or 10,000 BP. Gypsum Cave is a large limestone cave, 300 feet long and up to 120 feet wide, with five connecting chambers, sixteen miles east of Las Vegas. It was occupied by the giant ground sloth, its dung dating from 10,500 BP. Many stone dart-points and unusual basketry were found, dating from the human occupation of the cave from 9500 to 7500 BP. Leonard Rock Shelter, seventeen miles south of Lovelock, near the Humboldt Lake Basin, as well as the Lovelock and Humboldt Caves, contained atlatls and shell beads, mixed in with the bat guano, as well as cordage nets. Their dates averaged 7500 BP. Etna Cave, Caliente, was like Gypsum Cave. It contained projectile points, a mano, a worked crystal, a stone knife, two sandals, and four animal effigies made from split twigs, the split bits wrapped round and round themselves. Much later the cave was occupied by Basketmaker and Pueblo people, described in the next chapter.

Danger Cave, one mile from Wendover, on the western edge of Bonneville Salt Flats and just to the east of the Nevada border, is very important and the largest and richest as well as the best known of the Utah caves centred on Wendover. They are all in Palaeozoic limestone, with loess covered floors, and were excavated by J.D. Jennings. Danger Cave has 14 feet of stratified deposits which have yielded some 2500 chipped-stone artefacts, more than a thousand grinding stone fragments and many pieces of netting, mats and basketry. There are also objects made of wood, hide, bone and shell. The bones of food animals include those of mountain sheep, deer and antelope,

Danger Cave, Utah, USA. (Werner Forman Archive)

but there were no bones of extinct animals. The lowest layer was lake beach sand, followed by a layer dated at around 11,500 to 10,500 BP. The next contained bat guano, dated at nearly 10,000 to 9000 BP. There are no dates for the next layer but the following one gave 3819 BP. The final layers had dates down to 20 AD. Juke Box Cave is two and a half miles northeast of Wendover, with its black stylized paintings; twenty-five miles north of the town is Raven Cave. Other Utah caves are Black Rock, Deadman and Promontory. One of the two other major caves is Sudden Shelter, some 180 miles southeast of Danger Cave. This was a seasonal shelter or base camp, containing many stone projectiles, scrapers and other tools as well as bone and antler implements. It was occupied from about 8400 to 7250 BP, when artefact production increased until about 6500 BP; after this it was used on a lesser scale until about 4600 BP. Sudden is noted for some very good rock- and slab-lined fire pits. The last is Cowboy Cave, some 60 miles southeast of Sudden Shelter; together with Walters Cave, the three have yielded similar dates. Cowboy had many projectiles as well as fibre work, baskets, sandals, reed and bent twig figurines, worked wood, bone and shell ornaments, hairbrushes, hides and furs, animal skin bags, spindle whorls, clay objects and decorated pieces of stone. Its occupants certainly did not want for talent.

California has caves, containing bones and stone fragments, such as Mercer's, Potter Creek Cave, Samwel Cave and Stone Man Cave. There is also the famous Browne site. Colorado is best known for its cliff houses but there were occupied caves during early Pueblo times, such as Site 1205 on Mesa Verde, where corn, stone and bone artefacts and pottery were found; and also LoDaiska Cave.

One of the most famous of America's caves is Ventana Cave, in the Castle Mountains in the Papago Indian Reservation, some 75 miles south of Phoenix and west of Tucson, Arizona. Known as Papagueria, it is a large, very important rock shelter. The erosion of a mass of agglomerate at the base of a cliff, assisted by the protection of the overlying basalt, resulted in an overhang some 180 feet long. This is divided by a natural basalt 'wall' into two spaces: the northeast or 'lower' and the southwest or 'upper', the latter having a spring in it. Only this was occupied by man and by now extinct animals. It has a thick midden, which has revealed that the cave was occupied from about 11,500 BP until about 1400 AD. The Ventana complex was followed by the Amargosa and San Pedro up to 1 AD; then came the Hohokam and finally, in 1400 AD, the Papago, down to 1700 AD. The artefacts are crude because they are made from basalt – a difficult medium to work. They include grinding stones, showing the mixed diet of the people, adapted to a wide variety of vegetable foods, but also including marine shellfish, showing a link with the coast. The mammal bones were relatively few and mainly small; they included those of the wolf, jaguar, ground sloth, tapir and horse. The upper layers of the midden have grinding stones and pottery fragments, with an oldest date apparently less than 4000 BP. In northern New Mexico is Sandia Cave, near Albuquerque, which gave its name to the first of the three major point cultures. Famous also is Bat Cave, at the southwestern end of the Plains of San Augustin, between Magdaleña and Datil, a large amphitheatre-like rock shelter. Many artefacts have been found here, including more than four hundred projectile points, some of them of a type which has been named after the cave. They resembled those found in Manzano Cave in the Manzano Mountains, south of Sandia Cave, and in Gypsum Cave, Nevada. There is also pottery of the Mogollon type, described in the next chapter. However, Bat Cave, which should not be confused with the Bat Cave in Nevada, uninhabited but mined for bat guano, is most notable for the major discovery of corn near the base of Bed III, dated at around 5000 or 6000 BP. This is thought to be the earliest example of maize known, even older than the Mexican finds. It was very primitive, with both pop corn and pod corn, and the ear not enclosed in husks. The upper bed has examples of maize showing a progressive evolutionary increase in size of both cob and kernels. Tularosa Cave also had pod corn as well as more evolved types, and it too was occupied by Mogollon people. A similar cave was Cordova. Burnet Cave is a dry cave in the Guadalupe Mountains, 32 miles west of Carlsbad, which contained human cremations in baskets and twined woven bags; atlatl fragments; sandals;

ABOVE: Tularosa Cave, New Mexico, USA. BELOW: Cordova Cave, New Mexico, USA. (By courtesy of the Field Museum of Natural History, nos A93204, A93512, Chicago)

cordage and a projectile point, but no corn or pottery. There were caribou, musk-ox and marmot bones and the remains were dated at around 7500 BP. Over one hundred and thirty-five excellent Archaic split-twig figurines were found in Stanton's Cave, Marble Canyon.

The Friesenhahn Cave, Texas, has yielded the remains of pre-projectile, pre-Palaeo-Indian people, who used non-pointed and heavy choppers, scrapers and hammerstones. This is therefore one of the oldest caves in the USA, like Sandia probably well in excess of 12,000 BP. The Levi Rock Shelter is associated with the remains of mammoth, horse, sloth, camel, giant bison, tapir, dire wolf, glyptodon and mastodon. There is the Bonfire Shelter, of some 10,000 BP, and caves in the Hueco Mountains in western Texas contained ancient mats, baskets, and woven cloth garments, together with many tools for cleaning animal skins and for cooking, grinding and hunting. These show an advanced culture dating back to about 5000 BP.

Another possible Early cave is Jacob's Cavern in southwestern Missouri, containing a carved deer humerus dating perhaps to 14,000 BP. The carving was once thought to represent a mastodon but is not now considered authentic. Graham Cave, just north of the confluence of the Loutre and Missouri Rivers, is 80 feet wide and 60 feet deep. Most of the deposits are Archaic, from 8000 to 3000 BP, but some are older. A fireplace has been radiocarbon dated at 9700 BP and there are other dates back to 8000 BP. There is another interesting cave in Callaway County.

The Modoc Rock Shelter, on the Mississippi flood plain in Randolph County, Illinois, is between Modoc and Prairie du Rocher. It has been dated at about 11,000 BP, the same as the Barbeau Creek Rock Shelter. The Modoc was occupied from before 10 until after 4000 BP and there are thought to have been three phases: initial or Early occupation from about 10,000 to 9000 BP; local Archaic adaptation from 9000 to 5500, especially from 6000 BP; and specialized adaptation from 5500 to 4000 BP. In the last phase it became a seasonal autumn and winter home base, the occupants concentrating on hunting deer and waterfowl, with more projectile points than domestic or manufacturing tools.

Mammoth Cave, Kentucky, has already been mentioned as the longest cave system in the world. As well as being a major show cave, it is of great anthropological interest. Palaeo-Indian remains and artefacts have been found all round within a three mile radius from the cave entrance. Mammoth Cave has a Vestibule, the entrance area which was used as a camping site, where a complete split-cane basket was found. In 1875 explorers found an Indian 'mummy', a young woman whom they christened 'Little Alice', in Salts Cave, within the Mammoth Cave National Park, where it had dried out in the desiccated atmosphere. No pottery was found but there were gourds and mussel-shell spoons. The people who lived here used bark fibre, grasses and other stringy plants to weave fabrics for clothing, including moccasins. For torches they used reeds and the dried stalks of weeds such as still grow on the banks of the Green River, near Mammoth Cave. Armed with these, they ventured far into both Salts and Mammoth Caves to chip off and carry out the thin crusts of gypsum and other sulphate minerals; the marks of their activities are still there. Then in 1935 two cave guides found another Indian 'mummy', in Mammoth Cave, this time a middle-aged man trapped some two miles in from the entrance where a huge slab had fallen on him while he was chipping sulphate.

More radiocarbon dates made in 1957 show that the early Woodland Indians continued to live and work in Salts and Mammoth Caves from around 4000 BP down to between 420 and 280 BC. Mining took place mainly from late autumn to spring. The miners broke off gypsum, which they probably used to make white body paint, as well as mirabilite, which is salty, and epsomite, which is bitter, both for food seasoning and also, probably, because they are cathartic. All three minerals – and possibly others – may in addition have been thought to possess magic powers and they seem to have been traded widely with distant tribes for some 2000 years. Lee Cave, with the oldest dates of the group, was also mined. Pack rats lived here, as they did in Bluff Cave.

The Woodland people also worked epsomite in Wyandotte Cave, southern Indiana, 75 miles north of Mammoth Cave. The rock shelters of east Kentucky and south Ohio and the Ozark Bluff shelters of northwest Arkansas and southwest Missouri show similarities. As well as Mammoth and Salts, Kettle Hill Cave in southern Ohio has a 'mummy', found wrapped in a woven fabric shroud. In this cave were projectiles, scrapers, pottery, fabrics, corn cobs, pumpkins and gourds.

In the northeast, an inhabited cave near the rock shelter nine miles from Lake Champlain, in Vermont, contained artefacts. The Meadowcroft Rock Shelter in Pennsylvania contained carbonized plaited basketry fragments in its oldest layer, which were dated at 19,600 BP. Further south, there is the Stanfield-Worley Bluff shelter in western Tennessee, and in northeast Alabama, the Russell Cave, near Bridgeport, which was occupied from 10,000 BP until 1650 AD. Folsom tools, dating from 10,000 BP, were found in both caves to mark the end of the Palaeo-Indians, followed in Russell Cave by Archaic artefacts down to Woodland and Mississippian times. As well as bones, there were chert and quartz spears and projectiles, and abundant bone fish hooks, pins, awls or needles, necklaces, rings and lamps.

Well-known Mexican caves are Frightful, near the border with Texas, and the 9000 BP Diablo Cave, in Tamaulipas, and there are others at La Venta,

The entrance to the Cave of Hands can be seen at the base of this outcrop in the Chile Chico region of southern Chile. (Operation Raleigh Promotions Ltd)

better known for its Olmec colossal heads, which were occupied by pottery-making Indians.

Naj Tunich, in the remote lowlands of Guatemala, near the Belize border, is a superb, recently discovered, Maya cave. It is rich in artefacts and paintings, of which there are about a hundred, as well as petroglyphs. It was a sacred site for the Mopan Mayas, the abode of the underworld gods, used from perhaps 100 BC to 900 AD. There are signs of child sacrifice, ritual blood letting and intercourse. These are huge caves; there is an entrance hall nearly 500 feet wide and 100 feet deep, followed by a tunnel, the Passage of Rites, some 50 feet in diameter, which is nearly 1000 feet long before it divides into two. Here are many of the glyphs, some of them on stalactites. There is a pool of standing water and a second, empty pool. Needles, pottery, jade masks and other artefacts were found.

In the West Indies, eastern Santo Domingo (now the Dominican Republic), has pre-Columbian limestone caves which contained pottery and other artefacts, especially on Saona, an island off the southeast coast, and Salado, on the northeast coast. There are others in Haiti, with many legends attached to them; Cuba; Puerto Rico; and rock shelters in the Netherlands Lesser Antilles where there are petroglyphs.

There are caves and rock shelters on the Planalto in northern Brazil dating from 32,000 to 11,000 BP, one of the oldest being at Boqueirao do sitio da Pedra Furada. Large mammals are thought to have persisted until quite late in this region, and their bones are found mixed up with artefacts. In the Peruvian highlands, Guitarrero Cave contained lanceolate points dating from 12,000 BP. In the Andes, the Lauricocha caves were occupied in Neothermal times and fluted points were found in caves in Ecuador and Bolivia.

The famous Intihuasi Cave in northwestern Argentina was occupied by people who by 8000 BP were selectively gathering wild plants like acorns, piñon, grass seeds, edible roots and berries. These wandering bands of gatherers turned to shellfish along the shores as many of the mammals died out and, having discovered their palatability, left vast shell middens. The Cave of Hands in the Chile Chico region of Chile has wall paintings, many more than 8000 years old. Helped in 1986 by participants in Operation Raleigh, the cave is being reproduced for the Chilean Natural History Museum. The two most southern of the major caves in the Americas are also two of the most important. At the tail end of mainland Chile, just north of the Straits of Magellan, are Palli Aike and Fell's Caves. Here were found skeletons which have given radiocarbon ages of 9000 to 7000 BP, together with fluted and fish-tailed projectile points, dated at 11,000 to 10,000 BP, as well as the more primitive leaf-shaped points. The fish-tailed type are not found in North America north of Panama and Nicaragua. These Pampean people, living in Neothermal times, had guanaco as their main food source, using lances with bifacial triangular or square-ended lanceolate heads to hunt the animal. They also used grooved bolas stones, such as are still employed there, as an ancillary weapon.

CHAPTER 7

The Four Corners: pit dwellings, cliff dwellings and pueblos

T he Four Corners area of the Desert region of southwest USA –
where the states of Utah, Colorado, New Mexico and Arizona meet –
is the location of a remarkable development of rock dwellings. Man
came late, as we have seen, to North America and, as in other parts of the
world, he occupied caves. Many were open, natural caves, only slightly, if at
all enlarged, others were wholly artificial, excavated from the cliff face. Still
others were half-and-half: usually only stores and burial crypts were hewn
out of the rock at the rear while dwellings were constructed in front. Some
5000 years ago primitive farming spread from Mexico, where for the previous
5000 years or so folk who had earlier been foragers had learned to domesticate
the three staples – wild beans, squash and corn – to the Indians of Arizona
and New Mexico. As now, the land was very poor and there were few game
animals: only small mammals and nuts were available for food, encouraging
people to settle and take to farming. So, by 3000 BC, the Bat Cave people of
New Mexico were raising primitive corn, and it started to revolutionize their
life. This wild corn, now extinct, had cobs about one inch long with only a
few dozen kernels, with miniature ears and no tight husks to protect them
from birds and rats. Improving the strain was very slow, compounded by the
major problem of water: the only rain came from summer thunderstorms. So
they dammed streams, to conserve water, and improved their tools. By 300 BC
they had developed the first villages, the beginning of community dwelling,
in the valleys of the Mogollon Mountain range in western New Mexico.

The first settlers took their name from this range and Mogollon were
probably the ancestors of the present-day Zuñi Indians. They lived in the
region from 2100 BC to 1350 AD, their development being measured in five
phases. Their villages consisted of a few dozen pit-houses, a concept derived
from natural caves. The pit-houses were roughly circular or rectangular
excavations, two to three feet deep, with ramps leading down to the rough
floor, with overhead a superstructure consisting of a framework of stout posts
which could support a roof of poles, cross-laid with saplings, with interwoven
reeds and, probably, mud plaster on top to keep out all but the worst

rain storms. They were mainly round but also D-shaped, kidney-shaped or rectangular, the latter being the latest development. The earth pits helped to keep the houses cool in summer temperatures of over 38° C (100° F) – just as the kangaroo rats retreat to holes and burrows to keep cool – and also to keep them warm during the near freezing nights. The best known is the Pooit of Pines settlement in Arizona, near the New Mexico border, with some two hundred sites.

Neighbours of the Mogollon to the west in Arizona, since 1900 BC, were the Hohokam, also pit-house builders, the probable ancestors of the Pima and Papago tribes. By about 100 BC they had developed crude irrigation schemes, using dams, canals and ditches, to control and conserve flood water. This permitted the growth of larger communities. Their dwellings were large rectangular buildings, some of them true pit-houses, but later the pits became shallower so that the houses became, more literally, houses in a pit. Compared with the Mogollon, they had more elaborate ball courts and pyramid-like

Map of the Four Corners area, USA, showing the important sites and areas mentioned in the text.

mounds; the ball courts were used for a game which resembled football crossed with volley ball, using a rubbery ball made from the coagulated juice of the *guayule* plant. Both courts and pyramids – and their pottery – resembled the more sophisticated versions developed by the Aztecs in Mexico, including the motif of a serpent attacking a bird still to be found in the Mexican flag. They continued to become more and more civilized, up to about 1000 AD, parallel with the development of the Mexicans further south, although the mountain barrier between them must have precluded any suggestion of influence. The Hohokam artists learned to etch shells with a weak acid, using a vinegar prepared from the fermented fruit of the saguaro cactus, centuries before Europe discovered etching; they then traded the shells with coastal Indians from California. But the Hohokam never spread beyond their valleys.

North of both Hohokam and Mogollon, the Anasazi or 'Ancient Ones' began to settle around zero AD; as they developed, stimulated by the Mogollon and Hohokam, they absorbed both the earlier cultures, although in their early phases they had no pottery. They were the most widespread Indian group, whose modern descendents include the Hopi, present-day Pueblo Indians whose day-to-day way of life is very like that of the Anasazi; indeed, the Navajo, in whose reserve the Hopi live, call them *Ayakhini* or people of the *kivas* or underground houses. *Kiva* is a Hopi word for the circular underground rooms still used by some southwestern tribes for ceremonial purposes and known as *estufas* in Spanish. They were always built on the lower floors, their flat roofs being used as living spaces above, from which trap doors led through the ceilings to the interiors of the *kivas* below. They were used for secret meetings of a religious or ceremonial nature, each religious society having its own *kiva*: they were never shared. They were all equipped with ventilators of some sort, whose shafts were once thought to be either chimneys, entrances or passage ways, or even to be used for ceremonial purposes. Also, they each had a *sipapu*, a small hole in the floor to provide access for the earth-living spirits, both good and evil. The Anasazi are chronicled through three Basketmaker (about 400 to 700 AD) and five Pueblo stages (700 to 1300 AD). For example, the basin houses of Durango and the pit-houses were Basketmaker II, the fabled Pueblo Bonito was late Pueblo II, and the cliff dwellings of Cliff Palace in *Mesa Verde* (green table in Spanish), Chaco Canyon, Canyon de Chelly and southwest Utah were 'Classic' Pueblo III, of about 1100 AD. It was the Anasazi who first built the famous adobe apartment houses of the Four Corners region. The most spectacular are the cliff dwellings built into natural clefts high up steep canyon walls, as in Mesa Verde National Park, southwest Colorado, which they reached using toe holds carved in the cliffs. They are still in almost livable condition, even though the last inhabitants left 650 years ago. They also developed the multi-storeyed *pueblo*, meaning in Spanish town or village, which reached its zenith at Pueblo Bonito, in the River Chaco valley in New Mexico.

It is generally considered that natural caves and rock shelters led to the pit-houses and the pueblos and cliff dwellings grew out of these. Here chance played a part, for only in exceptionally arid areas, such as the Desert region of the southwest United States, much of Africa, and parts of Europe and Asia are there large and open enough caves to permit the building of cliff dwellings. Wherever there were suitable overhangs, such dwellings developed and the Four Corners shows this at its height. Fewkes compared the early North American caves and pit-houses with Matmata, and the later cliff dwellings and pueblos (especially the Hopi pueblo at Oraibi) with Médenine, Tunisia. He considered the changeover may have been due to congestion and the need for expansion.

The Anasazi had better farming country, needing less irrigation, than the Mogollon. It was mesa plateau country, containing some of the southwest's highest mountains, all good for the generation of rain. At first they built simple dome-shaped structures that, unlike the pit-houses of the Mogollon and Hohokam, were built around shallow depressions in the ground. They laid concentric layers of logs in a form of rail-fence arrangement, cemented with mud mortar. They lacked the normally essential fireplace, apparently heating stones outside and laying them in a pit in the floor; this may have been to reduce the risk of fire. But a few centuries later they turned to more conventional pit-houses, with a conventional central fire pit and a hole in the roof for the smoke. These had stone slabs arranged as a screen to deflect the wind from the fire.

Around 900 AD they started building pueblos, multi-chambered community houses on the flat mesa tops and in the valleys, with no cave component. The origin of these is unknown; they were like nothing in North America and not much like anything in Mexico. They were 'towns'; the biggest of the 'great houses', Pueblo Bonito, was built over the period 900 to 1100 AD. One storey tall at the centre, it rose to four along the curved rear wall and had more than 800 rooms and 30 *kivas*, arranged like a huge 'D' around twin plazas which were used for dances and similar events. The *kivas*, all on the lower floor, measured up to 20 feet in diameter. Twelve hundred families probably lived here. The smaller pueblos were like modular cube buildings. These had circular, semi-underground pit chambers, entered through an opening in the mud roof, which were the prototypes of the *kivas*.

What inspired the pueblo? Perhaps a lack of wood for building and an abundance of stone and adobe bricks, made of earth or clay and straw and sun dried. They were usually rectangular or tabular in shape, but earlier versions were cubical, with hand-rounded corners and no straw, ashes or charcoal being used instead. A third type, also in early use, were hand-rolled round bundles of twigs, with no corners or angles. Sometimes walls were constructed on the *jacal* method: rows of upright sticks supported the wall, with woven osiers, tied together, between them, to hold the clay or adobe plastering in place. For security, they could pull up a ladder behind them and become totally safe. Certainly security was the reason for the cliff dwellings, with access along precipitous trails, often including cliff climbs using only the toe holds. Cliff Palace in Mesa Verde sits in one huge sandstone cave, 325 feet long and 90 feet deep, with an arched roof reaching a maximum of 60 feet. From the cave to the mesa above is 100 feet, and down to the canyon floor below, 700 feet. Some villages were terraced, the terraces being some 30 feet wide, with houses built of blocks of sandstone, detached by the action of frost and water, together with mortar made from muddy clay; their rear walls would be up against the rock at the back of the cave. In front protruded the ladders from half a dozen sunken *kivas*. A lower terrace acted as a plaza, sloping down to an area used as a burial ground and rubbish tip where domesticated turkeys foraged.

Above, on the mesa, were the small fields, half an acre or so, reached by paths which were often mere toe holds, where corn or maize was grown along with low bean bushes and squash vines – pumpkin and crookneck – and also sunflowers for the edible oily seeds. They seem to have cultivated the miners' or Indian lettuce and also beeweed or bee balm, which was good for turkeys as well as humans and vanished with the Anasazi; it is related to the caper. Some piñon and juniper remained of the original forest cover, as it still does, growing in the red dusty soil. Rain averaged some eighteen inches per year, sparse but quite adequate for dry farming.

The villagers were short, stocky Indians, brown-skinned, with black hair, prominent cheek bones and slant eyes, very much like present-day Pueblo Indians such as the Hopis. Women were very important, since this was a matrilineal society for lineage and property. When a boy married he moved into his bride's house and the children belonged to the mother's social clan. While the young men hunted deer with bow and arrows, the girls and unmarried young men fetched water. This became a courting ritual: he would ask her for a drink and if she said 'yes', it also signified virtual agreement to a proposal of marriage.

A family house would perhaps have had five rooms, the largest, say, 8 feet by 10 feet, being the living-sleeping-dining-working area, with a fire pit in the centre of the floor. Disused rooms may have been converted into latrines. The family slept on mats of yucca fibre, rabbit skin or turkey down. There were pegs on the walls for hanging up bows and flint-tipped arrows, nets and snares. Three small rooms would have been stores, full of corn cobs, beans, squash, wild pigweed and goosefoot, much of it dried. The family wore loin cloths under a type of kilt, loose cotton tops, their feet bare or encased in simple rush sandals. They had polished stone tools and, in the later phases, pottery, but no metal: this was a Neolithic culture. They ground corn with small, cylindrical rubbing stones, *manos*, on large slanting grinding slabs fixed on upright stones, the *metates*. The staple diet was the *taco*: thin-rolled corn meal cakes baked on hot stones. With these, they ate – from the communal family pot – roasts or stews of turkey, venison, grouse or rabbit, with green beans and hominy (steeped corn kernels), all seasoned with mint, bee balm and wild onion, and salt from a nearby brackish lake. For a treat, they had piñon nuts, dried or toasted squash, and sunflower seeds; for a drink, a cordial made of sumac berry juice sweetened with prickly pear juice. They ate no fish: there were many trout in the streams but to catch them – let alone eat them – would be to offend the rain and water spirits. Women did light building work, such as plastering and painting. They also made beautiful pottery – black on a white background – mugs, pitchers, ladles, canteens, jars, bowls and dippers. One bowl was found with a southwestern horned toad painted on it: the paints were obtained from plants. Having no wheel, they used flat slabs of a special clay wound in a spiral to form a base and then again wound spirally upwards to make the walls of the pot. These were dried in the sun and then 'fired' in preheated stone troughs. The red sandstone

LEFT: An artistic impression of an attack on a village of cliff dwellers. RIGHT: Tower and cliff house, Valley of Rio Mancos, New Mexico, USA. (Peter Newark's Western Americana)

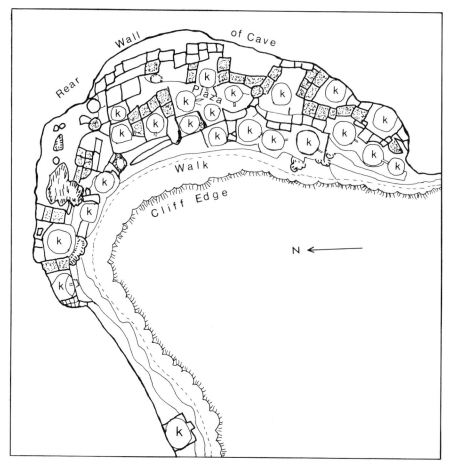

Simplified plan of Cliff Palace, Mesa Verde. The twenty-three circular *kivas* are marked 'k'. Enclosed areas are rooms, and the dots indicate rooms on the second, third or fourth storeys.

walls often bore petroglyphs and pictographs of human figures, hands, birds, mammals and 'doodles', as well as serious 'totemic' designs. Arts and crafts tended to be a slow business without benefit of metal but were very important. They had priests, usually married, who conducted rain dances and fertility rites; they believed in witches and malevolent spirits; they held ceremonies for treating sick people. The *kiva* was for men only: a sort of combined club house and chapel used for religious and other secret ceremonies – we might liken it to a Masonic Temple – but also as a work room. The men smoked tobacco in short lengths of hollow cane, and the smoke was used to invoke the clouds to produce rain. They gossiped and played games of chance. They produced cotton cloth from cotton which they must have obtained through trade with the people to the south: they had no cotton plants. They made bows and chipped arrow heads; produced stone axes, hammers and knives; bone awls and scrapers; ropes, jewelry and feather blankets; wove nets or baskets – this was a male job – and made ceremonial objects. The *kivas* were also, of course, used for more formal rain-invoking ceremonies and for the medicine men to perform their healing chants and rituals. The priest was also the village Sun Priest, with the vital task of determining when to plant the crops – for this was 6000 feet above sea level and spring frosts were a serious problem.

The Indians suffered from many ailments which can be recognized today; they include rheumatism and arthritis and many had very bad teeth. They often buried their dead in the back of the caves, but also in burial grounds outside, and those inside became mummified by chance, through dehydration and desiccation: no preservation was involved. The best example was 'Esther', a 19- or 20-year-old woman found buried in a crevice and so named by her discoverers.

At the time of their peak in 1200 AD, there were scores of cliff villages, and pueblos in the river valleys. Then, just before 1300, it all stopped. The houses were abandoned, and left unnoticed for six hundred years, when they were found by the settlers. Why, is not known for certain, but it was probably the generation-long drought that ravaged the southwest in the late thirteenth century, from 1276 to 1300, recognizable from the low growth rate of the tree rings. The people may have migrated, perhaps south to southern New Mexico and Arizona; they never reoccupied the pueblos, perhaps because other Indians had settled in the area. These might have been desert foragers from the Great Basin like the Utes, or hunters from the north, ancestors of the Navajo and the Apache. These latter – Athabascan Indians – were unrelated; for unknown reasons they came down during the period from the twelfth to sixteenth centuries. They were formidable people, armed with the strengthened, extra-springy Eskimo bow which shot further than those of the pueblo people. All these folk may well have deterred the Pueblos from attempting to resettle their old territory. But the newcomers soon settled in, picking up agricultural skills easily and bringing a new face to the Four Corners: unlike the gentle Pueblos, they were keen and effective warriors.

The sites

A clockwise tour around the centre of the Four Corners might serve to illustrate the extent of the Indian rock dwellings in the region, and provide further details of their more interesting features. In Utah the Anasazi lived through several phases in the Salt Creek area, at Horse Canyon among others. Their sandstone and adobe houses contained artefacts such as bows, pottery and corn cobs, and they left pictographs engraved in the desert varnish coating the rock boulders. Colorado must be the first choice for a visitor, to see Mesa Verde, which has given its name to the first national park to be created to preserve the works of ancient man. But there are other cliff dwellings in the state, common in the southwest although less grand than those of Mesa Verde. Some of the best include Sand Canyon, McElmo Canyon and Lost Canyon; the dwellings are large and small, rectangular and circular, great houses with towers, and cliff dwellings. All have underground *kivas* with ventilators, deflectors and mural pilasters.

Mesa Verde, in southwest Colorado, is in country of red Upper Cretaceous sandstone cliffs, canyons and mesas, with plenty of natural caves at the base and on the cliff sides. The complete formation consists of sandstone, full of water and with the caves at its base, overlying a layer of shale and coal, in turn overlying thick sandstone, overlying more thick shale. The whole massif was uplifted 60 million years ago, forming a plateau 1000 to 2000 feet above the surrounding country. The mesa top is scored with more than twenty canyons, all running north-south, with many small side canyons, in an area 20 by 15 miles in size.

Each cliff 'village' is a terraced apartment house, built into a cave or, better, large overhanging rock shelter, 50 or 100 feet deep, 700 feet up from the floor of the canyon. The people farmed corn, beans, squash and turkeys. Hundreds of ruins are now known, far more of them pueblos, on the tops of the mesas, than cliff cave dwellings. But there are three to four hundred cliff dwellings, in a better state of preservation than the mesa houses. The artefacts left behind include pottery, baskets, fabrics, stone and bone tools, turquoise and shell jewelry; there are burials and 'mummies', also in excellent preservation. But it took nearly twenty years – 1888 to 1906 – before they were protected, after years of looting, pillage and vandalism; the result was the Mesa Verde National Park. The park occupies only the northern half of the mesa; the southern half is part of the Southern Ute Indian Reservation.

Cliff Palace, on Chapin Mesa, was first discovered in 1888 by Richard, one of the Wetherill brothers, in a party of cowboys wintering their herds in the great Mancos Canyon, and shown the way by an Ute Indian. There were five Wetherill brothers, ranchers and traders, and they went on to become the region's leading cliff-dwelling discoverers and amateur archaeologists. Of the ten cliff dwellings visible, Cliff Palace in Cliff Palace Canyon, a branch of Cliff Canyon, in turn a branch of Navajo Canyon, on Chapin Mesa, was the largest. It had 200 rooms and 23 *kivas*, on four or more storeys, its size being dictated by the size of the cave; it was able to house some 400 people. The

Cliff Palace, Mesa Verde National Park, Colorado, USA. (Mesa Verde National Park)

kivas are mostly circular, although three are square with rounded corners, and generally some nine feet in diameter. The largest is nearly nineteen feet across and about seven to eight feet in height. The stone work is superb: the *kivas* always had the best masonry. Some adobe bricks were used but only rarely, as for the Speaker-chief's house. Both adobes and the mortar employed contained ashes and some rooms were plastered with sand or clay. There are mural paintings, some of them elaborate, with symbols like those of the Hopi. The doors and windows were just simple openings, the upper doors reached by ladders. There were jambs, sills and lintels but probably only sticks tied together or sheets of matting to close the openings. The roofs had rafters and the floors were of hard clay. Many fireplaces are found in the rooms but more were built in the plazas. There were corn grinding rooms and granaries, and burial and cremation was practised; it is interesting to note that nowadays only some tribes practise cremation, the Hopi and Zuñi not being among

LEFT: Spruce-tree House, Colorado, USA, showing entrance ladders to the *kivas*. RIGHT: Montezuma Castle, Arizona, USA, occupied by about fifty people between the 13th and 15th centuries. (Werner Forman Archive)

them. A large assortment of artefacts was found, including stone implements, grinding stones, stone game balls, sandals and baskets, woven cotton cloth, pottery, wooden sticks, bone scrapers and necklaces and a few ornaments: a turquoise ear pendant and a black jet bead, and some lignite beads and buttons. The seeds found included corn, squash, pumpkin and beans, as well as fragments of gourd.

Particularly popular is Balcony House. It has a splendid location, with the walls and roofs well preserved, and a spring at the rear of the cave. It is entered now by a thirty-foot ladder but this was not so in the Pueblo Indian days. They reached home by a path along a narrow ledge which then passed behind a boulder and entered a three foot wide rock crevice, 25 feet long. This was narrowed by the Indians by building stone walls on both sides; it ended with the Needle's Eye: a crawl on hands and knees. Balcony House has an adobe paved court with two storeys built on three sides of it; the fourth is a sheer drop, although the cliff dwellers even then had a low but sturdy protective wall. Three types of structure were built by the sixty to eighty people who may have lived here: houses, storage rooms and *kivas*. There were some thirty-five 'houses': rooms, some eight by ten feet in size, with few windows and only small doors; these average 16 by 24 inches in size and have sills two or three feet up from the floor. Some of the walls were plain, some plastered, some were adorned with red and white paintings. The roofs were low, made of pole and adobe brick. Each room housed a family, mainly for sleeping and housing possessions, while 'living' went on in the open courts. Under the upper doors are narrow walks or balconies, leading from room to room. There were plenty of stores: tiny rooms for corn, beans and squash. An open hatch in the court above is the only indication of the *kiva* below: there are two of these.

Of the thousands of pit-houses, pueblos and cliff dwellings, less than twenty-four had been excavated by 1948; one of the other important sites, Wetherill Mesa, was not touched for a further decade. Spruce-tree House, in Spruce-tree Canyon, running off the Navajo Canyon, is a cliff dwelling in a recess under an overhang, associated with Cliff Palace. It contains 114 rooms, fourteen for use as stores or mortuary chambers, and eight *kivas*; some four hundred people lived there. The north and south sections are divided by a street and there is a plaza; the walls were made of stone laid on mortar but some were laid dry and pointed later. Others include Kodak House, named after the photographic firm who did work there, Pipe Shrine House, Far View House, and Square Tower House in Navajo Canyon, built between 1204 and 1246 AD with eighty rooms and seven *kivas*, to house more than 125 people. On top of the mesa is the Sun Temple; no artefacts were found, since it was not a house but was used for ceremonial purposes.

Wetherill Mesa, named after the Wetherill brothers, lies three miles west of Chapin Mesa. A total of eight hundred and six sites were found on Wetherill Mesa between 1958 and 1960. The biggest is Long House, second in size only to Cliff Palace; others are Mug House – where many pottery mugs were found, Step House, Big Juniper House, Two Raven House and Badger House. Forty burials were found under Long House, and the remains of a large pit-house, nearly 16 feet in diameter, were also found under the area later covered by five rooms and a *kiva*; it was in use around 650 AD. Long House had a hundred and fifty rooms and twenty-two *kivas*, as well as one great *kiva*. The ratio of seven rooms to one *kiva* was little over half that in other cliff dwellings. Why was the number of *kivas* so large? Each religious society had to have its own *kiva*, but why so many societies? Perhaps the people from the small surface houses crowded in to use the Long House facilities. However, a look at some other ratios tends to confuse the issue further: after Long House, with 150 rooms and 22 *kivas*, giving a ratio of 7, there are Square Tower House, 80:7 = 11.4; Cliff Palace, 200:23 = 8.5; Balcony House, 35:2 = 17.5; and Pueblo Bonito, with 800:30 = 27. A different theory seems to be needed, although from seven to nine seem to be common ratios.

Step House had all its wooden beams missing except for one; one theory to explain this is that it housed doomed residents – the old and the crippled – who burned all the other beams. One of its *kivas* has been excavated; it was twelve feet wide, with six masonry columns to support its vanished roof beams. The fireplace was central, with a hole in the roof for the smoke. Fresh air flowed down a vent and round a deflector or stone baffle.

For water, the people of Wetherill Mesa dug ditches, half a mile long, arranged in a fan shape and all meeting at Mummy Lake – now dried up – which was their tank or reservoir, holding half a million gallons; the system drained 25 acres of hillside and had supply ditches to Spruce-tree House four miles distant and possibly to Cliff Palace, five and a half miles away.

On the Jemez Plateau of northern New Mexico, some 30 miles northwest of Santa Fe, are several groups of cliff and cave dwellings in a long mesa built of volcanic tuff. They are found on the Pajarito Plateau, in the Chama drainage area and in the Jemez Valley; they include, of course, the largest of the pueblos, Pueblo Bonito, in Chaco Canyon, already described, and the next biggest, Chetro Ketl. Like Cliff Palace, they are dated at 1100 AD. There is also the Anasazi Basketmaker Atlatl Cave.

The picturesque prehistoric ruins of Tsankawi, which is Tewa for Place of the Round Cactus, contain cliff and cave dwellings and also a great pueblo on the mesa, with perhaps 200 rooms on the ground floor and two floors above, each smaller than that below, giving a total of some 400 rooms altogether, with ten *kivas*, a large number for a population of three or four hundred such as may have lived here. Once again, occupation can be seen to have ended in a disaster. There are petroglyphs of animals and of humans bearing a tomahawk, and mummies, tools and household utensils were found here. At the pueblo of the Yapashi, Potrero de las Vacas, are two life-size stone panthers – pumas – cut out of the tuff, and nearby the Cueva Pintada or painted cave. At the Potrero de los Idolos are the remains of two more stone panthers. Tschirege, meaning Little Bird in Tewa, at Pajarito, is a huge pueblo with a large cliff village around it. One and a half miles to the south is Navawi, or Place of the Game Trap. Here there are cave dwellings with cut stone steps, and a bottle-shaped pit cut out of the solid rock, 6 by 3 feet across and 15 feet deep, as a trap for deer, bear and other animals. There are axes and hammers of granite, obsidian and flint. Ten miles to the north is Puyé, which for the Santa Clara Indians meant 'at the home of his forefathers'. People lived here in caves for more than a mile along the mesa. Some of the 500 rooms still show traces of plaster work and there are holes where logs fitted to support the balconies. Some carvings were found here and, with the skeletons of the inhabitants, samples of pottery, sandals and grindstones – both *metates* and *manos*.

Finally, two miles west of Tsankawi, is Otowi Canyon, site of the amazing cone-shaped 'tent rocks' or 'tent houses' which so resemble those of Cappadocia in Turkey. As well as natural cliff caves, which were often enlarged, and those that were wholly artificial, the unique white tuff cone dwellings, thirty feet high, owe their shape and preservation like those of Anatolia to the lava capping overlying the tuff, which prevented erosion from destroying them entirely. They are found half a mile above the main Otowi pueblo and some were lived in, like the other caves. Some of the artificial cliff dwellings were occupied well past the turn of the century. They have crude fireplaces near the door but few have chimneys. A little masonry is found here and there, for example casing doorways, and there were some porches. The main pueblo, below the cone houses, has five multi-storeyed terraced houses, with some four hundred and fifty rooms on the ground floor and ten *kivas*, which together with two hundred and fifty upper rooms give a total of some seven hundred rooms. Before moving west to Arizona, it should be mentioned that western Texas has large overhanging rock shelters, used by the Comanche Indians.

In Arizona, pride of place must go to Canyon de Chelly. Here there are the Navajo Blue Bell Cave, the Painted Cave and the Canyon del Muerto or Mummy Cave, divided into east and west coves, with four *kivas*, where pictographs and Navajo burial cists were found. There are artificial caves; multi-storeyed dwellings with artificial walls built in large natural caves; and many-storeyed pueblos – built singly, with a polygonal shape, scattered about, or in groups of one to three around a court. The White House is a small Anasazi pueblo. There are also individual family dwellings, again isolated or in groups, to make villages. The Casa Blanca is a good example; it was built in two parts, upper and lower, some 35 feet apart, the lower being some 50 by 150 feet in size. There are forty-five rooms and one ruin has three *kivas*. The walls, which were built on refuse, can reach 14 feet in height; they were defensive – some were chinked – but had no buttresses. The masonry was excellent and some adobes were used, as well as plaster. The roofs had wooden beams, despite the extreme scarcity of wood, and were the floors of the rooms above. Attempts at decoration included pictographs – abstract designs and more natural representation, such as hands. There were reservoirs, storage cists, and burial cists resembling dolmens. There are more dwellings in other nearby canyons.

The Canyon de Chelly buildings were late in the pueblo tradition and some at least are Hopi in origin. The earlier ruins of Arizona include those of Navajo, Keet Seel and Betatakin, and the famous Hohokam houses on the Gila River, near Casa Grande, as well as the Salt and Santa Cruz Valleys. They were built in mounds, not properly underground houses, of *caléche*, a

Cliff dwellings at Canyon de Chelly, Arizona, USA, dated c. 1300 AD. (Werner Forman Archive)

Cliff dwellings at Betatakin, Arizona, USA. (Werner Forman Archive)

local natural calcrete or calcareous cement, being too early for adobe, and were then plastered. They are claimed by the local Pima Indians. Some of the best pit dwellings in the southwest are the Old Caves near Flagstaff, Arizona. Here were rooms built of blocks of volcanic agglomerate, with a vertical descent hole leading to the *kivas* below which were excavated out of the solid rock. There are other good examples of pit dwellings near Roosevelt Dam and West Canyon, with its Inscription House. Also on the Gila River were the cliff dwellings, like Cliff House, Casa Blanca, cut in red sandstone by the Zuñi Indians. Access to their caves was achieved using poles with lateral teeth which they inserted into notches in the perpendicular rocks. There are good cliff dwellings near the Black Falls of the Little Colorado River. Single or multiple rooms are arranged here against the cliff wall, the rounded corners giving the structure its 'D' shape. There are more cliff dwellings at Walnut Canyon, cut in mixed limestone and dolomite, under- and overlying sandstone. They left fireplaces, wooden artefacts, pottery and corncobs, as well as bones. It has been suggested that some of the central Arizonan cliff dwellers had *hogans* or vestibules to their houses, like the present-day Navajo and Havasupai Indians in north-central Arizona. Just south of Flagstaff is Montezuma Castle. It dates from the thirteenth century when droughts forced the Sinagua Indians to move from around Flagstaff to the Verde Valley, and probably housed about fifty people; it is thought to have been abandoned in the fifteenth century. Lastly, there were the Maqui, who lived in sandstone villages on the mesas, only leaving when their land became barren through diminished rainfall.

Although outside the Four Corners region, the cliff dwellings of the Mexican frontier state of Chihuahua should be mentioned. These lie in the Sierra Madre canyons, 15 to 20 miles west of the Casas Grandes Valley, with its much pilfered mounds which were once the multi-storeyed, plaster-coated adobe Great Houses, near the adjoining state of Sonora. The Sierra Madre cliff dwellings are in groups in the Babicora district, built of wood and adobe, their inhabitants long gone. Their adobe walls, now one to three feet high, had boulders, twigs and vegetable matter to reinforce them. One such group is in Chico Canyon, with some fifty-five rooms; there is another in Garabato Canyon, with perhaps thirty rooms. The rooms had three types of fireplace: adobe platforms, with depressions like basins at their ends; at one end, against the wall; or semi-circular, against the wall. And three types of door: trapezoidal; or step-passage, with sills at various heights above the floors – about two feet eight inches from sill to lintel; or T-shaped, with sills flush with the floors, four feet six inches from sill to lintel. They had many small view holes in the front walls. The occupants stored corncobs in adobe bins; made basketry and red and black pottery, and grindstones (*metates* and *manos*).

Finally, the Eskimo of the Bering Sea coast of Alaska live in artificial cliff houses – not caves – which are thirty feet up, their backs firmly on bedrock but the porches and front rooms extending in front and propped up on long poles. There are some forty similar Eskimo dwellings on King Island, in the Aleutians. These have two rooms, an outer and purely verandah-like construction of poles and drift wood for summer use, and an inner, excavated rock room for winter, with a communicating tunnel several feet long. The Eskimo dwellings have prompted a German theory that a line of prehistoric dwellings runs down the west coast of America from the Arctic to Mexico, linking the underground ceremonial rooms in California and the *kivas* of the southwest.

CHAPTER 8

Tuff cones: monasteries
to farmhouses

The Biblically named Cappadocia region of eastern Anatolia, some 140 miles southeast of Ankara, spans approximately 3700 square miles over ten provinces of Turkey and has the city of Kayseri – a commercial crossroads since Roman times – as its capital. This one-storeyed city, with a fine railway station, was once the capital of the kings of Cappadocia; it was rechristened Caesarea Mazaca by the Emperor Claudius. It has splendid Seljuk architecture, madrasahs and tombs, fine old mosques and a medieval bazaar. Since early days the region has benefitted from modest mineral wealth: there was rock crystal, onyx at Avanos and a much prized white, translucent stone known as *phengis*. Cappadocia consists of a plateau, deeply dissected by the Halys River of old – now the Kizil Irmak – into uplands and *deres* or valleys, clustered round Mount Argæus, the extinct volcano, 12,373 feet high, now known as Erciyaş Daği and occupying almost the dead centre of Asia Minor, of which it is the highest peak. There is also another volcano, Hasan Daği. Still smouldering in the time of Strabo, at the dawn of the Christian era, the two volcanoes produced some 8 million years ago in late Tertiary times a vast outpouring of tuff, rich in zeolite minerals, and locally reaching more than 4000 feet in thickness – which covered the white freshwater limestone of Pliocene age and formed the plateau, extending northwest and southwest from Mount Argæus for 30 to 40 miles. The tuff bed is overlain by a layer of basalt lava, with some volcanic breccia, ranging from some four to twenty feet in thickness. It was the lava which was responsible for the formation of the astonishing cone-shaped masses of tuff – 'fairy chimneys' – by protecting them from total erosion.

The cones lie singly or in groups, thickly or sparsely, in valleys like Soğanli and Ürgüp Dere, running west from the plain at the foot of Mount Argæus, between the towns of Kayseri and Develi, to Nevşehir and Arapsun, a roughly equilateral triangular area with its sides some 14 miles in length. There are scattered examples extending southwards nearly to the Syrian border and eastwards to Malatya. They range in height from 50 to 300 feet; of this, the lava capping can constitute anything from three-quarters to

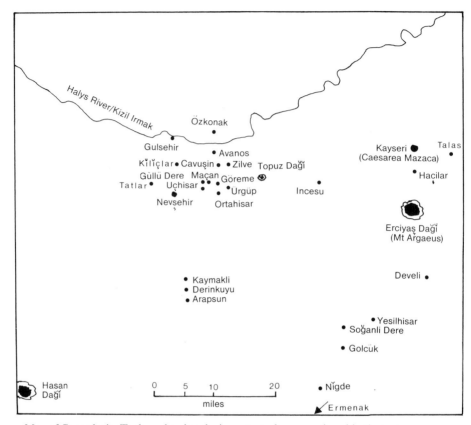

Map of Cappadocia, Turkey, showing the important places mentioned in the text.

nothing: it can be totally gone and some cones are more or less completely decomposed. West of Topuz Dağı, there is no more basalt, its place as a capping stone being taken by a dark pumice. There is no water on the plateau and it is very dry – flat, dusty, all heat and sand and utterly timeless – while the valleys are very fertile: surprising when there is virtually no proper soil, only decomposed pumice and tuff. Nevertheless, both fruit and vegetables are grown in the uplands as well as the valleys; the area is well known for its apricots, and grapes also flourish. From the top of Topuz Dağı, which is roughly in the middle of the plateau, can be seen the multicoloured cones and crags: white, cream, tan, ochre, pink, red and grey: there are said to be 50,000 cones.

The area has a history going back to 3000 BC, a thousand years before the time of the Hittites, when people first came to live in the cones and pyramids, perhaps at Aliçsar and Alacahöyük (?Catalhoyuk); this was the time when man had begun to excavate artificial caves and the area was culturally advanced in the seventh century BC. The peak was reached later, however, with fourth-century Christians hiding from their persecutors. St Paul travelled through on his so-called 'third journey'; the dark and dreary cave in Antioch (now Antakya), where he rested and spread the faith from 29 to 40 AD, might be regarded as the first Christian church. The first letter of St Peter to the dispersed Christians included the Cappadocians. There were at that time only two cities: Caesarea (Kayseri) and Tyana. In 200 AD Bishop Alexander went from his see in Cappadocia to Jerusalem and established the province as a centre of Christian theology, with splendid Byzantine sculpted, painted and plastered churches, especially around Göreme, monasteries with their refectories, kitchens and washrooms, as well as isolated hermitages and clusters of cells, shrines and tombs. In 300 AD, the early martyr Hieron (Hieronymus) fled until he was lured out of his hiding place and betrayed. St George was born here and the story of his encounter with the dragon still persists in the area. Then came St Basil The Great of Caesarea Mazaca, Cappadocia's most famous Christian, who ruled the community from 330 to 379 AD. He lived in the Greek-speaking village of Ortakieui, where St Gregory also dwelled: his farm can still be traced. Following the example of St Anthony and the other early recluses in the Egyptian and Syrian deserts, there was a powerful appeal in the monastic and ascetic life; the need for concealment from the internal conflicts plaguing the Byzantine Empire in the mid eighth century did nothing to detract from this, nor did the added persecution by zealous iconoclasts and marauding Arab tribes, with their threat of Islam, and the endless territorial captures and recaptures. Although many fled to more hospitable countries such as Italy, where they established their underground way of life in the south, founding settlements in Calabria and Puglia – and one estimate puts their number as high as 50,000, between 726 and 775 AD – many others established themselves in their unusual but strangely appropriate habitat and founded monastery after monastery.

For safety, the cone dwellers had high entrances, reached by rope ladders which could be pulled up after them, together with finger and toe holds cut in the rock to enable them to reach up to ten storeys. Some priests and hermits climbed up niches chipped into the sides of chimney-like shafts in the centre of the cones: the fairy chimneys. But others took to living deeper and deeper underground, as at Derinkuyu, Kaymakli and at four other localities, where between 20,000 and 60,000 people could withstand a siege. The Arab threat declined during the late ninth and tenth centuries, the tide turning in favour of Byzantium, when new bishoprics were created. But in 1071 the Emperor Romanos Diogenes was defeated, humiliated and captured by the Seljuk Turks, under their leader Alpaslan, at the major battle of Manzikert (Malazgirt) in northeast Anatolia. Roaming Turkoman tribesmen were now a problem and the Byzantine administration was allowed only limited freedom. Nevertheless, the Turks were generally tolerant of the culture and religion of the local population and in the three hundred years that followed the community was allowed to prosper and increase until in the thirteenth century there were some 30,000 Christians and more than three hundred underground chapels and monasteries had been hewn from the rock. Byzantium held on, surviving the fall of Constantinople in 1453 to the Ottoman Turks, who succeeded the Seljuks. But the slow decline from the fourteenth century affected the Cappadocian Christian settlement so that by 1500 few remained. The monasteries enjoyed a brief resurgence in the mid 1800s and a few Christians remained in the caves until 1922–3, when the Turkish-Greek mutual population exchange, coupled with lack of official support, made it virtually impossible to maintain the major sacred works of art, although private dwellings did not suffer in this way. Today, in fact, the quality of the work praised in the thirteenth century by the 'Synopsis Chronike' is still appreciated. Side by side with the holy men, the farmers cultivated the valleys where apricots, grapes, melons, tomatoes, beans, walnuts, plums, pears and apples flourished, together with cereals and other vegetables. Now the cone houses are occupied solely by farmers and still occasionally being excavated. But some people are afraid of the 'cave ghosts' that inhabit the reputedly haunted caves.

There were also the solitary abodes of the hermits, in a single cone with cell and chapel for the exclusive use of one lone anchorite or disciple, perhaps copying St Paul or Timothy, as at Zilve. Elijah fled here from the wrath of Jezebel, to drink from the brook and be fed by ravens. They had carved stone beds or couches, with stone bolsters, bedside tables, cupboards and cooking-stove ledges with a fire pot and fuel box. The altar might have had its three red painted crosses. One Paşa Baca cone was the abode of a Stylite. The first Stylite, Simeon, was born about 390 AD of peasant stock. He became a hermit and moved from one cone to progressively higher cones, ending up at the top of a 60 foot shaft. Here he lived for the rest of his life, giving sermons and attracting thousands of pupils and pilgrims. He founded the Stylite order of Pillar Hermits, and after his death a splendid monastery and cathedral were built around his pillar at Kalaat Saman. These are among the most famous relics of the region, reaching from Syria via Antakya (Antioch) and Alep (Aleppo). The next cone, nearby, was low, white and sprawling, with a stable cut into it, where nearby coenobites – members of ascetic convent communities – kept mules or donkeys for carrying water or for riding by the ascetics themselves, or for ploughing and working in the fields. Some hermitages were in groups, perhaps around a monastery, others were isolated. All the cells and chapels were elevated and therefore light and airy; the celibate ecclesiastical population may have reached a peak of around 30 to 40,000 at one time, apart from town dwellers and their families. The ridge of Kïlïçlar belonged to the monastic orders, with some anchorites as well. Although very rich in Byzantine ruins, this area is archaeologically young: only 1000 to 1800 years old as against the 5000 years of other parts of Asia Minor. There is a superbly frescoed church and the largest room yet discovered, in a bank, 32 by 21 feet in size, with a rock-hewn stove on one side for a huge monastic cauldron, a stable at the back and some splendid wine presses. The monasteries at Kïlïçlar and Göreme were cliff hewn while others, as at Bel Kilise, were carved out of a cone.

The recorded history of the region has been somewhat disjointed. Cappadocia was mentioned by Agatharcides in about 250 BC and later described by Diodorus and Strabo, whose *Soandus* may have been the southern village of Soğanlï Dere. The first detailed record was that of Leo the Deacon, who in his narrative of 959 to 975 AD labelled the inhabitants troglodytes, who lived in caves, holes and labyrinths. He considered the cone dwellings to be the most ubiquitous and characteristic habitat of the region and described the towns of Göreme (then Korama) and Maçan (then Matiano). The first western traveller was Paul Lukas, a Frenchman travelling at the behest of Louis XIV

Cone dwellings at Göreme, Cappadocia, Turkey. (Turkish Tourist Office)

who in 1718 described the troglodytic life of the region, estimating the underground population at 200,000. His excellent account was right in almost every detail, although it was strongly criticized by the German poet, Wieland. In fact, Lukas's only error was to believe that the cones had been built by man. The first record of the churches, chapels and monasteries was carried out by a young Jesuit, Father Guillaume de Jerphanion, between 1907 and World War I, when Cappadocia was sealed off to the world; his first volume and book of plates were published in 1925. The region was not reopened to the west until 1950, after the Government reputedly attempted to turn out the cave dwellers because of the unhealthy (carcinogenic) nature of the zeolites in the tuff. But now it is a renowned tourist area, and the area of some fifty squares miles containing the best examples of cone dwellings has been declared a *bolge* or official tourist zone. As usual, tourism brings its unfortunate side. The market town of Avanos, between the vineyards, is renowned for its pottery – the local clay is particularly suitable – and one of the three hundred or so cave potteries has established a Chamber of Horrors: a sample of hair from each visitor is hung up and an annual raffle held, with prizes given.

The troglodyte towns and villages have frequently been renamed. There is Ürgüp, a cliff-dwelling village of red rock, and Nevşehir of white; there are cones at Maçan (Avcilar or Martchan) and at Üdj Assarü, in the Göreme valley. Özkonak is the largest underground city in the region. Üçhisar, once Three Towers, is clustered round a rock pinnacle, while Ortahisar, which used to be Midtower, standing for fairy chimneys or *peri bacalari*, meaning occupied by spirits, is situated at the foot of a crag honeycombed with caves. There are Talas, Paşa Baca, Demiryi and Kılıçlar, which was the Valley of Swords. Soğanlı Dere has some sixty chapels, some of them with their natural rock cones above carved into domes. Güzelyurt, 15 miles from Ihlara, lies in a valley with dwellings from prehistoric times as well as interesting rock-cut churches, chapels and a mosque. About 60 miles from Göreme, on the Niğde road, are the underground cities of Kaymakli and Derinkuyu, dug down to nearly 400 feet below the surface, their rooms interconnected by tunnels, which were used as refuges from raids in Byzantine times, mainly between the late seventh century and 900 AD. Derinkuyu has disclosed older artefacts, however, such as a Hittite quern of around 2000 BC. They are equipped with ventilation shafts, wells, food stores and wine vats, as well as secret guardrooms, blind passages and trap doors for defence. There are palaces, chapels, wineries; now they are all equipped with electricity and water and people live there for six months at a time. Çavuşin has a large Byzantine church, like a Syrian basilica, which uses the rock pillar behind as its porch or narthex.

The cap of a large cone mound at Bel Kilise is the church dome of the monastery, one of only three decorated to represent a masonry cupola of coloured marble. The monastery occupies all ten floors of the cone, the church having the top areas, with wine press, kitchen with rock-cut stove and chimney, refectories with stone tables, below. The monks' cells are in between. There is a monastic cemetery at the rear, with the graves cut in the rock. The anchorites in the cone cells of a typical monastery might descend a rope ladder once a week to collect their ration of black bread and olives, oil, raisins or dried figs, and to attend monastery prayers. One of them collected some valley soil each time he came down, with which he made a little hanging garden, watered by a rock-cut cistern, to grow onions, radishes and fennel.

The cone dwellings are perhaps 100 to 200 feet high, with many windows. Like most cave dwellings, they are cool in summer and warm in winter. Inside, the rooms may be ten feet high and have a door and windows, a fireplace and cooking stove, divan beds, tables, cupboards, niches and shelves, all carved out of the tuff walls. It was easier and cheaper to dig caves in the cones in a land where wood was so scarce. In 1919 it was reported that one man could carve a chamber 25 feet long, 13 feet wide and 10 feet high in thirty days. In some towns and villages, such as Garin, the houses reach ten or twelve storeys. Long ago Turkish farmers learned the art of cave-cutting from the Christians, making four inch grooves to outline a rectangular block in the wall which is then split out and kept for building external walls and facades. To reach the higher entrances, there are ladders reaching up chimney-like shafts. Inside, the ceilings are arched – a feature of a great many European caves – and the kitchen and living room are continuous, while the bedrooms are usually reached by more ladders.

A typical cone house has a spacious living room, with rock-cut divans around three sides, a rock-cut fireplace and flue – although not all cave homes have chimneys – and, in winter, a roaring fire. The stone divan beds have straw or wool mattresses, the walls are hung with rugs and the floor has Turkish carpets, today, perhaps, with plastic sheets beneath to keep out the ubiquitous dust. There might be the hareem next door. Upstairs, there are two small but attractive rooms with windows, now used as stores, set in a garden with a poplar, looking like an Istanbul mosque with its domed roof. The cone houses are whitewashed and those that have no chimneys, such as in the Kiliçlar valley, resembling American Indian *tepees*, require the sooty rock to be chipped off every year, enlarging the houses in the process, before a new coat of whitewash is applied using a besom (bundle of twigs) brush. In 1962 a farmer paid the equivalent of $500 for a five-roomed cone house near Üçhisar.

As another example, a cliff dwelling in a gorge has a front entrance opening into a saddle room, followed by stables for horses, mules, asses, goats

Cone dwellings at Ürgüp and Göreme, Cappadocia, Turkey. The cones in the right-hand picture contain several storeys of dwellings, as can be seen by the number of windows. (Turkish Tourist Office)

and oxen. Then there are steps up to a terrace in a large hollow in the rock wall, like a domed open-sided court, with a rolling stone disc to shut the door. From the terrace all the rooms open: stores, stable, hareem and male guest room, with striped rugs, blankets and ripening melons hanging from the ceiling and a rock-cut shelf for copper, pewter and pottery vessels.

The village of Maçan, with the town of Üçhisar in the distance, is notable for the spire-like points of some of its cones, a result of weathering once the capstones are lost. In early days a Christian bishopric, it now has modern flat-topped houses. But a house near the village had a front door 13 feet up and a bedroom that was once a chapel. It had the usual arched ceiling, raised altar and Christian crosses on the walls; the monk's wall niches were used as shelves and cupboards. Above and below were other rooms and stores, one of which was once a mausoleum, with four graves. On the very top was a church. The people here live exactly as other Turkish people live in ordinary villages; only their houses are different, with vineyards on the roofs although the threshing areas in front of the house entrances are completely normal. There is a Greek temple here, and also a well-preserved church with facade, doorway and vestibule, leading to the cave interior which has many frescoes of Greek saints and Byzantine columns and arches.

Another interesting example of an underground house is that of the Imam or prayer leader of the village of Maçan. The stable is the old house, at the back, with the barn in the inner part of the stable; both are old caves. There are now three roofs, one below the other since the new house was recently built out in front. There is a courtyard, a cistern, a latrine; also a kitchen, reception room and guest room. Their use varies seasonally between winter and summer. In emergencies, the caves normally used as stores can become refuges, being less vulnerable to natural disasters like earthquakes, where the family can live while the new house is repaired.

The house combines home, workplace, sometimes public meeting hall: the village has no hall, only the mosque and schoolhouse. There are the stable, straw barn, tool shed and agricultural store. There is a guest room for weddings and feasts; in the richer, more influential households, this is the social centre. The family home is the preserve of women and children, where female but not male friends and relatives will be received and entertained. Before a marriage ceremony, the bride-dressing takes place in an inner cave-room in her father's house, before she is bidden farewell by her female relatives and becomes a member of her husband's household. The house is therefore divided up between men, women and animals. Bedding is stored in cupboards during the day and the rooms are used throughout the twenty-four hours. But not throughout the year: each zone has winter rooms and summer rooms, in equal number, with stores common to both. The caves are used in winter for warmth, and to save fuel, but also in part in summer for the coolness, when ventilation is employed to control temperature.

Üdj Assarü, or Castle of Üdj, once called the Three Castles, is a mass of tuff in the Göreme valley near Golkundra. One estimate and photograph placed the number of cones in the area at 50,000. Some were never excavated for dwellings although it is not known why: they seem to provide first class material. Some are genuine cones, others have been called obelisks because of their straight-sided prismatic shape, apart from a little pointed conical cap, causing them to look like rockets. The entrances to the dwellings when they were high up were by two vertical and parallel rows of offset finger and toe holds. Some of the cones contained up to nine storeys of dwellings, countable from outside by their windows. The stairs were internal sets of finger and toe holds, arranged up chimneys. One five-storey cone could house four families. The chambers were spacious, with shelves and niches carved in the walls for storage. The small cones were used for granaries and pigeon houses. There would also be a fruit drying area and in front of the cone a wheat threshing area.

Ürgüp is a village built around a great pumice hummock. As well as cones it has cliff houses, with gabled balconies and arched doors, wooden windows, iron grille work and painted walls in a typical two-storey house. The people live and sleep in front, using the dark rooms at the rear as stores. The facades look like normal houses but are just 'fronts', built of quarried blocks of tuff, with most of the houses occupying the caves behind. The domed mosque sits on the top of the hummock which is the original plateau before erosion. Unlike the cones, these houses can be enlarged at will, but are prone to the occasional huge boulder breaking away and rolling down onto the village, crushing people and houses alike. Tatlar is a similar village, without cones, and another cliff village is Soğanlï Dere, a complex with thousands of chambers, churches, chapels and graves. It spans a gorge, the Onion Valley, with the cliff dwellings built on a terrace on one side, while on the other is a high cliff of early monks' cells, up to sixteen storeys high. There are very few cones and no temple or church facades such as are found at Maçan.

Some of the farmers are Christian but many are Moslems, all living as any other Turkish peasant community. They are typical agriculturists, rising early, using donkey carts for many purposes, keeping also some cows, goats, sheep and horses in the lower parts of the caves. Blindfolded donkeys or mules are used to turn the grindstones. The grazing is common to all but one family may own several caves. Like their monastic forebears, they grow apricots, grapes, pears, walnuts and other vegetables, as well as red poppies and some wheat, although the cereal yield is low. Most of the grain is grown and the cattle raised in the valleys and the neighbouring flatlands. The women, who wear baggy trousers called *salvar*, work hard, carrying water, working with donkeys, shearing sheep. They also spin and dye the wool, and weave rugs and carpets. Few people are rich; in some villages, families may live seven to a room, including a grandmother. Cows and chickens provide meat and sheep brains are a luxury. Their food includes frequent shish kebabs, rice pilaf and *börek*, a local sort of lasagne; superb mint salads with fried squash; onions; yogurt and dried apricots; apples; raisins; eggplant; and grape and rose-petal jams. Wine – the white is very good – is cheaper than water, and they also have vodka, brandy and raki (aniseed). They use oil lamps, bottled-gas cookers and lemon-lime cologne. The young people get married after the harvest is safely in – not during or before it – when it is too hot for anything to grow, let alone for men to work it.

A remarkable feature of Cappadocia is the number of pigeons and doves:

they are kept in their thousands, both for food – their eggs and flesh are eaten, although only in certain towns and villages – but mainly for their guano, which is harvested annually as a fertiliser and is what makes cultivation in the valleys, on soil that consists almost solely of disintegrated tuff and pumice, so successful. Thousands of old churches, monastery cells and houses have been turned into pigeon lofts, the entrances to their holes painted red or white; when they take to the air, the birds resemble a swarm of locusts.

The churches

The principal glory of Cappadocia is found in its churches. There are more than seventy rock churches, as well as the many monasteries, hermitages and chapels, mostly dating from the tenth and thirteenth centuries of the Byzantine and Seljuk periods. Many are built on an inscribed-cross plan with a central cupola supported by four columns. There were subterranean refectories, wine presses and cemeteries with graves cut in the floor, and tombs hewn in the narthexes of several of the churches. Many of the paintings are superb and some show the quandaries and battles of the monks over whether or not to portray Christ and his saints.

There were three early church phases: Early Christian (500–700 AD), Iconoclastic (700–850) and Archaic (850–950). There were three-aisled

Frescoes in the Tokalï Kilise church, Göreme, Cappadocia, Turkey. (Turkish Tourist Office)

Karanlïk Kilise, the Dark Church, at the open-air museum, Göreme, Turkey. (The J. Allan Cash Photolibrary)

basilicas, and one-aisled basilicas with a single apse. There were churches with transverse vaults, cruciform churches, one triconch church, at Tağar, and cross-in-square churches.

Most of the sixth-century churches in the Göreme valley have been defaced over the ages by Moslems and vandals but one, called 'The Apple Church' after the apple tree outside, is now an open-air museum. The display includes churches, chapels, monasteries, nunneries and hermitages, as well as homes. The tiny, relatively young Elmalï Kilise, the Church with the Apple, at Göreme has among its preserved wall paintings the Last Supper, the Crucifixion and the Resurrection painted, amongst other colours, in red, ochre and blue, as well as Daniel foretelling the Kingdom of God and David's advice to his son, Solomon. There is also the chapel and monastery, with its stone table, benches and abbot's seat of honour.

Nearby is Karanlïk Kilise, the Dark Church, typically Byzantine, with a dome-shaped central room full of angels, archangels, apostles, prophets and martyrs surrounding Christ. The images stand on columns in the apses, look down from small domes and lean in from the roof vaulting. Soğanlï Dere gorge has Christian monk and hermit caves carved in the cliffs, where the monastic community grew up between the fifth and tenth centuries. Here is Belli Kilise, the Church of St Barbara, the only rock-cut church whose pointed dome set on a high drum can be viewed from the 'exterior'.

Güllü Dere is one of the apricot-growing valleys between the cones, where the Christian period reached its peak between the tenth and twelfth centuries. The frescoes in Analipsis Church include the three wise men from the east with gold, frankincense and myrrh, and also Judas, with St Peter, after kissing the Lord in Gethsemane.

Tokalï Kilise – the Church with the Buckle – is the largest and most interesting, with thirteenth-century fresco paintings on narthex arch and nave walls. Scenes are by the priest-artist Constantine, showing eight saints in a row; the angel appearing to John the Baptist; the angel appearing to Joseph in a dream; Joseph with Mary on a donkey on the way to Bethlehem; Jesus meeting John in the desert; Jesus being baptized in the River Jordan; Jesus and his tempters; Matthew at the receipt of custom; fishermen disciples on the Sea of Galilee; and the marriage feast in Cana of Galilee. Tokalï Kilise church also has countless graffiti, with autographs going back to 1650.

The other churches include Carïklï Kilise, the Church with Sandals, which has footprints painted under the Ascension; Yïlanlï Kilise, the Apocalypse Church with the Snake, showing the dammed in the coil of serpents; and Sümbüllü Kilise, the Hyacinth Church.

Çavuşin has the church of St John the Baptist, with its vestibule and Great Pigeonhouse. At Güllü Dere there is the Church of Three Crosses, at Cemil, St Stephen, and at Ihlara, Ağaçaltï Kilisesi (the Daniel Church). And near Maçan is Kïlïçlar Kuşluk or Church of the Virgin Mary, with its frescoes of Christ and the Apostles still intact.

Finally, and this has to be a mere footnote, there are similar cone-shaped structures, some thirty feet high and known as 'tent rocks', hewn from a similar sort of white tuff formation in Otowi Canyon, Pajarito Plateau, part of the Jemez Plateau in New Mexico, half a mile above the main pueblo. Some of these were used in the past as dwellings.

CHAPTER 9

Houses in – and over – the ground

T he southern part of Tunisia includes a region containing some remarkable types of rock dwelling. It stretches from Gabès in the north to Dehibat in the south, and from Matmata east to the Libyan border, beyond which, in the past, Jews also lived in caves and holes in the ground. The local people are Berbers, originating in Saharan north Africa, from Egypt to Morocco, and described by Herodotus as Libyans and by the Romans as Barbarians; never prepared to accept domination by Carthage or Rome, they nevertheless made alliances acceptable to both sides. When the Arab conquerors arrived, they also accepted Islam, but when the eleventh century brought hordes of the Beni Hillal, laying waste to all around them, the Berbers took refuge in the mountain tops. The French Foreign Legion, working in the area around the turn of this century, thought that they developed three or even four types of rock dwelling.

One of the two most interesting, sometimes called *matmatas*, derive their name from the town of that name. Matmata, 28 miles south of Gabès, lies near the northern end of the Matmata Range, running southeast for some 95 miles through the limestone Houaia Mountains southeast to Dehibat. Between the deeply eroded and ragged peaks – the area was used as a location for the film *Star Wars* – there is a deposit of loess up to 65 feet deep. Consisting of clay with enough gypsum to act as a binding agent, it provides a firm and stable but easily worked material for excavating rooms that will not collapse. Here, and in the neighbouring villages of Beni-Aissa, Hadège, Techine and Beni Zelten, among others, some of the people came down from the mountains some three hundred years ago and developed a type of troglodyte dwelling that survives to the present, virtually unchanged, with a new lease of life from the interest it arouses in the visiting tourist.

On a level piece of ground a pit or hole is dug, some 65 feet in diameter and up to 30 feet deep, with vertical sides. This is the central courtyard or patio, with palms and other trees and a central cistern to collect as much rain as possible, reached by a long sloping ramp, wide enough to accommodate camels. Tool sheds and stables for the animals – horses, donkeys, goats and sheep — are dug into the walls of the passage; the living and sleeping rooms, together with store rooms, granaries and stables, form a lower level excavated into the sides of the courtyard. A higher level, sometimes only accessible by a rope, contains more store rooms. Cereals are poured into the stores from above through a narrow conduit and the grain keeps perfectly for years in the granary rooms. For quick access to the courtyard, there are ladders or stone

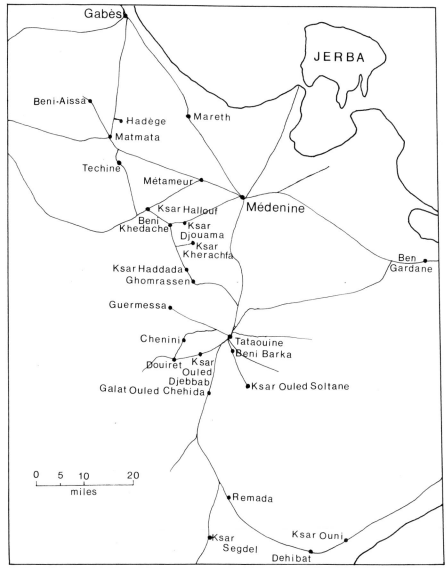

Map of southern Tunisia showing Matmata, the Ksars and other places mentioned in the text.

135

steps leading straight down into it. Here would be women weaving material for burnouses and woollen shawls or making mats from esparto grass, children playing and chickens scavenging, while fierce dogs keep guard. Piled high are esparto grass grain baskets. Life proceeds as it has done since the days of Christ.

This pattern would be the same in the Matmata villages and in the mountain villages or oval and horseshoe-shaped towns. There would be a Mosque, domed *marabouts* or shrines of the holy men, and the ruler might be a Caid or merely a sheik. Early this century, some 5000 people may have lived in caves in Matmata; in some cases a family living in one cave could have numbered a hundred individuals. A sheik's cave would in days past have had whitewashed walls and doors of palm tree planks pegged together with olive wood. There would be some European furniture and fine local carpets. A splendid row of large, pottery Ali Baba jars would contain water and olive oil. Next door to the sheik, in the next cave, lived his wife and family, although this practice is not observed in all communities. When a young man wanted to get married, he would need to give his bride's parents presents of goats, sheep, olive oil, wheat, barley, a fez, slippers and so forth. A more modest underground home would have a rectangular principal living room, again whitewashed, with the curved or arched ceiling that is always the rule. There would be furniture and shelves dug into the walls and also, perhaps, skeleton shelves made of twigs covered with plaster to form a trellis of varied geometric designs. At the back of the cave would be narrow benches with rows of holes to take provision jars, while in the middle of the room the bed would have on one side the same open lattice work as the shelves. Beni-Aissa and Techine provide excellent illustrations of such furnishings, and Matmata now has two hotel-restaurants formed by joining up caves and preserving as much of the traditional construction and furniture as possible.

Why did the people live in *matmatas*? Their ancestors fled to the mountain tops to live, as we shall see, in caves which they could easily defend and whence they could roll stones down onto their enemies. The lack of food and water probably drove them down to the plains; here there were no natural caves, but being used to such a way of life, they built their own on a pattern suited to the environment. Many young men would go off to Tunis where, if they were lucky, they would do well for themselves and return to their troglodyte village to marry a local girl and settle down happily. This pattern is still followed; Tunis is full of civil servants from the troglodyte region, as well as news vendors from Chenini and fritter makers from Ghomrassen.

Cave and earth dwellings the world over keep warm in winter and cool in summer, a fact certainly appreciated by the Berbers. They are mainly farmers, herding flocks and cultivating some wheat and barley. Their olives

Pit dwelling at Matmata, Tunisia. (C.M. Dixon)

are famous, as are their figs, but date palms are few. Water is the major problem and the meagre rainfall – some 8 to 12 inches per year in the hills – is conserved by dams to feed the *oueds*, river beds that are usually dry, which then irrigate terraces built on the same level and enclosed by mud walls. There are underground oil factories, which have two working areas. In the first, runner mills driven by camels, sometimes blind, grind the olives. The resulting paste is then pressed by a huge olive-tree trunk, operated by a winch, and the oil is collected in stone basins or jars in the ground.

To the south of the *matmata* region is another area, centred on Médenine. This is possibly Strabo's Mapalia, home of the nomadic tribes of North Africa, or it could be Libya, according to Herodotus. But Mapalia is almost certainly further north in Tunisia, south of Mahdia, which is south of Sousse,

137

Ksar of *ghorfas*, Médenine, Tunisia. (Tunisian National Tourist Office)

around El-Alia. In Médenine there are cave-shaped structures made of stone and local cement, reaching up to four or five storeys. These are *ksars*, roughly rectangular assemblages of small cells called *ghorfas*, many without windows, packed side by side, one on top of each other, looking out onto a common court and connected by a system of projecting stones and stone steps. Strictly speaking, these are not rock-cut chambers; however, they are so bound up with cave dwelling and the use of underground rooms that they can be deemed to belong here. *Ksars* were used as granaries in times of trouble, and also as refuges, and in peaceful times as market places and social centres, for trading and meeting, but they were only occasionally lived in. They were used by the nomads of the plains between Mareth and Ben Gardane, to store and protect their harvests. The *ksars* could be enlarged or united to protect the granaries of an entire tribe: in the case of Médenine, more than five thousand *ghorfas* around twenty-seven *ksars*, some built up to five levels high, were united. Métameur, 4 miles northwest of Médenine, has grain storage *ghorfas* on two or three levels, around two courtyards, and there are others at Ksar Djouama, three centuries old in parts but possibly originally dating to the fourteenth century; Ksar Hallouf; Ksar Kherachfa, built around 1700 and still used as a collective granary, with *ghorfas* on three or four levels; and Ksar Haddada, now a *marhala* or inn, with the *ghorfas* converted into bedrooms. Some *ghorfas* are now little shops, selling Bedouin silver jewelry.

These were the *ksars* of the plains but they are also found on the mountain tops, where they are more complicated and of an earlier date than those of the plains. Three sides are set flush with the cliff, the entrance being on a narrow ridge joining the peak to the outside world. This has an archway, with a heavy door, leading to a central square surrounded by the *ghorfa* cells which are laid out all round on as many as four floors. To the left and right of the entrance are the blacksmiths' and woodworkers' shops, repairing ploughs and making camels' pack saddles. *Ghorfas* were added as required, simple cradle-vaulted recesses 13 to 16 feet deep and 6 feet high. The top ones were reached by a primitive outside staircase and the builders of these upper cells imprinted their hands and feet and sometimes their names and the date in the rough stucco. The outer walls of the *ghorfas*, rounded at the top, are attached to the next to form a long bare wall, surmounted by irregular battlements. The stone, the patina of the plaster and the weathered walls all merge into a single ochreous colour which makes it very hard to spot a mountain *ksar*: a very simple but effective form of protective camouflage.

Perhaps the most beautiful mountain *ksar* is Ouled Soltane, up a zigzag road and with several hundred cells on four or five levels around two court-yards, one fourteenth-century and both still in use. Others are Ouled Djebbab, now an inn, Beni Khedache and Chenini, with built-up cave entrances in tiers in the curved cliff face and an underground mosque, old olive presses and a communal bakery. Above and beside the mosque at Chenini are some ten curious tombs, over 12 feet long. Christians took refuge at Chenini from Roman persecution and the tombs are those of some of them who were walled

Inside a pit dwelling, Matmata, Tunisia. (Tunisian National Tourist Office)

up in their caves by the soldiers. They continued to grow, so the story goes, to awake four centuries later, be converted to Islam, and eventually die and be buried in twelve-foot tombs near the Old Mosque. Still further south, beyond Remada, are more mountain top *ksars* such as Ksar Segdel, with its amazing mural decorations of boats, and the almost inaccessible fortress refuge of Ksar Ouni, with a twelfth-century underground mosque.

But perhaps even more amazing are the *kalaâs* of the region south of Tataouine and used as fortress homes, together with fortified granaries. The *kalaâ* at Guermessa is almost inaccessible, a fortress over seven hundred and fifty years old with a fortified granary some 150 feet below built over eight or twelve storeys. Below this are cave dwellings, side by side along the cliff, the excavated material used to form a platform in front, which provides both courtyard and path. Some two thousand people live here, noted for their fierce and warlike nature. Their caves, largely man-made, are used for three months of the year, the remaining nine being spent in a nomadic existence. Water used to be a problem for some people, reached by a three-mile walk along a zigzag path to springs 1800 feet below. To ensure a happy marriage, young husbands and their friends climb up to the top of the *kalaâ* and indulge in highly dangerous games, hopping on one leg, for a full week. They have to carve the imprint of their feet and the date of their marriage into the rock to ensure happiness. There are other examples of *kalaâs* at Beni Barka, which is fourteenth-century, Ksar Oedim and Galat Ouled Chehida. In the same region there are also more recent granaries used by both Berbers and nomadic Arabs.

As well as *matmatas, ksars*, and *kalaâs*, southern Tunisia has in its central region, around Ghomrassen, other troglodytic communities. The town of Ghomrassen, with its vaulted granaries, also has very large and deep caves in which, in the early part of the century, some three thousand people lived. Other mountain towns and villages, some 1000 to 1600 feet above the valley floors, such as Douiret and Chenini, resemble beehives. The houses here are generally all the same: there is a courtyard in front with a small entrance hall, and a vaulted granary above. Around the courtyard are small outhouse buildings, including the kitchen, while the living rooms are dug deep into the high cliffs.

It is not surprising, amongst this wealth of troglodytic dwellings and associated structures that the early French soldiers found themselves confused when they tried to decide how many variations on the theme they could identify. Tunisian underground dwellings have been compared with the pueblos of the 'Four Corners' region of the USA, and even with the cone dwellings of Cappadocia in Anatolia, Turkey. But surely they should be regarded as unique.

140

CHAPTER 10

Recent cave dwellers
in Europe

F rom historical times onwards, as we have seen, far more is known
about the way of life of troglodytes and cave dwellers generally. For
most instances, there are records and we are no longer in the realm
of purely circumstantial evidence backed up by legend and myth. Although
there are examples from every continent, by far the majority are from Europe
and Asia. And in Europe, most were in France, although the last known cave
dweller in Great Britain only abandoned this way of life in 1974. For a world
survey of genuine cave dwellers, within historical times, and remembering
that Cappadocia and Tunisia have already been covered, we can start in Great
Britain.

Rather surprisingly – or perhaps not, in view of the climate – not many
people have lived in caves in Scotland, except as a refuge, and for the most
part were only transient residents.

The cave in flaggy Old Red Sandstone on the north side of Wick Bay
was frequently occupied during the last century by tinkers, coming from the
large town of Wick. They worked at tinned iron: the men cut, shaped and
hammered the metal, the women soldered it. They were not true Gypsies but
vigorous, if not strongly built, people of varied 'West Island-Caithness-
Southern Scotch' ancestry. In the great cave on the south side of the Bay,
about 10 feet high and 6 feet wide at the entrance, only extending now for
about 70 feet before being blocked by a rock fall, twenty-four more tinkers –
men, women and children, in four families, with numerous dogs – were living
in August 1866. They slept on straw, grass and bracken, with dirty blankets
or matting, on stone beds; on one, a couple and many children lay naked. All
their furniture in fact was stone and they had few clothes. Their supper,
cooked on peat fires, probably consisted of porridge, oatcakes and treacle.
The last inhabitant – the MacPhies – only moved out in about 1940 and may
have been the last occupants of an 'open' cave in Britain. There is another
large cave nearby, some 15 feet high, 30 feet wide and 60 feet deep, that was
also lived in.

Occasional use was also made of caves on the Caithness and Sutherland

Two views of a dwelling at Vale's (or Crow's) Rock, Kinver, England. (L. Dunn)

coasts, such as that at Ham, in the parish of Dunnet, also by tinkers. There are two caves at Archerfield, near Haddington in East Lothian. Both are natural but had had paved hearths built and in one a walled-up front with a door, a window and an oven. Possibly both had been inhabited since Roman times because fragments of Samian ware were found amongst the shards. Certainly, they had been occupied over a long period. Smoo Cave, after *smuga*, hole or hiding place in the language of the Vikings who discovered and named it, is in Durness, in Durness Limestone. It is vast; one of the largest in Britain, measuring 49 feet in height and 99 feet in width. It lies at the end of a sea inlet 800 feet long, which could possibly have once been roofed over. There is now a wooden bridge to the inner cave, where the Allt Smoo waterfall drops 70 feet into a pool. There have been suggestions of prehistoric occupation, and connections with the supernatural, but almost certainly the cave was used by smugglers.

In the Edinburgh mining suburb of Gilmerton, an early eighteenth-century blacksmith called George Paterson lived in the Cove, an underground house which he spent six years hewing with a pointed tool out of solid sandstone. It was complete with stone beds, tables and chairs, together with a large punchbowl and a forge. Here he and his family lived happily for some thirteen years, while he worked away below and tended his garden up above. He was exempt from rates but because of the punchbowl and some pipe-like

142

holes found piercing the rock, he was charged with supplying liquor on the Sabbath. There was a narrow passage, barely three feet high, believed to lead to Craigmillar Castle, which later drew and amazed the crowds. However, it is now thought that the Cove could never have been dug in six years and must be pre-1724, possibly 2000 years old, and might even have had later Masonic connections.

In July 1488 a bastard girl child was born in an open cave on the bank of the River Nidd in Knaresborough, near Harrogate in Yorkshire; her unmarried mother was permitted no other shelter. The child grew up there and at the age of twenty-four married Tobias Shipton. She wrote poems and – as Old Mother Shipton – became a noted prophetess who besides foretelling many local events, prophesied the defeat of the Spanish Armada and that Sir Walter Raleigh would bring back from America a 'new leaf' – tobacco – and a 'strange root' – the potato. She died in 1561 and her magic well was opened to the public in 1630: the first show cave.

The area around Buxton, in Derbyshire, had many lime works for producing quick and slaked lime for mortar, plaster and limewash for building. It was easier and quicker to carry coal to the limestone rather than the other way about, and burn it along the limestone ridge of Grin Low. This produced vast spoil heaps of ash, shale and rock, out of which the poorly paid eighteenth-

Interior of dwelling at Holy Austin Rock, Kinver, England. (D.M. Bills)

Rock House at Kinver, England. (L. Dunn)

century lime workers would excavate rooms to make small cottages – the ash or lime houses. The heaps still contained some quicklime which, under the action of percolating rainwater, would slake and carbonize, to consolidate but not over-harden the heaps so that they could be easily worked. This saved paying rent for inferior accommodation in the villages around Buxton. The cottages had walls, dividing them into rooms which could be, for example, 7 or 10 by 14 feet and 5.5 feet high. They had windows, fireplaces and a chimney; one central chimney hole served for the whole house or even sometimes for a group of houses. Some had dry-stone masonry and massive doorposts. The houses were grouped in the hillocks in clusters of, say, ten, partially roofed with turf and heath. There is one group on a farm in the village of Dove Holes, north of Buxton, where until the mid 1970s herds of seventeen or so cows were wintered in one of the houses. Another was near Pole's Hole, now Poole's Cavern, on the north slope of Grin Low. Nevertheless, despite the saving in rent for housing that would probably have been little better, both British and French observers commented at the time that the people lived like savages – or even like moles and foxes – in wretched and disgusting conditions.

An account of the English sandstone caves can begin with East Retford, near Nottingham, on the edge of which was the hamlet of Bolham, in what is now Bolham Lane, running alongside the River Idle. There is a line of caves in a cliff of red desert Keuper Sandstone in which people lived, working mainly in Bolham Mill. Otherwise, there were no houses: all the inhabitants lived in the caves, with their own circular rock chapel, mentioned in the Domesday Book. Some 12 feet across, it has a pillar dividing the entrance. The chapel, which was vandalized in the 1960s, is in the Manor garden and there is a house in the yard behind the mill – nineteenth-century and the fourth mill to have been built on the site – with a fine brick chimney. The mill owner, who lived in the Manor above the cliff, had two passages dug, some 35 feet long, down from his garden and up from the mill, for him to walk through to his office; they failed to meet by some few feet. The present owner of the lower tunnel now plans to grow mushrooms in it.

Around Mansfield, north of Nottingham, are many caves which were lived in mainly by the nomadic makers of besom brooms from heather which they gathered from the moor and forest. Sneyton, also near Nottingham, had rock dwellings, cleared away for the railway extension. Richard Manford lived for most of his life in a cave near Hawkstone, near Market Drayton in Shropshire, until he was eventually found dying by the roadside on 10 May 1910.

One of, if not the most, interesting groups of rock dwellings in Britain are those between Bridgnorth and Kidderminster, in the soft red Triassic Bunter Sandstone in the area. They are found in Bridgnorth; along Kinver Edge, a sandstone cliff on the Worcestershire and Staffordshire borders; and in the villages around Kinver. Outlying examples further north in the Ironbridge area are the pair of caves at Higford Mill, near Beckbury, between Telford and Wolverhampton, now used to store coal and garden tools, and another at Worsfield. Bridgnorth has a group of large 'closed', walled-up caves forming a row on the edge of the town, each measuring twenty to thirty feet in width, depth and height. There is also the 'open' Hermitage, a group of three large caves near Hermitage Walk, where Cyril Taylor can recall living until 1928. His mother's family had lived there for many years, ever since the local landlord decided to take steps to stop poaching in the area – the game keeper's cottage was too far away. The caves were equipped with doors, windows, double cooking range and fireplace and the new tenants moved in, ready to patrol the woods. Mr Taylor's grandmother lived there from 1898 to 1911, when the family moved to a house in Birmingham and retained the caves only as a chicken house. However, young Cyril preferred living in the caves to the back-street cottage and used to camp there at weekends. In 1918, when he became redundant, at the age of fourteen, from his job at the Birmingham Mint he moved there permanently, living off the land until, in November 1928, a pheasant was found in one of his rabbit traps and he was evicted. He claims to be the last caveman of Bridgnorth and possibly the last 'open' cave dweller in England!

ABOVE: A member of the Fletcher family outside his dwelling at Holy Austin Rock, Kinver, England. (Birmingham Reference Library) BELOW: Painting by Alfred Rushton of the interior of the same dwelling. (Northampton and Dudley Breweries)

Holy Austin Rock today.

Kinver Edge is a large sandstone ridge, now a popular country resort for the area, containing a string of former cave dwellings that have been well described by D. M. Bills and others. The most northerly is the best known: Holy Austin Rock, a large knoll near the north point of the Edge, supposed once to have been a camp of Penda, the Anglo-Saxon King of Mercia from 632 to 655. It has been hollowed out on three levels to provide several little cottages – possibly six – containing small whitewashed rooms with passages and stairs, chimneys, fireplaces, shelves and windows. The Shaw family lived at Holy Austin for over a hundred and fifty years, until 1935, and the last occupants were rehoused in about 1950; however, the Rock House Café remained in business until 1967. Nearby, on the other side of the ridge, is Astle's Rock, once containing a pair of rock houses which were later converted into a museum that remained open for twenty years. About a mile southwest of Holy Austin is Nanny's Rock; this is smaller but also extensive, a warren of five rooms with window spaces and a chimney, now much covered with graffiti. It was never 'converted' like Holy Austin but was lived in by recluses and known also as Meg-o-Fox-hole. At the southern end of Kinver Edge is Vale's or Crow's Rock, another cave dwelling on two levels inhabited until the early 1960s by Jack Leyland, a skilled besom broom-maker. Other inhabited caves and rock houses in the area are Gibraltar Rock and Samson's Cave, and those used as storerooms include the Stag Caves.

Nanny's Rock, Kinver, England.

The cottage fronts of these rock houses were usually built in brick up against the cliff and the other rooms scooped out of the rock behind them. They had doors and windows – the grooves and hinge marks are still visible – and, of course, chimneys; there were kitchen, bedroom, storeroom and stable, and the cottages were neat, both warm and cool, dry and comfortable. They were lived in by nineteenth-century iron workers, who preferred them to the crowded city cottages and tenements rented to them by the iron masters for a substantial sum. Many were lived in for centuries, for example by besom makers and mole catchers. There are numerous legends concerning them; giants were said to have lived in two of the caves and Holy Austin Rock is supposed to have been occupied by the first Christian missionaries, including an Augustinian friar. This is the legend which inspired Sabine Baring-Gould to write his romantic novel (see p. 238).

The villages around Kinver are full of old cave houses, the most picturesque being at Drakelow, including the part formerly known as Blakeshall. Most were built partly into the rock with the other main rooms added in front; in the early years of the century rather unattractive red and yellow brick chimneys were added, one of which twisted wormlike to avoid the overhanging rock. Some were lived in until the 1970s; the last was vacated in 1974. However, several of the brick-built cottages still have kitchens, bathrooms or garages that are partly caves, and a tramp is said to occupy an empty

148

cave from time to time. A further group of former cave dwellings is visible in the car park of the Queen's Head, Wolverley.

Much further south, men lived during the reign of Charles I in caves in the ravines about Lydford, just west of Dartmoor in south Devon. They were called the 'Gubbins' and had a king called Richard Rowle. In 1878 the Cornish Magazine reported that two shellfish gatherers – Irish widows aged between fifty and sixty – had worked for thirty years along the shore of Whitsand Bay, between Lore and Downderry, collecting limpets for sale in Plymouth, some ten miles away. They lived in a small cave just west of Seaton, close to Downderry, in Cornwall: a mere cleft in a shady cliff. How they survived, with the minimum of bits and pieces, defies description. They slept on sloping rock or wet sand, in front of a driftwood fire. They used a couple of old iron boilers as cupboards and smoked short, malodorous pipes which they kept on rock niches. In good times they made some fourteen shillings a week between them, but in bad? During freezing southeasterly gales in winter they took refuge in a disused pigsty nearby. Many stories exist of smugglers living in caves in Cornwall and Devon and, in the eighteenth century, an old stone-cutter once lived with his wife and children, some of whom were born and died there, in an artificial granite 'cave' near the Cheese Wring on the Cornish moors. It measured some twelve feet in depth and was rather less wide, with a vast 'capstone' roof' weighing many tons. On the side of the entrance was carved 'D. Gumb 1733'.

As if to keep the troglodytic flag flying, when a recent applicant for planning permission to build a house in southern England was refused, he built instead a Tunisian-style *matmata*, digging a circular court below ground level, leading off from which he excavated the various rooms of his 'house'.

As we have already noted, France is probably the country with the longest history of troglodytism and cave-dwelling in the world. After the Cro-Magnon people were replaced by *Homo sapiens*, their caves in the Dordogne region were taken over and occupied through the Middle Ages right up to the turn of the century. In the other major French cave-dwelling area, the Loire-Loiret region, where the local chalk, known as *tuffeau*, is particularly amenable to excavation, the practice survives to this day, with quite a few people living in caves with walled-across entrances.

There are many old caves along the River Loire which were used for stores, with new houses built in front of them for occupation. The Aquitani of Caesar's time lived in caves and Boyd Dawkins noted that whole French villages, including the church, were sited in enlarged, extended and modified cave systems. Aquitaine was originally the triangle now corresponding roughly with Gascony: from Bordeaux – Burdigala, the centre of ruling power – up the Garonne River to the Mediterranean and back along the Pyrenees to the

Bay of Biscay. It was later extended to the River Loire, making – as Strabo said – nonsense of the name, but it then included the Dordogne. Thirty miles west of Chinon, on the Vienne River, is Dénéze-sous-Doué, famous for its souterrain, mentioned in a later chapter, its sixteenth-century sculptured cave and La Fosse, the seventeenth-century cave dwellings still occupied by farmers. Other sunken cave rooms are found at Doué-la-Fontaine, south of Saumur. A few miles further west are the troglodyte houses and caves of Louresse-Rochemenier, in Main-et-Loire, first used as refuges in the ninth century and later, in medieval times, as dwellings. Many pigeons were kept there, recalling Cappadocia. Some caves are still used as homes by farmers and others have been restored and are now preserved, with a peasant mushroom-growing and rural-life museum.

In Chinon, in Indre-et-Loire, there are troglodyte houses above the wine *caves* in the ridge high up above the town, near the cave where a pious sixth-century hermit – one of many such monastic recluses – had his cell. Radegund, the wife of King Chlotar I, consulted him about her intentions to leave the court and take the veil. She did so and had an oratory built, which was later enlarged into the St Radegonde Chapel. The present cave dwellers are known as *Les Marginaux*, the troglodytes who succeeded the vagabonds and outcasts who once lived in the two rows of caves in the cliff above the River Loire. The rock, known as *millarge*, is a gritty yellow limestone. It is harder than *tuffeau* but less porous and more frost resistant. The Château of Chinon is made of it and the caves owe their existence largely to quarrying. Many of the tunnels and galleries around it, secret routes into the Château from a good few miles distant, have been filled in. There is a chapel and a 'Museum' cave next to it. Thirty of the caves in the upper row are still occupied, while the lower row is abandoned; thirty years ago all were lived in. The caves are owned by individuals, by a 'troglodyte cooperative' and by the State. In the past, when a suitable cave became available, anybody could occupy it, put up a door and after thirty years claim legal ownership. Of the present generation, most have inherited their caves from their families, although some are rented.

The people are of Gypsy origin and used to live off the land, eating dandelions, chestnuts and wild lettuce, but they also cultivated gardens and kept chickens and rabbits. Now they are scavengers, choosing to live there for freedom's sake, with high wire fences and Alsatian guard dogs. The caves are 10 to 13 feet across and up to 33 feet deep, and some are sub-divided, but the whitewashed rooms are difficult to enlarge because of the type of rock. They have a kitchen with a fireplace and a bread oven, a bedroom and a store behind. They hunt around for firewood but use calor gas for cooking and some have modern heating. Their food now consists of rice, eggs, milk and potatoes, with some chicken and rabbits still. Some of their stews are delicious.

The walls are exposed rock, showing the pick marks, sometimes whitewashed or patterned; the floors are tiled, cemented or of beaten earth. There are alcoves and niches with shelves for storage, with wooden furniture and old rugs. The houses are generally clean although damp and humid, sometimes with water trickling down the walls. However, they are easy to heat compared with wattle-and-daub houses and there is never any freezing. The temperature is higher than outside – in winter nearly 20° F (8° to 9° C) higher inside the caves – and they are much cooler in summer. Some occupants take pride in ownership and have small gardens and letter boxes, but their washing is grey and the rubbish tips smelly. There are no water closets, only primitive lime-filled pits which are later covered over with more lime; frequent disinfecting is necessary. Personal hygiene is limited; few have bathrooms or even running water and most people get their water from deep – 100 foot – wells or, far more frequently, from the public taps where water-fetching is a social event; people do their laundering there as well. The people vary, of course. Some are suspicious, with fierce guard dogs, others friendly. One old man thought of giving in and moving out, one old woman did go but came back to 'her cave'. One 'handicapped' family had a retarded woman, now in care, living with an older man and wheeling a pram containing a large doll to replace a dead child. One family, with a terrier, had members who were in the Resistance during World War II. When they are ill, the District Nurse is always called out – her services are free and she is always well received. The patient may go to hospital, probably turning out to be dirty and usually returning to his or her cave when cured.

Some men work, gardening or hay-making or brick-laying, but only when it suits them; a few have small pensions. They tend to support their young people, who do not want to work, conform or integrate. Despite limited money, alcohol is a major problem and they love parties: in the summer they get drunk on wine, singing all night, brawling and fighting and becoming very noisy. This would not be tolerated in normal housing, even though the town is friendly towards them, and they would need special estates – unacceptable segregation. But they do not want to live a normal life with other people and the District Nurse regards caves as preferable to the town's slums; the people are fiercely independent, with their own way of life. The police prefer it, too, only climbing up if it becomes really necessary because, even if fights do lead to the occasional major accident or even death, there is never any evidence. But their numbers are down, since few young people want to stay in the caves and as they become vacant, the Council boards them up. Everybody seems to want to study them; this account owes its thanks to one such investigation.

And now? Bourgeois renovation! The upwardly mobile are buying up the caves along the Loire, at Vouvray and Montrichard, for weekend cottages, where they copy the troglodytes except in their very different style of living; bathrooms and central heating are added and some caves used as games or play rooms.

There are many other examples. Along the River Loire, at Villiers, in Loir-et-Cher, a newly-cut front to a one-room cave house, complete with door and window, had sculpted above it the 'aces of hearts, spades and diamonds, an anchor, a cogwheel and a fish'. On the other side of an untrimmed rock buttress was the next house, also newly fronted. Trôo, on the Loir, is a once-walled, half underground town on a hill, resembling Og's city, described in the next chapter. It has a Romanesque church and was fought over by the Catholics and the Huguenots. It is like a sponge, the chalk cliffs perforated with passages, halls, some of them circular, with many storerooms and stables. Most of the houses and cafés were all or partly underground. Holes in the ground led to lower galleries of rooms via a rope or a ladder, with chimneys sprouting everywhere. Some cave entrances had ledges only a few feet deep – nobody seemed to feel giddy – and ten or twenty feet wide. Rubbish was left to dry in the sun or be washed away by rain.

Also on the Loir, and formerly walled, was Les Roches, above Montoire. Most of its houses were hewn from the chalk, with a church, perched on the crags on a narrow road, squeezed in between. The rock houses have living rooms, kitchen, cellars and stables, complete with doors and windows, carved into the stone. The chimneys ran up and through the rock and are protected from the rain by brick breastworks. The pretty sixteenth-century Château de Boydan is half rock-hewn; the Chapel of St Gervais wholly so, with an inner and an outer chamber. The window wall was cut too thin and fell away, revealing the remains of spirited frescoes of a hunting king and huntsman with horn and boar-spear. Nearer to Montoire on the left bank of the Loir is Lavardin, high up the hill in a dense wood, a troglodyte hamlet. The Grotte des Vierges was the principal 'building', with a main chamber complete with chimney and window, and was once a hermitage. It had subsidiary buildings, once occupied, and its own circular six-foot-deep grain silo, as well as a wine cellar. Nearer to Vendôme is the Château de Rôchambeau, now replaced by a modern mansion but with rock-hewn auxiliary rooms and also the Roi des Halles, the cave where the Duke of Beaufort hid when he escaped from Vincennes prison during the Hundred Years' War. There are more caves, including a hospital, at Lisle, further up the Loir above Vendôme and in the Quartier St Lubin. In Vendôme cave houses high up the cliff were occupied until recently. Above Tours and Marmoutier on the Vouvray road is La Roche Corbon, once a troglodyte village, again with many pigeonries.

In Main-et-Loire and part of Vienne there were many underground

Cliff dwelling, Main-et-Loir, France. (French Government Tourist Office)

villages. In this valuable vineyard land, the owner would wall his property round using stone, quarried from a pit; he then dug into one 'wall' of the pit to make a cave house under his vineyard, looking out from his door and windows into his quarry. He bored a hole upwards for his chimney and built a square block of bricks around it. Thus, all that could be seen of the hamlet or village was a series of chimneys sticking up out of the vineyards. The dry moat around the fine medieval castle at St Leger, near Loudun, is dug out of rock and from this fosse many houses were excavated outwards. Along the Loire from Tours to Saumur, along the Loir, and at Duclair and elsewhere on the River Seine, are numerous cave dwellings, until quite recently inhabited. Most were very poor, reached by exhausting sinuous tracks, although some had scraps of gardens or terraces, with hanging greenery. They had chimneys and windows, and some even had embellished facades.

At Bourré, Loir-et-Cher, the beautiful *tuffeau* chalk, much sought after for building, is quarried and the quarrymen built their villages in the old workings or dug them out of the actual rock. At Ste Maure, on the Tours to Châtellerault road, is the troglodyte village of Courtineau, complete with chapel, hewn out of the distinctive estuarine rock. At Villaines, Indre-et-Loire, the cliffs are pierced with the caves of the basketmakers – neat, comfortable and well furnished – and the streams below used to be lined with willows and bundles of cut osiers soaking to preserve their suppleness.

The village of Ezy, in the River Eure valley of Normandy, had a strange settlement extending for rather less than a mile along the railway, where numerous underground dwellings, built on three storeys with horizontal platforms before them, were constructed and occupied by the owners of the vineyards covering the hill above them. The vines failed, the buildings were abandoned, and the caves were used only for occasional traditional drinking and dancing festivals, such as Easter Tuesday. Little taverns sprang up between the caves to support this ritual, but they too fell into ruin around 1860 or 70. Whereupon, some eighty miserable men, women and children, all social and moral outcasts, moved in, dressed in rags, sleeping on dry leaves and living on thieving, begging and the scrounging of discarded food and furniture. Their main possession – which they all had – was a wooden crook used for lowering into the common well whatever utensils they might possess, to draw up water.

Similar cave settlements could be found along the Dordogne and Dronne Rivers. St Emilion, in Bordeaux, had eighth-century troglodyte houses, as well as rock-hewn churches. At Cuzorn, between Périgueux and Agen, the fine and much-quarried rocks have natural caves and those dug out as quarries, yielding halls and galleries that were until fairly recently lived in. At Brantôme, on the Dronne, many houses backing onto the rock were normally built out in front but with their owners' workshops – blacksmiths, carpenters, tinkers, tailors, cobblers – in caverns behind. La Roche Beaucourt, between Angoulême and Périgueux, had a nest of cave houses in a rock called l'Argentine, with floor silos and wall cupboards. Aubeterre on the Dronne had subterranean stables and storehouses and even some rock-hewn bread ovens. Near Brive, in Corrèze, there are some sandstone caves which were inhabited since the Upper Palaeolithic and some of which were lived in well into this century. Those at Lamouroux have mural paintings. The caves do not run deep into the rock; they are square cut, on several storeys, with holes cut in the floors of the upper stages for ladders, or with narrow access cornices. They had partially walled-up entrances and wooden doorways, shelves and cupboards, all hewn with picks with a triangular point. They had the usual rooms for living, with others for livestock, stables, storerooms, silos and pigeonries. Commarques had a completely rock-hewn stable. Many of the cave dwellings had cisterns, with plugs, and basins, and one had a well. Opposite Les Eyzies there used to be an hotel-tavern, part-cave, part-gallery, called l'Auberge du Paradis. It was reached by a ladder in a grotto, and the kitchen was rock-hewn; so too was the bedroom once allocated to an American honeymoon couple. Grioteaux is a hamlet on the Beune, a tributary of the Vézère, built on a terrace overhung by the cliff and thus – like Mesa Verde – a cliff hamlet. Above it, reached only by a ladder, there was once a rock-hewn chamber with

LEFT: Base of the castle at Les Baux-de-Provence, France. RIGHT: Family group outside their dwelling on Sacro Monte, Granada, Spain in 1953.

a wooden gallery in front of it, used by the community as a hiding place for their valuables in times of trouble. The River Célé, flowing into the River Lot, has the village of Sauliac, in an amphitheatre of fawn and orange-tinted limestone where, surrounding the castle, which is buried in huge oaks, the houses were a mixture of faced caves or buildings glued onto the rock face. This was once in the heart of the Hundred Years' War territory. La Laugerie Basse, on the right bank of the Vézère, known for its Cro-Magnon shelter, has very old cottages whose back rooms are cut deep into the rock, with lean-to roofs added in front.

Les Baux-de-Provence, in the Chaîne des Alpilles, had partly rock-hewn houses in the fifteenth century in the Grande-Rue; the base of the castle was also rock-cut. Some 25 miles east of Orange, in the Rhône valley of Provence, religious wars led some hundreds of people in the hilltop village of Barry to excavate caves in the cliffs and use the soft stone to build part of their houses out in front; they ended up two-thirds within the cave, one-third outside. The painstaking carving on the lintels and mullions of both houses and chapels alike suggested a date in the 1600s, but some could have been much earlier. One couple recently reoccupied one of the caves and opened it as a troglodytic bistro.

Cave dwellings in volcanic rock were found in the Auvergne and the Cevennes, such as those in the tuff and agglomerate in the Vivarais. At the

Balmes du Montbrun, a crater 300 feet across and 480 feet deep forming part of the Coiron, near St Jean le Centenier, has many artificial cave dwellings including a chapel and one cave said to have once been the prison. This settlement was lived in until around 1800. The Grottoes de Boissière are twelve in number, on the side of the Puy de Châteauneuf, overlooking the Saint Nectaire to Marols road, in the Puy de Dôme. All are dug out of tuff and of similar size, although one is larger, 28 by 12 by 7 feet high. Below the caves, on the hill slope, are small fields and gardens, built on terraces and with dry-stone walls. Also in the Puy are the Grottoes de Jonas on the Couze, near Cheix, found in stages ranging up to a height of between 90 and 120 feet. The mountain is precipitous, the tuff porous, but sixty remained out of the many more there must once have been. They were probably prehistoric but were lived in during the Middle Ages when the tracks linking the stages were built and protected by walls with parapets. They include a castle and a chapel, and a remarkable spiral staircase, all rock-hewn. Artefacts ranging from flint tools to bronze weapons to coins and statuettes were found.

At Ceyssac, in Haute-Savoie, a ridge of harder than usual tuff from the volcano La Denise which survived erosion by the River Borne, thus providing security, was excavated into a troglodyte village in five superimposed storeys. There were stables with mangers and rings for tying up cattle, a vast circular hall and rooms with seats and lockers hewn out of the rock. There was also a subterranean chapel with an early Romanesque doorway. The Polignacs built a castle on the topmost spike of rock, reached only by a flight of steps cut into the rock face. The people gradually moved to the flat land and built normal houses and a modern and unsightly church. More volcanic cave dwellings occur along the River Borne, such as the fourteen at Conteaux, in Haute-Loire. Here the largest is divided into three rooms, each 45 feet deep by 11 feet wide, although the usual size was from 28 to 36 feet deep. The vaulted roof is usually over 6 feet high and a single roof opening did service for all three as a chimney.

So cave dwellings were clearly very common in France as, relatively speaking, they still are. They were dug, or found naturally, in the *tuffeau* and the normal chalk, in limestone, sandstone and volcanic rocks. In addition to those mentioned, there were others in Var, Bouches du Rhône, Aveyron, Gard, Lozère, Cantal, Charente and Vienne. They were so common in Perigord that the place-name *Cluseau* frequently occurs, meaning a lived-in cave with a walled-up entrance, door and window; ordinary grottoes, whether lived in or not, were known as *roffi*.

The so-called *Heidenlöcher* or pagan-holes at Goldback, overlooking Lake Constance in south Germany, were excavated in a cliff of loess – wind-blown loamy dust – rising perpendicularly some 23 feet from the lake and formerly reached from a narrow path skirting the lake shore. The former stairs disintegrated badly and were replaced by stone. Only seven caves remain at Goldback, many more having been destroyed. They consisted of a series of rooms, chambers, cellars and niches, connected with each other by hallways and stairs extending for some half a mile. The rooms are of different sizes and shapes, some with groined arches, others with flat ceilings. Some had columns, pilasters, architraves, cornices and springers, others were plain, quite unornamented. Nearly all had stone benches, niches and window and door openings with grooves for frames and the remains of wooden dowels. Other niches and rifts in the cliff mark former cave dwellings.

The first cave, entered by an arched doorway, is 10 feet high with niches near the entrance. The second has two windows and a chimney, with a niche opening into the third cave which is 6 feet high and nearly 7 feet wide. The fourth, 7 feet high, has a groined ceiling and a stone bench at the opening. On a lower level is the 'chapel', with seven steps down to a path which bifurcates to lead to the open or to the fifth cave, which has two stone columns in the middle supporting gothic arches. Two more caves – numbers six and seven – also have niches and benches and extend down to the surrounding meadowland level. No one knows when, why or by whom the caves were built. There is no record and no artefacts have been found to explain them. There is just one single stone image of, perhaps, a sitting man, carved in quartz rock, possibly of Celtic origin or even, if it represents the God the Father figure, Christian. It is thought likely that the early, simple caves were enlarged and added to over the years as Celts, Suevians, Romans and Allemanni lived there in turn; the name 'Heidenlöcher' is ascribed to the Romans. In 1760 the city council of Ueberlingen ordered the destruction of the majority of the caves because of their occupation by tramps and vagabonds; when the new road was built between 1846 and 1848, many more on the lakeside went, leaving only the seven, which were well looked after as a tourist attraction.

There are inhabited caves in Malta, especially in the north, and in Italy, caves at Settinango, near Florence, at Lucca, at Pisa and in Umbria have been lived in during historic times. However, the best known by far are those of Sicily. The whole southeast corner of the island is full of underground cities, Val d'Ispica being the most famous. There are Siculiano, Caltabelotta, Rafadalle, Bronte and Maletto. Although known as *Ddieri*, they were not tombs but habitations, as their oil and corn handmills testify. The Val d'Ispica is a narrow eight-mile-long limestone valley between Modica and Spaicaforno, lined both sides with tool-marked artificial grottoes. Some have ten or twelve rooms in a line, seldom more than 20 by 6 by 6 feet high. The stream in the valley bottom provides water and irrigates wild figs and oleanders. Higher up

The caves on Sacro Monte, Granada, Spain.

grow acanthi, wild artichokes and festoons of cactus, shading the grottoes. These were on several levels, reached by finger and toe holds, steps or ladders with, on the very top, a ledge or gallery reached by another ladder, with a magnificent view. Here the women would promenade and gossip or the whole village could take refuge, hauling up the ladder behind them. One dwelling, on three storeys, was called the Castle and the total number of dwellings was reckoned at over fifteen hundred. None appeared to have any ornament, just rough holes for doors and windows. Rings found hewn in the stone in some of the rooms must have had some purpose. Fragments of Samian ware and carved marble were found, probably of later date than the construction of the dwellings. Some contain graves which were probably both earlier and later than the houses. Nowadays shepherds still occupy some of these caves, as they do those in the Cammarata Mountains, which are well supplied with streams. Roman slaves once hid here, two thousand years ago, and now shepherds live for weeks on end during the lambing season, using a mixture of rock and imported wooden furniture.

In the Barrio de Santiago, beyond the Santiago Church Road in Guadix, east of Granada in Spain's Andalusia, lives a colony of Gypsies and non-gypsies in a quarry-like, rather moonscape area which forms part of the treeless foothills of the Sierra Nevada. Here there are caves dug into the easily worked mixture of clay, loam and limestone which forms the Villafranchian (Calabrian) conglomerate and *costras* or crusts, which overlie the Pliocene conglomerate, sands and limestones.

158

The people are *gitanos*, descendents of the Gypsies who came from India 500 years ago to be tinkers, coppersmiths, peddlers, horse traders and fortune-tellers. Some roamed the country, some settled in Granada – then a very rich city – and moved into the Albaicín, the old Moorish falconers' quarter, or else scooped out shelters on the slopes of Sacro Monte. Thirty or so years ago people climbed up Sacro Monte – second to the Alhambra, across the valley, as a tourist attraction – to visit the caves, where the people performed for them. The caverns and taverns were full of gleaming copper vessels; some caves were poor and squalid but many housed prosperous dancers and singers, with baths, electric light and telephones. No longer; the people now are fierce, with guard dogs, and tourists are warned to keep strictly away. Further north, some 50 miles south of Madrid, is another troglodyte town at La Guardia, where people live for choice, complete with kitchen fires and chimneys, their *cuevas* cool in summer and warm in winter. In 1957 they cost 700 pesetas ($14) for a small cave and 10,000 pesetas ($200) for a large one; this might perhaps be £100 and £1400, respectively, in 1987 English money!

Still others settled in Guadix and most of the people here are friendly, and welcome tourists. Guadix – meaning Valley of Life in Arabic – has what must be one of the world's largest present-day troglodyte populations, numbering between ten and twenty thousand, occupying approximately one square mile. The Barrio de Santiago has its own roads as well as stores, taverns, schools and churches, some – once all – underground; the chapel had its spire above ground like the chimneys. Now it has a square with a church

Church and houses at Guadix, Spain.

in the centre. Gypsies often venerate Sara, the Egyptian handmaiden to St Mary Salome and St Mary Jacobe. Many of the cave houses have their porch or front room built out, looking in some ways like a normal house. Inside, they have arched doors and ceilings for strength, whitewashed walls – occasionally, some are papered – and tiled, lino-painted or well-tamped earth floors. Storerooms are just left bare-walled and floored. There are no passages, the rooms leading one into another, there often being as many as half a dozen. The furnishings are attractive, some of the double beds quite miraculous with their drapery. Electricity, with all its wires surface-channelled, provides for television, refrigerators and fridge-freezers. Calor gas is used for cooking, hams are smoked, and there are plumbed-in sinks and washing machines. A far cry from the past, when there had been only one tap between three families, although the latrines are still relatively primitive; nor are baths much in evidence. Again, an almost constant temperature – never too hot, never too cold – is enjoyed. Outside, the cave houses can be an absolute delight, with street numbers, little flower gardens, the occasional trellis with its vine, plenty of flowers and a good few vegetables. There is the odd cow, donkey or mule and abundant dogs. But perhaps best of all are the chimneys: these are everywhere, sticking up where no other sign of life is visible, indicating cave after cave beneath. They are exactly like the chimneys of the 'Lost Boys'' underground houses in 'The Never, Never Land', in *Peter Pan*.

The Canary Islands – off the coast of Morocco and volcanic, arid and tropical – include Tenerife and, in particular, Gran Canaria, the third largest island, nearly circular and 592 square miles in area. In these two islands, colonies of Canarios, fierce and curious stone-using farmers, descended from the tall, light-skinned Guanche (or Guanchos), perhaps related to the Berbers of North Africa, who originally inhabited the island in the fifteenth century, lived in caves in the high cliffs. They are mainly clustered in the fertile valleys of the northern half of Gran Canaria, where as many as twenty entrances can be found on a single hillside, surrounded by terraced farming. Sunny slopes were obviously preferred; north-facing caves are noticeably damp. All were hewn from the soft volcanic tuff, which is also mined as a building stone, the quarries resembling those of Caen in Normandy.

The majority consist of one or two simple rooms, probably often volcanic blow-holes in the tuff later enlarged although some are entirely man-made. They are said to be clean and comfortable, warm in winter, cool in summer. The interiors vary; the rooms are nearly seven feet high, with rounded and unfinished walls, although later caves had squared-off walls and rectangular entrances, with walls painted white. Older caves had stone-hewn beds or beds made of rubble, and roughly hewn shelves and deep niches to 'contain vessels of milk or water'. The doors were simple, made of wood, with primitive windows. But since the islands were conquered by the Spanish in 1463, the use of caves as habitations began to decline and now the majority are empty. Many have now been abandoned and bricked up or are used as stores or for livestock, although some have been incorporated into surface houses which have electricity and running water. As well as forming the church, caves were also used for ceremonies and burials; one abandoned cave on a hill, with three entrances, might have been used as a communal meeting place, possibly for religious ceremonies.

The most impressive cluster of caves on Gran Canaria is the Cenobia de Valerón – Convent of Valeron – on the north coast, near Guía, west of Aracus; it is now protected. High in the tuff cliffs, below a magnificent basalt arch more than 80 feet high and nearly 100 feet wide, nearly 1000 feet above sea-level and overlooking the coast road, are 298 pre-Hispanic caves. Each is simple, hewn with stone tools on various levels with stone-cut steps and abundant graffiti. Signs of joist holes suggest an earlier superstructure. The colony is said by Guanche tradition to have been a pagan 'convent', where the daughters of noble families spent their youth until the age of thirty–five, when they were free to choose between marriage or monasticism. Certainly it was a community; possibly it was a fortified village, but it may later have become an outcast colony for the sick. The Cenobio was declared a national monument in 1978. A few caves are still lived in Minorca, in the Balearic Islands, where one has been converted into a bar, and in Madeira.

Quite a few of the Greek islands have caves that have been inhabited at one time or other. One well-known example is Thira (or Santorini), the southernmost of the Cyclades. In Hellenistic times there was a natural cave, with masonry additions, which was the sacred place of the cult of Heracles and Dionysus; otherwise, there was then no underground living. In early medieval times the island formed part of the Byzantine Empire until pirates took it over from a weakened empire in the late twelfth century; it remained in their hands until Crusader forces restored order in 1244.

Overlying the tuff are flows of basaltic lava and the junction between the two was used later for deep, narrow houses and storehouses, buttressed by the pumice-like *thiraki-gi* rock which is particularly good at withstanding earthquakes. Nevertheless, seismic damage is noticeable in the island in the number of abandoned buildings. By the eighteenth century the growth of underground dwellings had reached the point when local bye-laws had to be introduced to prohibit owners from enlarging their houses if there was any risk of them touching their neighbour's, and from planting trees in gardens that were over a house. The inhabitants of the island are still reluctant to plant flowering shade vines on their terraces for fear of damaging adjacent cave dwellings or cisterns.

LEFT: Dwellings on the shore at Santorini, Greece. (The MacQuitty International Collection)
RIGHT: Caves at Matala, Crete. (Paul Henderson)

Typical dwellings in the island developed from excavated cave to semi-subterranean dwelling to barrel-vaulted masonry house. As mortar they used 'theraic cement', a mixture of lime and pozzolanic earth similar to the Roman cement made from the volcanic ash mined around the Bay of Naples. As is common practice, the excavated blocks of stone were used to build strong facades and cave-shaped outer rooms, whose vaults supported terraces for drying crops. The typical house had two rooms with a thick masonry wall between, one room in and one out of the rock. The latter had a door with a window above and one on each side. Kitchens, latrines and stables would be housed in outbuildings, the kitchens often having ventilating shafts which served to ventilate the whole house. Diurnal temperature variation in these houses is, as usual, very low: $5°$ F at the furthest point inside as against $30°$ outside. The climate of Santorini is very moderate but there is enough of a winter, and a hot summer, for the inhabitants of these semi-troglodytic dwellings to appreciate their natural insulation.

Further south, in the Greek island of Crete, lepers lived in caves in the cliffs of sandy limestone on the south coast of the island at Matala, south of Phaistos and just north of Akra (Cape) Lithinon. The area is literally dotted with caves but they were never occupied by any other people until, after the lepers were moved to the tiny island of Spinalonga, just off Crete and recently abandoned when the remaining patients were transferred to the mainland, after which hippies moved in the 1960s and had to be cleared out.

Caves have been lived in in Cyprus, Bulgaria and Poland and, in the Crimea, from Cape Kersonese to the Bay of Ratla. The hills here consist of layers of limestone alternating with clay and hard shale; these erode easily and the clay washes out to form great caverns in the sides. Although liable to collapse when unsupported, they have been used as dwellings. The Rock of Inkermann – the ancient Celamita – runs east of the town beyond the marshy Chernaya valley and was converted into a vast quarry, threatening the old troglodyte town in the cliffs. This had rooms big enough to hold 500 people, linked with a warren of underground galleries. The rocks of Djonfont-kaleharri are also honeycombed with caves, inhabited until the early part of the century; some were open, some had screening walls, and the domed church stood beneath an overhang. In Amasia, Armenia, there were caves with a vertical entrance, reached by a ladder down a 'well': some people 'closed their door' by rolling a large circular stone across.

Xenophon discoursed on the troglodytes of Armenia. He described how Polycrates, an Athenian captain of a company of troops, asked for leave to undertake a private mission and set off, with some of his best men, to the village which had been 'allotted' to Xenophon, after he had been fêted everywhere he went. Polycrates found underground houses, reached through a hole like a large vertical well but opening below into spacious chambers. He surprised the headmen and villagers and found seventeen young horses being raised there as a tribute to the king. The animals - goats, sheep and cattle, as well as horses – had a ramp to enter but the people used a ladder. They had stores for vegetables, wheat and barley and made a wine from the latter, in which floated malt grains and sections of reed. These were pulled out and used as 'straws' for drinking the wine. It was very strong, as Polycrates discovered, very much an acquired taste, frequently needing the addition of water.

Cave house at Drakelow, Kinver, England. Chimneys were
added at the beginning of the century.

CHAPTER 11

Recent cave dwellers in Africa, Asia and North America

T here are examples of recent and contemporary cave use and dwelling in Africa, apart from the extraordinary houses to be found around Matmata and Médenine in southern Tunisia, the subject of a separate chapter. At Ras Ashagar, meaning 'Bald Head', there is a vast cathedral-like limestone sea cave near Cape Spartel, near Tangier, Morocco. It is used between day-time tides by gnome-like men of possible Riffian ancestry from the village of Mediouna, some three miles away, who come armed with kerosene lamps to extract millstones for crushing grain: the hard porous limestone is particularly well suited for this. In between, they are said to practice some rather dubious ancient and secret rites in the caves.

There were whole cave villages in Egypt. In the district between Mansa-Sura and Cyrene, mountain grottoes reached only by ropes housed families, some members of which were born, lived and died in them, without ever going out. The Tibu people live around Tibesti, typically at Uweinat, in southern Libya and northern Chad, west of northern Sudan. Here they occupy stone shelters, some hollowed out of ledges on the walls of wadis. These are some eight feet in diameter, with a gap for a door and no roof. The remains of fires, bones and other refuse abound. There are many other round stone huts on rock terraces, with roofs of branches. Socotra, the frankincense island off Somalia and now part of South Yemen, has Bedouin cave dwellers living about a thousand feet up a camel trail up the Motaha Gorge, where they live off their herds. The effects of war are found again in northern Ethiopia, where the Eritrean rebels are known to be living in caves in the mountains.

In Mali, in the remote village of Sanga, some 800 miles east of Dakar, some 250,000 Dogon people live along the ninety miles of escarpment called the Cliffs of Bandiagara. These 600-foot sandstone cliffs are cave-ridden; some of the houses are caves while others cling to the edge of the cliff, made of mud with straw-hatted granaries. The people very cleverly build – or rather use – staircases up natural fault-fissures in the rocks. They place great store on the spirits of their dead elders, the theme of their *dama* ceremonies, while

LEFT: A Dogon compound along the Bandiagara Cliffs, Mali, Africa. RIGHT: A village and caves along the Bandiagara Cliffs, Mali, Africa. (Werner Forman Archive)

their diviners predict the future from the study of, for example, fox tracks. The Mitumba Mountains in Katanga, in southeast Zaïre, contain cave dwellings, of which the principal cave is at Mokana, northeast of the Juo falls on the Lufira River. The caves are up to twelve feet high and very dark, reached by clambering round a chaotic mass of large rocks. Large trees growing in the entrances usually mark their location. This might be the region referred to in his letters by Dr Livingstone, in which he said that in central Africa there were vast caves capable of housing whole tribes, their household goods and their livestock. Elephants go after salt into the Kitum Cave on Mount Elgon, close to the Ugandan border with Kenya. They seek mirabilite – hydrated sodium sulphate or glauber salts, a mild laxative – and also natrolite, a zeolite. Humans live higher up, at about 7000 feet, where an African farmer might live in one half of a divided cave and his cows in the other, with a brush wall across the entrance. Cave men have left their traces in other caves nearby.

There were several types of cave dwellers in Asia Minor. Some had masonry houses but granaries and stores in caves behind. Less advanced groups lived in Cilicia Tracheia, in a valley named Bakluzan Dere in a pass in the Taurus Mountains, some 10 miles north of Ermenak, in modern Turkey. They improved their dwellings, building strong masonry walls round the entrances, but did no agriculture and were somewhat unfriendly. Their entrances were high up perpendicular cliffs, reached by long, but light, poles which they could pull up after them for virtually perfect safety. Those – the sick and aged – who could not manage this were strapped to the backs of active men. Less unfriendly people, but living a cruder way of life during the long summers only, were widespread around Lycaonia. Others lived at Serai, north of Karaman, near Ermenak, where the alternation of layers of rock and clay led to many cavities which were easy to excavate but which the inhabitants did nothing to improve. The famous tuff dwellings of Cappadocia, in Anatolia, form the subject of a separate chapter.

In the Hauran, on the east side of the Zanite hills in Palestine, was Edrei, the subterranean labyrinthic residence of King Og of Bashan. This Amorite king, who 'was not taken in the Flood' and 'reigned in Ashtaroth', was conquered by Moses and Israel in the battle of Edrei. He was huge: his iron bedstead in Rabbath, capital of Ammon, was said to have measured 9 by 4 cubits, perhaps 15 by 6 feet. One approached Edrei down a sloping passage to reach some twelve rooms, now used as stalls for goats and stores for straw. The passage became smaller and smaller until it reached a 'well' several feet deep, which dropped into a city with broad streets with dwellings on both sides. There was a market place, with shops in the walls, as in modern Syrian cities, and a great hall. The whole was spacious, sweet-smelling, with fresh air and a mild temperature. There were very few roof supports and only a few fallen columns: a model for any modern subterranean dwelling. There were other caves in the limestone cliffs of Palestine, such as Jayonim Cave in Israel and the Grotto of Adonis in Lebanon. Haua Fteah, in Cyrenaica, is used for shelter in winter by up to eight families and their flocks and herds. Several caves in the Middle East are still in use. Carleton Coon found two families of Dervishes from Sultanabad had set up house in Belt Cave in northern Iran. They had come to the shore to spend the winter in the cave, complete with their dogs and donkeys but also bringing less welcome visitors – fleas and TB.

But by far the most important examples of modern cave dwelling in this region is the Shanidar, in Kurdistan in northeast Iraq. This was the cave occupied by the first 'Flower People', Neanderthal men who in about 60,000 BP honoured the graves of their dead with bunches of wild flowers. Here, in 1953, Ralph Solecki found a community of Kurds living during the winter in the main cave known as Shkaft Mazin Shanidar – the Cave Big Shanidar. The cave is in the Gali a Shkafta – the valley of the cave – and is reached by a two-hour walk up a steep path on the east side of Baradost Mountain from the village of Mergasur. The cave is one of several in the area, in the Cretaceous Qamchuga dolomitic limestone. It has been occupied on and off since about 100,000 BP. The modern Kurds living there have been taking refuge from conflicts with their central governments since the days of the Ottoman Empire and now of the state of Iraq. In 1970 a US radio broadcast announced that the Barzani Kurds were leaving the cave to resume occupation of their villages.

Solecki found the people belonged to the Shirwani tribe and came from the villages in the Mergasur Valley where there are no caves. They occupy five or six caves in the Shanidar Valley during the winter from November to April, returning to their more open homes in the early spring. They are Sunni Moslems, a conservative sect, although there may be some Shias among them. The caves in the Rowanduz area to the south contain plenty of hearths, with soot and other evidence of prehistoric occupation, but have nobody living in them now; their only use is as shelters for animals.

Traditionally, the Shanidar cave was once owned by Khuder Agha, from the village of Korka, near Mergasur. The wily Khor Pasha of Rowanduz, builder of roads and fortresses, was supposed to have taken refuge here, with his army. The Turks met him in battle in about 1837, blasting into the cave with cannon while Khor Pasha's men fought back with flintlock rifles. This was not the last time the cave was to be used as a refuge; fragments of artillery shells suggest a more recent bombardment, supported by signs that hunks of stone had been knocked off the ceiling. Some of the stone walls had a tar deposit about a sixteenth of an inch thick which had seeped locally into cracks as deeply as three-quarters of an inch.

The Shanidar cave is shaped like a rough triangle. The opening is 82 feet wide and 26 feet high, the interior soon widening to a maximum of 175 feet while the ceiling vaults to a jagged crevice some 45 feet high, before dropping down to a height of 25 feet. The ceiling then slopes gradually right down to the floor some 130 feet in from the cave mouth. The interior is fairly dry and dusty but has at least one major drip at the rear. The slope in front of the cave, with its slowly increasing debris, is steep, slanting down to a gully about 140 feet below with an intermittent stream and stagnant pools in the summer. In the wet season the gully fills up and water is plentiful, with an accessible capacity at any one time of some 265 gallons. The women carry the water on their backs in goatskin bags. In the dry season the only supply is from a spring called Kani Petka, 440 feet above the cave, which takes a seventeen-minute climb up a winding path. On the slope in front of the cave, while looking for Palaeolithic traces, Solecki found a mottled black flint with translucent grey edges and curious signs of wear on the edges. His Barzani porter recognised it as a strike-a-light flint of that period, called by the Kurds a *berdeste*. With his piece of wrought iron, from his pocket, he immediately produced sparks. The flint-and-iron are used to ignite 'punk' or dry pulverized cloth.

On each visit the present-day occupiers build some fourteen small and flimsy huts in the rear of the cave, where black soot hangs down in thick

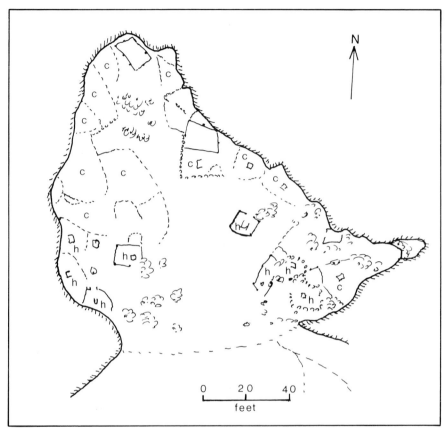

A simplified plan of Shanidar Cave. Corrals, some of them converted houses, are shown as 'c' and houses with hearths as 'h'. (After Ralph S. Solecki)

strands of cobwebs. They are made from poles and brush and in some ways can be seen from the upper fossil layers to emulate their prehistoric predecessors. Despite all the dung and straw around the cave, the huts are kept very clean. There are six householders, including the head man, down to a lowly rock-breaker and his family. The houses are single-roomed, built – understandably – without too much regard for weatherproofing. Solecki found eight houses with hearths, and a further four with hearths that had been converted to corrals; the remaining two huts had no hearths. The number of houses occupied at any one time varies from five to seven although the twelve houses with hearths could house in all some ninety people. Seven were in use; they averaged only 150 square feet of floor space, because living space was probably sacrificed to housing of animals. This is thought to be the case because the rule of thumb is to allow about 108 square feet per person. The cave held forty-five people, requiring 4850 square feet but the available floor space was much bigger: 11,685 square feet.

There are animal stalls and corrals with hitching posts and tethering stakes arranged around the sides of the cave; the floor littered with straw and much sheep, goat and cattle dung. Amongst the debris Solecki found two worn pestles and mortars, two broken pottery jars, a worn-out basket, a twig besom broom and other bits and pieces, including a piece of scented wood used as a snake repellent. The whole cave was dusty, its ceiling covered with hard, shiny travertine except where locally darkened by soot. Bird feathers were everywhere and swallows were darting about. The occupants obviously had stone-bordered open fires but sometimes they lit a large communal fire, burning cakes of earth up to a foot square and composed of humus and dung prised up from the floor of the animal corrals; these burn for days with a hot blue flame. They bury no dead in the cave – unlike their Palaeolithic predecessors – but in graveyards in Mergasur or Shanidar villages.

A typical family arriving back at the cave in the autumn consists of two young men, two small boys, an elderly man and two young women, with three donkeys. The old man lights his pipe with a strike-a-light flint; all are tired and ragged, and the donkeys have raw welts. Another family comprises an old man, a middle-aged man, three teenaged boys, a young boy and a girl. They have seven horses, two colts and four donkeys. The two mothers, completing the two families of eight people each, turn up later carrying all

Interior of Shanidar Cave showing shelters. The cave can be seen in the background. (Ralph S. Solecki)

the copper kettles and pots and the weaving materials, including spindles and cloth. Then comes another woman, with a baby and a little boy, and their dogs, the first to be fed. Finally, two more girls arrive with the supplies. Boulder mortars are used for feeding the dogs and pounding the meal. Goats, chickens and a calf appear, followed by more people. The final cave population is forty-five and the animal count about two hundred, all needing to be taken out in the morning and brought back in the evening. There are ten horses, four donkeys, forty-one cows and calves, a hundred to a hundred and fifty goats – but no sheep – seven dogs and about six chickens.

The people devote little attention to washing and many have foot wounds. They spend their days collecting wood for fuel and goatskins of water, in cleaning and preparing food, in weaving and, of course, collecting grass fodder for the animals. Wheat is ground in highly-prized querns made of igneous rock, some fourteen inches across, the upper stone rotating round a wooden pin fixed to the lower, stationary stone, but mortars are used to grind acorns. Unleavened nan bread is baked from their own wheat outside the cave on a round sheet of metal over an open fire. Goats' and cows' milk is used to make *mastou,* watered 'leban' or yogurt; spiced with scallions and chilled with mountain snow, it makes a delicious drink. The Kurds' food consists of milk, sour milk, butter, cheese and *mastou*, with wheat bread, dishes made from the flour of acorn nuts or *balot*, and grapes or raisins from across the Greater Zab River. Meat is an occasional treat. There are plenty of carp in the Zab, but the Kurds do not fish. They gather pistachio nuts in five-gallon tins but these are to sell, not to eat.

Apart from their copper pots and kettles, they use a few pottery jars, the metal sheet for bread-making, some knives, an axe, a brush knife, goat-hair ropes, bedding, sacks, goatskins for carrying water and other liquids, and a few wasp-waisted glasses, carried in special boxes fitted with holes, for drinking tea. In cold weather they wear animal-skin slippers or moccasins, with the hair inwards. Amidst the continual dust, smoke and dirt flying about in the cave and the endless human and animal racket, the men knit socks while the women weave, carding wool on a board fitted with three rows of three-inch spikes, making headdresses and skullcaps.

Caves have been occupied in India, especially by the Dravidians in the south. In northern Pakistan, the Gandharan Buddhists of about 200 BC to 200 AD followed Mousterian people in the Sanghao Cave near Mardan, which measures 120 by 40 feet under the overhang, and herdsmen in Hunza use caves in summer, as do shepherds in Sicily. In China the Dunhuang Oasis cave site on the Silk Route had the 'Western Paradise' painted on its walls. Peter Fleming wrote in 1936, in *News from Tartary*, while travelling on the Lunghai railway, from Chengchow to Tungkuan, to get to Sian (Xi'an) in

A temporary shelter belonging to the Veddas, Sri Lanka. (Bury Peerless Picture Library)

Shensi (Shaanxi) province: 'There was a kind of prehistoric look about this land, through which the train snorted laboriously, like an antediluvian monster. There were few houses, but many habitations. The terraces above us and the gullies below were riddled intermittently with man-made caves — caves with doors and tattered paper windows, above which a black and tapering smear commemorated on the yellow sandstone the house-fires of many generations. The men and women who emerged from these catacombs were thin and ragged; sun and smoke had made their faces black and they seemed strangely un-Chinese, mopping and mowing on those narrow ledges.'

The film *Yellow Earth*, shot on the Yellow River in Shaanxi province, in the same part of the extreme northwest of China, depicts an empty Arizona-like desert; this is the centre of the loess belt which, with Henan and Gansu provinces, contain most of China's myriad caves. The time was 1939, when the Communists and Nationalists were both fighting the Japanese, and people were living in caves. A soldier who is collecting folk songs to adapt for marching is quartered on a family of peasants who did not know there was a war on. Fifty years ago began the 6000-mile Long March which lasted one year. Ninety thousand men of Mao's army set off across the Great Snowy Mountains for the town of Wuqi, in Shanxi province, in retreat from Chiang Kai-shek's Kuomintang Nationalist army. Their goal was a 'town' of seven families and one bachelor, destined to become the centre of a complex of caves dug deep into the earth to house Red arms, clothing, paper and shoe factories. Here, at Yan'an, Mao Tse-tung was among those who for nearly ten years settled in a cave. These caves became museums, whilst the general store served four thousand inhabitants. Now, however, forty million people are said to have once more taken to living in caves in hillside terraces in Shaanxi, and in Gansu, some of them equipped with running water and sanitation. This is one of the measures taken to help solve the housing problem and it has been so successful that cave hotels are to be built, based on a Neolithic village near Xi'an, site of the terra-cotta army.

The Negritos of Malaysia and Thailand settled there some two to three thousand years ago. They shelter in groups overnight in caves and overhanging rock shelters, sometimes living in jungle caves which they decorate with drawings, such as those near Lenggong in Perak, north Malaysia. They also make their own shelters from ferns lashed to saplings. They have a bamboo

Cave 10 at Yun-Kang, Shanxi Province, China. (Werner Forman Archive)

LEFT: Mao Tse-tung at his mountain stronghold, Yan'an in 1942. (Peter Newark's Historical Pictures) RIGHT: Yun-Kang Caves, Shanxi Province, China. (Werner Forman Archive)

culture; from bamboo they get digging sticks, pots and cooking utensils, blow-pipes, quivers, poison-tipped arrows and darts, fishing equipment and musical instruments. They also have wooden mortars, gourds, combs, fibre and rattan 'clothes' (rags), bracelets, girdles and headdresses. They mainly hunt small mammals, roasting the meat in a cleft stick, and gather roots, tubers and fruits; occasionally they grow maize and hill rice. Their leader is the *halak* or shaman and their religion is one of good and evil spirits, which can live in birds and animals and be propitiated by sacrifices.

Present-day cave men

J. S. Kopper wrote of three groups of Palaeolithic hunter gatherers still living a Stone-Age life in the modern world. This must be one of the most remarkable aspects of cave dwelling in all its history – if not of anthropology as a whole: the survival for tens of thousands of years of the way of life of Cro-Magnon Man in three separate countries. The first are the Tasaday, living in Mindanao, in the Philippine Islands. The second are the Toala of Sulawesi, formerly the Celebes; and the third are the Veddas of Sri Lanka.

The Tasaday are a tribe of twenty-eight Manubo Blit people, speaking Manubo Blit: it means both the people and their Polynesian dialect, which is a variant of the Austronesian language. They live in the extreme south of Mindanao in an area of mountain rain forest, covering some 600 square miles at 3500 to 4500 feet above sea-level, in a group of three caves in the razorback ridges where helicopters cannot land. Their land is bordered by that of the Tboli, Ubu, Blit and some six or so others of the total of sixty tribes to be found in Mindanao. The first Philippine people were Negritos and there are still some tribes and groups of them in the islands. In Palawan Island, west of Mindanao, people lived in the Tabon Cave, where stone tools of 52,000 BP were found, much better ones of 22,000 BP, and so on up to 2500 BP, when metal took over. People migrated into the islands around 6000 BC (8000 BP); in the eighth and ninth centuries AD Arab and Asian traders arrived and in 1521 Magellan, from Portugal, was the first European to land. Mindanao remained the least explored island until the 1960s, when timber cutting and then farming opened it up. It is thought that as well as the Blit, the Tboli, Ubu and other tribes, including the northern Higa-onon, 'probably had ancestors who lived in caves'. No other caves are lived in now although there is another cave nearby big enough for about six people. A story concerning the Tasadays' ancestors relates how they once carried a small cave around as a shelter, on bamboo poles, whenever they travelled. Until one day it grew, and they could not carry it any more, so it remained where it was and the Tasaday stayed in it. Was *this* the site? They did not know! When asked, were there any other groups like them, they replied in the affirmative, pointing away in different directions: the Sandukas and the Tasafangs. They – the Tasaday – had always lived in caves.

Who are they? One theory was that they are a group of Manubo who fled into the forest a few decades ago, perhaps to escape a plague, and then retrogressed. But now it is thought that they are the originals, a splinter group isolated for some four hundred to a thousand years since the other tribes became 'modernised'. Recently a scheme was drawn up to protect this very gentle, harmless, happy, gregarious, totally self-contained people in their own forest, by turning it into a reservation 'around' them.

The caves are in the grey limestone which forms the main rock mass, protected by quartzite conglomerate above it. They are reached by clambering over rock slabs and huge ferns, amongst roots and rattan, up a 10-foot rocky incline, to a ledge some 4 feet below the cave's lower lip, whence one can look in. They face towards the stream and are entered through a curtain of leaves. The caves face east or northeast, thus catching only a few hours of morning sun when there must be better orientated caves in the area. They all have arched entrances, some 15 feet high and 35 feet wide. The largest is huge, well-lit, some 175 feet across, 50 feet deep and 75 feet high. Inside it is full of arches, the biggest being a rock overhang with jagged ledges and niches.

Then two more caves some 25 feet higher up, used for sleeping in. All but one of the Tasaday slept in the larger of the two, some 30 feet deep and 50 feet across. The last man slept in the smaller cave next door, reached by a 20-foot honeycomb of niches. The walls of the caves are eroded here and there, like plaster, and there are orange, ochre, green and grey-white mineral patches.

The Tasaday are a very gentle people and do not use, or even recognize weapons or war; nor do they hunt. They make fire with a wooden drill rolled between their hands, to ignite tinder-dry fibres. This ancient technique has been almost forgotten by the other Philippine tribes. They climb vines, saplings and slender tree trunks like monkeys, entering their cave in this way and having no need to depend on ground trails through the forest. As well as sharp bamboo knives and digging sticks, they have limestone stone axes or choppers with which they open fruit and also rotten logs, to get at the grubs. They make edge-ground stone scrapers and hafted stone pounders in some quarter of an hour, honed on a flat, stream-washed rock, using a circular motion.

When first found, some twenty or thirty Tasaday squatted in two groups, separated by a rock buttress, around their fires or on rocky shelves in the big cave, with its glistening dark brown walls and ceiling, except where blackened by the fires. The babies suckled – they are nursed for three years – and the children ran about, urinating on the floor. One family was living in a space some 8 feet square, 64 square feet, another in the other bay. But the available space would allow 65 square feet per person, which is lavish and twice the minimum suggested by one anthropologist. They do not use numbers but on this occasion counted off – correctly – the twenty-seven people in their group. These included ten men, five with wives, in seven families. Women are in short supply, they said; the children are mostly male, which perhaps explains it. They wear loincloths and sleep on bamboo platforms, mounted on six or eight inch diameter logs notched into large boulders, which they enlarge as necessary. The caves are more or less as the water action left them, with no improvement or decoration; the Tasaday use natural shelves in the rock to keep their stone axes and other few possessions on. They have no 'division of labour': each does what he is best at. They have no leader, all deciding on courses of action together. They are patrilineal and have no sense of property, sharing their stone axes and, now, their *bolos*. They are frightened of thorns and poisonous snakes, and of thunder – the Big Word. They respect a bird whose call acts as a warning for them. They don't know if they have souls, knowing only about dreams – although not what dreams are. They have one musical instrument: a *kubing* or bamboo jew's harp.

The Tasaday use their caves primarily as a base; they are sometimes left empty when the group goes off on a foraging trip for three or at most four days, sleeping away. Otherwise – and they prefer this – they forage locally over something like 10 square miles within a 5-mile radius for two or three hours daily, always returning before dark. They eat well when away but not when foraging locally; their diet is then very frugal. Sharing seems to be limited to local forage and token food brought back from trips away. Their diet consists of the occasional trapped deer – although the deer had been friends of their ancestors and, until recently, as we shall see, they would not harm them – small mammals, birds, palm grubs and, from their streams, tadpoles, frogs, fish and crabs. Not many plants are eaten and these are mainly tubers and roots: yams, *ubud,* which tastes like artichoke, and the palm called *natok* (or *natak* or *natek*) which gives a sort of rice-like starch from which they bake little cakes. There are also flower petals – especially a red and yellow variety, berries, wild bananas and the fruits of ginger and rattan, with very occasional green vegetables. They sometimes eat the *bikin* or *biking* vine (a large starchy, potato-like root or tuber), *basag* and *camote,* but they have no use for *pandanus* or screw pine, although other groups use the spirally wound-up leaves. The caves are full of bats, swifts and spiders, but the Tasaday do not touch the swifts, their eggs or their nests, which last from year to year. They cook – in families, not groups – by wrapping the food in orchid leaves and placing it close to hot coals; they then serve it on banana leaves. They carry water in lengths of hollow bamboo.

Then two things happened. Firstly, a Manubo Blit trapper, Dafal, found them in 1966 or 7 and tried to advise them, especially on how to trap game and hunt using a bow and arrow or a *bolo* or steel knife; however, they were not particularly interested, although the *bolo* was useful for extracting the grubs from logs and the pith from their two favourite trees. Secondly, a journalist put forward a story that the Tasadays' Stone-Age way of life was really a stunt, thought up to encourage tourism. One anthropologist supported this idea, suggesting that the caves were really a sacred place of the Tasaday and not their home, and that they rejected offers of 'stone age' gifts such as *bolos* and hand axes, wanting instead salt, cloth, beads and electric torches. The lack of 'patina' on the walls of their caves was suggested as possible evidence of their recent occupation. However, whereas the first was fact, the second was mere speculation; I prefer to believe in Kopper and John Nance, who wrote a book about the Tasaday.

The Toala or forest people of Sulawesi, formerly Celebes, are the few remaining of the original inhabitants of this part of eastern Indonesia, enslaved by later peoples and now surviving in scattered, isolated enclaves. Their tribe was reduced by an epidemic to about a hundred people, then living in the highlands of the southwestern peninsula, near Makassar. Their language is a dialect resembling that of the Bugines, probably in the Hesperonesian group. Until less than sixty years ago, they were hunter gatherers, killing and preparing shellfish and the other wild fauna – which was unique – with flint tools. They then went through a transitional metal and ceramic phase until now, when they cultivate 'half-wild' maize in small clearings near their caves and keep chickens and dogs, operating a system of barter with adjacent groups. Their marriages are monogamous and they are certainly patrilineal. Several families live in a cave, with perhaps five individuals in an average nuclear family; thus, some fifteen people might have occupied Upper Tjankondo Cave. This typical cave is 260 feet above the valley floor and 1400 feet above sea-level, oriented north-northwest with a mouth 65 feet wide and an occupied portion 20 feet high and 20 feet deep. This floor area of about 1290 square feet works out at about 86 square feet per person, close to the figure of 108 square feet per person often quoted for prehistoric occupations although Kopper quoted 65 square feet for the Tasaday. The Toala had built two- or three-room huts of pole and thatch close to their cave dwellings, presumably as 'spare rooms', when group numbers exceeded cave space. They could have built – but did not – these huts closer to their new agricultural activities, suggesting a definite preference for cave dwellings. The total population in a Toala group occupying one cave and a single hut would number about twenty, close to the hypothetical twenty-five suggested for a Palaeolithic hunting group.

The Toala improve the interiors of their caves. For example, they erect platforms out of poles above the floor on which the inhabitants cook, work and sleep, thus avoiding the cold and damp floor of the cave. The platforms have walls that almost block the cave entrances, keeping out the rain. Both these devices could have been used by Palaeolithic cave dwellers; certainly huts were built by Lower Palaeolithic people in southern France and skins were widely used across cave entrances to control the flow of air. The Toala seem to have no strong preference for the direction in which their cave entrances face; out of seven investigated, five faced northerly, one east and one to the west. This conflicts with the common view that the south and east are preferred because they thus face into the warming sun. However, the hot climate may have come into this, coupled with the Toala's own cave modifications; the Tasaday also occupied caves facing east and northeast. The Toala appear to conduct no burial practices although some human bones were uncovered, and no cave wall-paintings or engravings have been reported.

The last of Kopper's three so-called Palaeolithic hunter-gatherer groups are the Veddas of Sri Lanka, described here out of geographical order for that reason. they constitute a distinct ethnic group, divided into Veddas, Village Veddas and Coast Veddas, all speaking a Sinhalese dialect which includes remnants of the vocabulary and phonetic traces of their own, originally Indo-European, language.

Only the first sub-group – Veddas – have remained relatively unaffected, both physically and culturally, by the Tamils and Sinhalese. These 'pure' Veddas are now confined to several areas in southeast Sri Lanka, although they were once much more widespread. Like the Toala, they too underwent an economic and cultural transition, perhaps seventy years ago; before this they hunted large mammals and reptiles, dug yams and gathered honey. They were divided into six major and several minor hierarchically ranked clans, each controlling its own defined hunting territory. Within the clans were hunting bands, each holding and strongly defending its own lesser territory. Band membership may have consisted of one to seven extended families, the families each numbering seven to ten persons, giving band groups of some seven to seventy individuals. Their descent is matrilineal, possibly borrowed from the Sinhalese, with cross-cousin marriages preferred, thus having the effect of uniting bands from different clans through blood links. On marriage, the new husband would move into the bride's family home. The Vedda religion is described as a cult of the dead, with shamans as the principal agents. Bodies are laid out in their own caves, which are then left empty for ten to twenty years; on reoccupation, the bones of the previous occupiers are not buried, merely discarded.

The use of caves – which are rock shelters rather than deep caves – seems to have been cyclical, following group movements which in turn were controlled by supplies of available game. During the driest periods of the year a single family would construct a temporary shelter near a water source. In the caves or rock shelters themselves, improvements often included the building at the front of a roof apron or extension to extend the 'dripline' outwards, or a 'door' of hides, wood or bark might be constructed to keep out the rain and even the dew. One typical rock shelter at Pihilegodagelge is about 35 feet wide, averaging 7 feet in depth from dripline to back wall, giving a floor area of about 237 square feet. It has an average height of about 5 feet. If five extended families lived here, each of some seven individuals, they would have some six and a half square feet of floor space each, so far below the normal minimum spaces reported that a new theory on occupation density seems necessary. This shelter, incidentally, faced west: not the most popular orientation from a solar point of view. Under these crowded conditions, each family must have had its own clearly defined living space, which was then respected by the others. Cooking is communal but family fires are often maintained for warmth and to provide light. The Veddas decorate their caves with mainly zoomorphic and anthropomorphic paintings, in which man is the only easily identifiable species; they make no deliberate attempt at representation or abstraction. As in Australian aboriginal art, no care is taken to preserve the paintings, which were apparently renewed spontaneously and at random. Unlike the people of the Gibson Desert, the painters are often women and attach no significance to their work, other than to provide a diversion which pleased them. For pigments they mix ash and charcoal with saliva, applying it with a forefinger, a technique providing little permanence.

Towards the end of World War II, 21,000 Japanese hid in caves, blockhouses and pill boxes in Suribachi, Iwo Jima, and fought on for a month after the US Marines had landed in February 1945. The caves are hot from volcanic sulphurous steam. One had an entrance hardly bigger than a rabbit hole; when recently revisited, prior to the island being returned to Japan, the caves were found to be full of old rifle ammunition, live hand grenades, land mines, small artillery shells, rusty helmets, rifles, long-dry canteens and so forth. Two brown coloured skulls were also found. Further north, the Bonin Islands, of which Chichi Jima is the largest, which have also been returned to Japan, have hill caves used by the early settlers in the middle of the nineteenth century to hide from the drunken crews of the whaling ships when they came ashore. More recently still, American prisoners-of-war were held prisoner in caves in supposedly neutral Laos, on the fringe of the war in Vietnam. Fishermen still live in caves in Easter Island during their two-month fishing season, as did their prehistoric ancestors.

In America some Hopi and other Indians live in houses resembling the pit, pueblo and cliff dwellings of their predecessors, although most live in adobe houses, and southern Californian Indians still use underground ceremonial rooms similar to *kivas*. In northwestern Mexico, the Tarahumara live in caves on the Sierra Madre plateau, at the head of a blind canyon. The principal cave is some 50 feet above the ground and is a rift, some 7 to 8 feet wide and 14 to 15 feet deep. There is an outside gallery where concrete walls and floor, doorways, and loopholes for arrow fire have been built. Access to the cave is achieved by zigzag finger and toe holds cut into the rock face. The Tarahumara live in the caves in the winter, probably for warmth; at other times they usually occupy wooden shacks.

Skeletons have been found in the concrete floor, wrapped first in wool, then in fine cloth, then in coarse cloth and finally with coarse matting. One of the skulls had some hair and dried flesh still adhering to it. With the skeletons were *ollas*, burial goods comprising fine-ground corn meal, small corncobs, weaving implements, bows and arrows, and black pottery.

CHAPTER 12

Burrows

This chapter is about all those man-made subterranean chambers for which neither dwelling nor any religious or burial function was ever the primary objective or intention. It may have become the secondary use to which many burrows were put, eventually, or from time to time, but it was never the first function. They have also been called 'subterranea', both in the titles of books and as *Subterranea Britannica* – both the journal of the Federation of Subterranea Brittannica and part of the name of the society itself, since it was founded in 1974. Burrows comprise the wide assortment of underground chambers, rooms and passages built for some other purpose, known or unknown. Many must have been built or dug for ritual ceremonies of some sort. Many would have been refuges, in the widest possible sense. Of the other possible functions, some can be listed: castles, forts, prisons, shelters, hide-outs, grottoes, follies, factories, stores, stables, ice houses, 'traps' and pitfalls. They include especially *souterrains* – a splendid word, from the French for underground chambers; *fogous*, from *fogo* or *fougo*, late Cornish for cave or underground chamber; and *erdställe*, the German, literally, for earth stable. Nearly all were subterranean or semi-subterranean but a few are above ground and still carry these names. Also included are *hypogeum*, plural *hypogea*, meaning underground chamber or subterranean tomb. In this chapter the first meaning mainly applies, to include refuges, stores and even dwellings. Under the second meaning, chambers dug as communal graves or for funeral cults are implied, rather than straightforward sepulchres. All these burrows were used extensively as air-raid shelters during World War II.

The Bible is full of stories of people hiding in caves. So, too, in Palestine and especially in southern France – from the Romans and the Saracen Moslems and from their own countrymen – folk were always taking refuge in caves. In 759 AD, to escape the conquering Pepin the Short, of the Empire of the Franks, the people of Quercy in France hid in a dozen named caves on the banks of the River Lot; eight on the Célé; more than eight on the Dordogne; and between the rivers, some seven more, ending up at Vers, among the cliffs spanned by the Roman aqueduct. In Germany the mountain called Quadersandstein spanning Adersbach and Wickelsdorf, on the border between Bohemia and Silesia, is riddled with rocky peaks and fissures, with a crystal clear rivulet, the whole known as 'the petrified forest'. It was used by people hiding during the Thirty Years' War of 1618 to 1648, between France and the Habsburg powers of Austria and Germany, again in the Seven Years' War, and again in 1866 to escape the Prussian army of the Elbe.

Souterrains are widespread in France, as always well to the fore if not clearly in the lead in matters concerning underground chambers. They are common in Brittany and in the west-central areas centred on the Loire–Loiret valleys; they are virtually absent in the east. Their most probable uses – apart from cult or ritual centres – were as hideouts and refuges and as stores and stables for livestock. Wherever natural refuges presented themselves, or could be contrived, high up on inaccessible cliffs or in easily defended depths, man made use of them. When they were absent, he patiently and laboriously and often painfully excavated them below the surface of the land. Sometimes such refuges were constructed beneath a town, whose walls and ramparts failed to provide sufficient protection, in the form of an underground labyrinth of passages, chambers, halls and storerooms, where the townsfolk could seek shelter or protect their possessions against attack.

Such a town was Saint Macaire on the River Garonne. Others were Alban, in Tarn; Molières, in Lot; Bourg-sur-Garonne; Aubeterre; and at Ingrandes-sur-Vienne, where there were three groups of hiding places.

At Château Robin, Indre-et-Loire, in the Touraine there are two rows of caves in the 60-foot chalk cliffs, the upper of which were used in prehistoric times. The lower caves were exposed by road widening and were greatly feared by the locals as the abode of the devil. So they were explored and, although nothing came to light other than some Gaulish pottery in the upper set of chambers, the caves were found to be complex and extensive and to have many of the characteristics of a *souterrain refugé*, including the marks of the picks used in the digging. The usual plan was to have an entrance opening on to a low and steeply sloping passage, down which an invader could only run, doubled up, only to land up in a 20 to 30 foot deep bottle-shaped well in the floor, immediately behind which was a door, strong and barred, leading to the actual refuge. The defenders, of course, would cross the well with a plank bridge. As an extra welcoming device, a side chamber had slots through which pikes, spears and swords could be thrust, commanding the doorway. There would be little hides on each side for ambush, and two exits, and ventilation shafts to provide air and to guard against the enemy attempting to smoke out the defenders. These refuges had grain silos, lamp niches and other essentials to help withstand a siege. The Château de Fayrolle, near

Riberac, on the Dordogne, was typical. Another was St Gauderic, in the very friable lacustrine sandy marl of Carcassonne, entered, in the middle of a field, by twelve steps and a long corridor, with nothing to indicate its presence. A third was near Fauroux, a village near Roquefort and Lugasson, in Bordeaux, a fourth at Cluseau de Fauroux. Many or even most of the castles of France had souterrains, where – *noblesse oblige* – the feudal lord must protect his vassals and their property, as well as his own family and immediate circle. This was the case at Vendôme; Lavardin by Montoire; Paulin, St Sulpice and Montvalon-Tauriac, all in Tarn; Anterroche Castle, Murat in Cantal; the Count of Armagnac's castle at Salles-la-Source, Aveyron; the manor of Gâtines at Contigne, and also Doué-la-Fontaine, both Maine-et-Loire; and many more, all equipped with granaries, silos, kitchens and other necessities. At Brantôme, in the Dordogne, there is an ancient abbey with souterrains beneath. These buildings have recently been put to use once again, for purposes such as a garage and a fish farm. Other souterrains lay under churches.

In Picardy and Artois are many more huge underground networks, some with a hundred or more large rooms, such as those at Gapennes, between Aussy-le-Château and St Ricquier; Domquer; Hiermont; all around Arras and Amiens, between Roye and the sea and by the Somme – such as Naours – and the Authie.

Arguably, the three most interesting souterrains still in good condition and open to visitors are in the Loire-Loiret region: Dénéze-sous-Doué, La Roche Clermault and Châtres-sur-Cher. Dénéze-sous-Doué is near Saumur, 29 miles west of Chinon. It has a chimney, beams and was used for wine-making and storage. Mousseau Dénéze has heads, figures and monsters carved in the chalk-like rock. La Roche Clermault is a seventeenth-century château with souterrains beneath. These were religious refuges; they have carvings, including leopards. They were used, too, for slaughtering sheep, with depressions on the floor linked together to collect the blood; it is not clear whether these were for ritual sacrifice or religious initiations. At Châtres-sur-Cher, Barbarant, south of Blois, the souterrains cover 200 square yards, and the deepest is some 33 feet, hollowed at different times out of chalk and clay. The furthermost chamber, reached through bottlenecks and a secret passage, was a chapel containing triple altars arranged as a cross, dated 1870. There were wall niches containing figurines and statues, the heads of some of which have been mutilated or cut completely off: a symbol of sorcery or witchcraft? There are bones, pottery fragments and a great deal of associated folklore; for example, that the chapel contains the tomb of a sixth- or seventh-century AD Barbarant chief. It was used up to the early 1900s, perhaps as a witch sanctuary, and then perhaps for male initiation ceremonies. The souterrain at Châtres-sur-Cher can be compared with those at Bourbonnais, Limousin, and with some in Germany and in Catalonia, in Spain.

A recent French book on the subject, sub-titled 'Shelters for the living or for the spirits?', suggests that souterrains were the prehistoric alternatives to above-ground tombs and shrines and attempts to link them with surviving 'caveman' instincts and sentiments. The late prehistoric rock-cut and above-ground tombs are seen as ancestral to the later underground catacombs, cemeteries and shrines and the book goes on to discuss their use in Christian times.

Souterrains are also found widely in Ireland, the Orkneys, the Shetlands and Scotland north of the Firth of Tay, and to a lesser extent in Iceland – told about in the same Saga as those of Aquitaine – and Scandinavia. There is a souterrain under Scarborough Castle. They are common in Cornwall where, as already stated, they are known as fogous. In Germany, erdställe are restricted mainly to the Danube area of Bavaria. Probably dating from the late Bronze Age, they were used as dwellings, workrooms, shelters and refuges, hideouts, stores, religious centres and later as quarries and water catchments, up to the thirteenth and fourteenth centuries. A narrow hole opened from a courtyard, cellar or shed to a tunnel leading to a labyrinth of four or five tiny rooms and galleries. The galleries were lower than the rooms and the holes connecting them had a diameter of about one foot four inches. The roofs were vaulted, with cupolas or pointed arches. An example at Eidengrub, Cham-Roding, in south Germany, has many low narrow rooms with only a single entrance and too little air for a refuge: its use is therefore not known. Erdställe are known also from Pfaffenschlag in Czechoslovakia, where they were built as late as the thirteenth century. There were also pits called 'loess holes' in the loess-covered coastal plain of central Germany. The connection, if any, between these and erdställe is not known, but the latter are certainly not related to the huge souterrains of northern France. There are pit dwellings at Jesso. Christian refugees hid in 1822 in the Cave in Melidoni, to escape the Turk Hussein Bey, but were finally suffocated by smoke from a large fire. In the same year the Cretan Christians, also revolting against the Turks, hid in the mountain labyrinth of Gortyna and, besieged for months by guns and smoke, managed to survive. Arabs in colonial Algeria used to hide in caves but often suffered death by smoke suffocation at the hands of the French.

In Britain, souterrains and fogous were built only in groups and always associated with settlements, especially those enclosed by the small earthworks called *raths* in Ireland and *rounds* in Cornwall. Elsewhere, isolated souterrains are rare also. All are stone built and date from the early Iron Age, to which they are limited in Ireland, Cornwall and Brittany, but in other areas some are medieval. They were almost certainly ritualistic in original purpose and vary enormously in design, ranging from simple curving passages, with or without subsidiary chambers, to the elaborate arrangements of passages and chambers to be found in Ireland. All are dry-stone walled, with roofs constructed of stone slabs. Iron-Age, Roman and post-Roman artefacts and pottery have been found in them, with medieval and later pottery in those that have stayed open. The earliest – all Iron Age – come from Ireland, Cornwall, and some, such as Castle Law, Glencorse, south of Edinburgh, from Scotland, while there are Roman and later examples in Scotland and Ireland which underwent reuse during the early Christian era. The best-known example of the Cornish fogous is found in the Iron-Age village of Carn Euny, near Sancreed, west of Penzance. It is semi-subterranean and was built in two stages, including a 'creep'; first an entrance passage and a circular chamber with a fireplace, and then a later, curving passage, with finally a small subsidiary passage. The chamber and later passage are corbelled and vaulted and roofed with granite capstones. It was occupied from the fifth century BC to the second or third centuries AD and is comparable with the souterrains of Brittany. This kind resembled dolmens; other examples are found at Halligye, in the Lizard, and at Trelowaren. Another type was found at Porthcothan, excavated out of the rock, with a passage leading to the sea, and was perhaps dug by smugglers.

Of the several thousands of souterrains in Ireland, large groups are found in the northeast, east, west and southwest, and smaller groups in the northwest; there was a large example called Landnama Bok. The most common type in

Fogou at Carn Euny, Cornwall, England. This is the best-known example of a Cornish fogou.

County Cork, where there are, in all, some 500, is dry-stone built but others are earth- or boulder clay-cut or tunnelled and a few are rock-cut, of which the best example is at Duniskey. The stone-built chambers were built in an open trench or made use of a natural cave, cleft or fissure. Some Irish souterrains may have included wooden constructions, while others were incorporated into the walls or ramparts of ring forts and similar constructions. They are also divided up according to the arrangment of their chambers, cells and passages. The usual plan is based on rectangular chambers, circular cells and long, narrow galleries and passages: there can be rectangular stone-built chambers and galleries; circular chambers that are stone-built, earth-cut or clay-built; and earth- and rock-cut chambers that are not lined with stones. There are others in Waterford, and a newly discovered early Christian souterrain at Carnmore, County Galway, is L-shaped, with three chambers. Various theories have been put forward as to their uses. Certainly, ritual ceremonies would have been predominant, with other possible uses such as domestic storage, the concealment of valuables, refuges, temporary or even occasionally permanent dwellings, the sleeping quarters for ring forts and – later – anchorites' cells.

If there is one single area of Britain which can rival France for the sheer volume of its man-made underground chambers it must be Nottingham. In his life of King Alfred, written between 900 and 1000 AD, Asser says that the old name for Nottingham was Tigguocobauc, meaning 'houses of caves'. The city is a mass of them – there are more than a hundred – and most are very old, well known from medieval times, although none are known for certain to be Saxon. One might be a mid-Saxon *grubenhaus*. They were all carved, mainly between the thirteenth and nineteenth centuries, out of the soft, friable Triassic Bunter Sandstone – easy to hew but no good for building stone as it is so easily damaged by water and frost. Their main function was not generally for dwelling. It is thought that they were used mainly for brewing and malting; for the tanning industries; for the storage of, for example, fish and wool; as quarries and mines, mainly for sand; rarely, for communication; for pleasure, mainly for drinking, gambling and cockfighting, and other leisure activities; as puticoli, catacombs and burial vaults; possibly as churches; and, very much later, as air-raid shelters.

There were caves on the 'old way to the gallows'. They were used as refuges by Roman Catholics in the time of Elizabeth and James I, and by Dissenters – the Puritans – during the reign of Charles II. But a few were definitely lived in, lit by tallow candles placed in niches, with vent-holes for smoke and their own wells, fitted with finger and toe notches. The cliffs on the south side of the castle rock were greatly favoured, and also the area around Cliff Road further east, and the caves hewn primarily as dwellings were always above ground. Monks lived in communities, there were hermits dotted about, and townspeople, such as tanners and dyers, whose trade required a great deal of water, chose to live underground. For water they dug *scoop-wells*, holes down through the floor of their living apartments, equipped with steps, until they reached water which then formed in little pools. Some of these caves were lived in temporarily, from time to time, and some were adopted for dwellings as a secondary use. Until the authorities finally cleared most of the Nottingham caves of their inhabitants, in about 1820, the deeds of transfer of property had customarily described the tenements as *below* or *above* ground. The last tenant was a sand-man, who stabled his ass in another cave behind.

The caves are found in so many different areas that it is difficult to put them in a sensible order. Nowadays, the most important single excavation is thought to be Mortimer's Hole, under the castle, surrounded by other caves and rock-cut arches opening on to Brewhouse Yard and the green which surrounds the castle rock. The two cave areas for which guided tours are organized are the old Drury Hill, now Broad Marsh district, which includes Severn's, the old public house on Middle Pavement; and Bridlesmith Gate, an area of large caves including an ice house. The other frequently mentioned area, the old Farmer's site in Old Market Square, once housing a leading draper's, is now closed since it is too close to large modern buildings. Long Stairs and Short Stairs are both famous as rock-hewn stairways, and under the Shire Hall are rock-cut cells and dungeons.

There are four pubs with caves beneath them. The best known, perhaps, Ye Olde Trip to Jerusalem Inn, dates from 1189 and is the oldest tavern in England. Its cave is not now open to the public. Ye Olde Salutation Inn, dating from 1240, is open and has an elliptical cave once used for brewing with a bench all around on which were placed the beer casks. The Lion Hotel, also open, has a cockpit in its underground cave, and another brewing room. The cockpit is thought perhaps to be too low – cocks fly upwards when fighting – and too small to hold an audience, but it could have been used to keep the birds in, to exercise them and to hold fights for very small, exclusive audiences. The fourth, the Bell Inn, is also open. Other areas with caves below include the Mansfield Road, with Robin Hood's cave, church and cemetery; Friar Lane, where there are many, including one with a manger; Goose, Warser, Castle, Hounds and Wheeler Gates; Park Tunnel; Angel Row; Hollowstone; Plump Street; Long Row; the Angel Caves under Stoney Street and Queen Street Post Office. There are also two hermitages – Sneinton and the Park – on the east and west edges of the city.

Mortimer's Hole is more than a thousand years old, pre-dating the castle and discovered by William I in 1068 after he had started to build the Norman

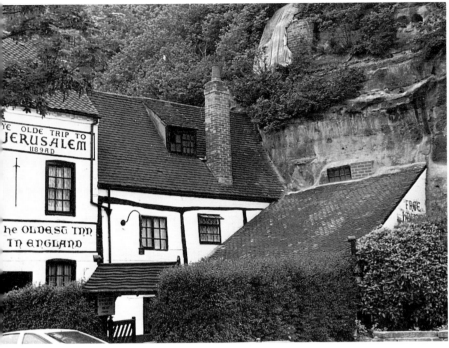

LEFT: Ye Olde Trip to Jerusalem Inn, Nottingham, England. This is the oldest tavern in England. RIGHT: The exit from Mortimer's Hole, Castle Rock, Nottingham, England.

castle. It was built on Castle Rock, separated from the Saxons camped to the east beyond the present site of St Mary's Church by cliffs and water, and became a 'mid-English castle' in the 1100s. The Hole was a secret passage, now within the castle bounds. It had stone steps down and a tower built over it, with a stone which, when pressed, opened the door. In 1327 King Edward II's wife, Isabella, met Roger Mortimer in France – Edward's inclinations left him uninterested in his Queen – and they planned to overthrow the King, when Isabella would become Regent. The plan succeeded; the King was captured, imprisoned, deposed and revoltingly murdered. Although the 14-year-old Edward III succeeded to the throne, the real power lay in the hands of the Queen, Mortimer and the Council of Barons. Three years later, however, Mortimer was arrested in the Hole whilst holding a Parliament in Nottingham, and hung, drawn and quartered. The castle started to fall down in about 1500 and was last used in the Civil War by some of Cromwell's men. The Royalists found out about them and captured them halfway down, where they had mounted two cannon. The Hole had a bakery and a brewhouse for the soldiers' bread and beer in the west stairs, where there were also a chapel –

ABOVE LEFT: Park Hermitage, Nottingham in 1810. ABOVE RIGHT: Sneinton Hermitage, Nottingham in 1810 and BELOW in 1972. (Nottingham Local Studies Library)

sometimes known as the Monastery or the Papists' Hole – and a guardhouse, with King David's Dungeon at the bottom. There is a piece of metal in the ceiling of the west stairs, the story being that it is the end of a pike, left there by a startled soldier who leaped into the air one day when he was disturbed. The castle was finally pulled down after the Civil War and replaced in 1670 by the Duke of Newcastle's mansion; he used part of Mortimer's Hole as his wine cellar. The mansion was taken over by the Council in the last century and is now the Castle Museum.

Drury Hill, near the Broad Marsh centre, is no more, having been incorporated into the viaduct. The caves here date from the fifteenth century, where they were used for sheep- and goat-skin tanning – these animals being cheaper than cattle. The skins were first kept in London for a year, until the price went up, which cannot have made the tanners' job any the more pleasant. One cave was an illegal brewery, complete with a malt kiln, and one later became a drinking house, with a well. Another – for this was the red-light area – was a gaming room: there was a hole down from the road through which warning pebbles could be dropped. Another, once thought to be a cockpit, is now considered to be too small, like that under the Lion Hotel. The Industrial Revolution brought more people to the area. Many lived in tiny one-up, one-down houses, but others opted for the caves. In the end,

Rouse's Cavern, under Mansfield Road, Nottingham, in 1926. (Nottingham Local Studies Library)

the Drury Hill caves, like the rest, were air-raid shelters in World War II and one was used as a solicitor's office, resplendent with an iron safe.

There are some caves, mainly in southern England and many in the Chalk, which have had a variety of uses, nearly all of them unusual. The St Clement's Caves in Hastings, Sussex, in the soft white Ashdown Sandstone, cover about three acres. There are many legends about them. They may originally have been mined for glass sand in the seventeenth century and the sand smuggled to Belgium. They are decorated with many paintings and are believed to have harboured many unsavoury characters. They too were used in World War II as a huge air-raid shelter. There is to be a ceremony in the caves in 2066 to mark the Battle of Hastings. Nearby there is the Bo-Peep Cave in St Leonards' Sandstone and the Westerham sandstone mines in Kent. The Chislehurst Caves, also in Kent, were possibly mined for chalk by the Romans; certainly they are all man-made. It has been suggested that the Druids used them, and had altars and other ritual paraphernalia there. In the Civil War Royalists hid in the caves and in the Napoleonic Wars, flints for the rifle flintlocks were knapped there. One chamber might have been a denehole, on which there is more later. The Chislehurst Caves were used as ammunition stores in World War I and as air-raid shelters in World War II, accommodating up to 15,000 people. Many ghost stories exist about these caves, such as that of the woman who was murdered there by drowning two hundred years ago.

The Hell-Fire Caves, in West Wycombe, Buckinghamshire, are a quarter-of-a-mile long and dug into the Chalk. The chalk was used by Sir Francis Dashwood in 1748 to make a road from West Wycombe to High Wycombe to give unemployed farm workers work during a failed harvest: 'my sole reason for making the road is the welfare of the villagers. I am determined that they shall have employment.' They received one shilling a day. The caves have an unusual, perhaps symbolic plan, possibly linked with the Eleusinian Mysteries of Ancient Greece, and include the mythical, underworld River Styx. They contained a hidden cache of coins but their main claim to fame was their association with the Hell-Fire Club, founded in 1746 by Philip, the first and only Duke of Wharton as the Knights (or Brotherhood) of St Francis of Wycombe or the Monks of Medmenham. The President was the Devil – a chair was always put ready for him – and the club existed 'for ladies and gentlemen of the highest circles to promote sacrilege'. In fact, it did nothing of the sort but the members enjoyed shocking the outside world. They included the Chancellor of the Exchequer, the First Lord of the Admiralty .and the Governor of Bengal. The ladies dressed as nuns, wearing a badge inscribed 'Love and Friendship'. After nearly twenty years of secret meetings in Medmenham Abbey on the River Thames, the eminent and somewhat alcoholic members' secret was revealed and they transferred their meetings to the caves in 1763. Benjamin Franklin first visited the caves in 1772 when staying with the Dashwoods at West Wycombe Park.

A somewhat similar story concerns the Blackheath Caverns in Kent, which were not Celtic, as was once alleged, but were excavated by the local lime burners as dens for drinking and entertainment. They include Jack Cade's Cavern, the refuge in 1450 of the Kentish Rebel.

Some time before 1800, Blind George the fiddler and his dog ventured one day into the chalk cave under Anstey Castle mound, near Buntingford, in Hertfordshire, where no one had been before. Some say they never returned, others that although Blind George was never seen again, his dog emerged, tailless and with all its hair singed off. Their bones, or just the old man's perhaps, were found in the cave in 1902 or 4 by an old man called Skinner. The cave is now below the water level of the moat and has never been found again. It is believed to have been a chalk adit or 'heading', leading to an exit about a mile off at Cave Gate. When a tree blew down recently, the exit was found but the tunnel had been blocked by a rock fall after a short way; all has now been filled in.

There are also the grottoes and other follies, the grottoes usually decorated with the scallop shell, emblem of St James the Great. He was commemorated on 25 July by London's children with the cry 'please remember the grotto' – a collage of mirror-glass, flowers, picture cards and scallop or oyster shells – with a coin. Following the lead of Alexander Pope, whose grotto in Twickenham, begun in 1718, was the first truly subterranean grotto, the poet and essayist John Scott had a huge grotto of tunnels and chambers excavated in a chalk hillside in the gardens of Amwell House in Ware, Hertfordshire, completed in 1773 at a cost estimated at some £10,000. The rooms are mostly lined with shells, flints, mirrors, spar and Wookey Hole stalactites, and include a Consultation Room, a Committee Room – right at the centre – and a Committee Room No. 2, a Refreshments Room, Robing Room, Pillar Room and Council Chamber. There are also a Gothic arch, ventilation shaft, niches and seats. One theory maintains that it afforded a possible escape from smallpox and other diseases, of which it is known Scott had a pathological dread.

A grotto at Margate, in Kent, was found in 1834 and is still a mystery. It has been variously assigned to the Romans, Mithras, Danes, Persians, Phoenicians, Essenes, Moors, Tibetans and Cretans, as well as the Druids! It could have been a Rosicrucian Society temple, of the Brothers of the Rosy [or Red] Cross. Like Scott's Grotto, it is decorated with shells. More caves at Margate, highly decorated with carvings, include Nash Court and others, found by mistake in 1798 by the gardener in the grounds of Northumberland

House, and thought to be a medieval chalk mine. There are the Eastry caves, decorated with paintings, that may once have been smugglers' caves and were possibly used as tombs. There is a grotto at Goldney, in Bristol, and an underground labyrinth at Hawkstone, in Shropshire. A problematical underground 'temple' at Caynton Hall, near Beckbury, between Telford and Wolverhampton, was built in about 1780, presumably by the Hall's owner, W.J. Yonge. It lies on the edge of a disused quarry in red Lower Keuper Sandstone, completely hidden in a wood between the Hall's grounds and the road. Its entrance is a vertical cleft, resembling a large badger sett, and inside it extends for some thirty feet between cylindrical pillars, pediments and capitals, giving three crescentic galleries, with apertures and recesses, and ending with an apse-like room in which 'ecclesiastical' niches have been carved.

The word 'denehole' has already been mentioned. Also known as 'dene holes' or Danes' pits, their use is not really known but since they are all found in the Chalk, it is thought very highly probable that they were early chalk mines, all excavated by man as rooms and never as tunnels. They correspond with some, but far from all, of the French souterrains, such as those in Picardy and Aquitaine, which are also in the Chalk. They are found principally in Suffolk, Essex, Berkshire and Kent; there are good examples at Darenth Wood, near Chislehurst, East Tilbury, Crayford and Little Thurrock. At Bury St Edmunds in Suffolk there is one chalk-mine tunnel. Deneholes may have been used as hiding places when the Danish Vikings' ships appeared over the horizon but would originally have been chalk mines or quarries, for chalk was exported at a very early date from the Thames to Zealand, now Sjaelland, in Denmark, and onwards elsewhere, and it was needed at home also for agricultural use. Deneholes must have been used and reused as refuges and grain stores and so forth; plenty of bones and artefacts have been found in them and the hermit of Dumpton, in Kent, lived in one. The condemned cell in the hangman's cottage at Rye, in Sussex, was rock-hewn.

Variations on the theme of souterrain are the megalithic Orkney 'earth house', constructed of Old Red Sandstone and roofed with Caithness Flagstones, typified at Newark Bay, consisting of a stone-lined rectangular tunnel leading to a small chamber, and the semi-subterranean settlement of Skara Brae. The earth house at Culsh, near Tarland, west of Aberdeen, dated at the second century AD, is about 6 feet wide and high and 30 feet long, and was perhaps used as a store. Related or synonymous underground stone habitations were the post-Iron Age, pre-Viking 'weems' or 'Picts' houses' of Scotland and the Hebrides; most of these, again, are of unknown age and use but were probably pre-Roman refuges or hiding places or even burial places.

Pre-historic refrigeration – snow and ice stores – may be the explanation for 'pits of no obvious function' such as those of Palaeolithic age in Jersey and the Ukraine. Neolithic examples are found at Eaton Heath, Norwich, and there are Bronze Age, Iron Age and Romano-British examples. Ice houses are known to have been in use by the Chinese since the first millenium; the Greeks and Romans had them and finally they came to Europe. Britain discovered them late, possibly a reflection on its climate. The first-known British ice house belonged to Charles II, who had it dug in 1665 at Greenwich after his gardener, Rose, had been on a visit to Versailles. Ice houses were dome- or globe-shaped and known as 'cup and domed'; circular; rectangular; or, rarely, tunnel- or bell-shaped. Some were of stone but far more commonly they were of brick, cement or lime rendered. Naturally, they always had the entrance on the north side and few were larger than 30 by 20 feet, while most were smaller. An example is the Temple of the Winds at West Wycombe, in Buckinghamshire, and there is a possible ice well at Tadworth, in Surrey. One of the earliest-known examples in the USA was in the grounds of Thomas Jefferson's innovatory home at Monticello in Virginia.

There were, of course, wells and also potato caves or *hulls*, 20 to 40 feet long, 7 feet high and up to 7 feet wide, dug in Cornwall out of rotten granite (*growan*) for storing root crops, such as those found at Burrator.

Hideouts

In the fine tradition of Ali Baba and his gang, in the days before Marbella and Rio de Janeiro became fashionable, caves would have been high on the list of suitable hideouts for any robber gang. There is a good example to be found in the story of Humphrey Kynaston, the somewhat wild second son of Sir Roger Kynaston of Hordley, near Ellesmere, who had embraced the York faction in the Wars of the Roses, neglected his duties and allowed the castle of Middle, a Crown property of which he had been made Constable, to fall into ruin. This was partly due to Humphrey's shortage of money following his father's choice of the Yorkists. So Humphrey took to robbery and was outlawed in 1490, the fifth year of the reign of Henry VII. He fled from Middle and settled with his horse in a narrow cave in a cliff of New Red Sandstone at Ness, near Bass Church, overlooking the Shropshire plain. He cut himself a flight of steps about halfway up the 70-foot cliff and then excavated two chambers, one for his horse and one for himself. The latter had a hearth and a slanting-upward hole as a chimney, and a circular window by the door; in the buttress between the two he cut two niches, perhaps for a lamp. At the base of his steps is a trough, perhaps designed for oats or corn for his horse, since no water exudes from the rock there. Although he was pardoned in 1493 – and no further wild behaviour has appeared in the family since – he did not die until 1534. A later hand carved 'H.K. 1564'.

In the time of James I in the early seventeenth century, the notorious Sawney Beane dwelled with his wife and many children in a huge cave on the shores of Galloway, in southwest Scotland. Here, for twenty-five years, they lived as cannibals, robbing, killing and eating the pickled and salted bodies of travellers, until at last they were caught and executed. Late in the reign of James II another brigand is said to have lived with his wife and family in a den called Feruiden or Ferride's Den, in Angus. They, too, practised cannibalism, for which they were burned, apart from the youngest daughter of twelve months. However – strange to relate – she was condemned for the same crime when she grew up. Less of a monster was the burglar who terrorized the neighbourhood around Dunterton, on the Devon side of the River Tamar, where he lived in a cave in about 1780, entering the houses he had selected down the wide chimneys current at the time. White Woman's Hole, near Leighton, East Mendip, in Somerset, was the workshop of a Roman counterfeiter. The sad Icelandic Saga of Grettir the Outlaw tells of his nineteen years of outlawry, two of them – 1022 to 1024 – spent in a freezing cave. The lava cave of Surtshellir in the same country housed twenty-four robbers in the thirteenth century.

In the early nineteenth century, a group of murderous brigands lived in the vast grotto of Lombrive, Ariège, in France. There was a robbers' den called La Crouzate on the Causse de Gramat in Lot, and the famous cavern at Gargas, near Montzéjeau, in Hautes Pyrenees, was occupied ten years before the French Revolution by a stonemason, Blaise Ferrage, who forwent his trade to seize, murder and, unlike his prehistoric predecessors, eat young girls. He sometimes treated men in the same way until after three years he was caught and, in 1782, executed by being broken on the wheel.

Henry Leichtweiss was born in 1730 at Ohrn, son of a forrester in the service of the Duke of Nassau. He was apprenticed as a baker but was caught appropriating trust money. So he took to a vagabond's life, together with a girl he had seduced, living for seven years in a cave which he had dug, until he was caught, put in the stocks, and finally hung. The rock labyrinths at Adersbach and Wickelsdorf in Bohemia also served as robbers' dens for men such as Alt and Babinsky in the early nineteenth century.

In 1858 a miller named Ebel, out to collect firewood from the Pyritz Forest near Soldin in Prussia, chanced on a robber's 'cave', a roofed-over pit well equipped with tools and stores including a well-stocked cellar full of wine, champagne and brandy. The robber, Carl Friedrich Masch, had disappeared but was found later to have set up in a similar only larger 'cave' pit near Warsin; this one even had a small library of books. He was caught and executed in 1864, having committed twelve murders over eight years and made several other attempts. He was one of the last criminals to live in a cave.

The Cave of Adullam, now identified as Aid-el-Ma, in Palestine, was one of many in a round, 500-foot hill. Here, and at Maon, David hid from Saul, after being recognized at Gath, where he had first fled. He became the leader of some four hundred fugitives, turning them into a gang of freebooters. There are many such limestone caves in Palestine. 'Lot went out of Zoar and dwelt in a cave.' There was the cave of the five kings at Makkedah, and the rocks, pits and holes where the Israelites hid from the Midianites in the time of Gideon, and from the Philistines in the time of Saul. Samson hid from his enemies in a cliff cleft at Etam, and Saul hid at Engedi. Obadiah hid the Lord's prophets in a cave; the robber hordes lived in caves above the plain of Gennesareth; the Gadarene demoniacs lived in sepulchral caves; and Josephus and his countrymen hid in the cave of Jotopata during their final struggle.

Refuges

Rock and cliff refuges differ from souterrains because the latter were burrowed into the soil, with concealed entrances. In fact, their aim was total concealment, if possible, because they also needed to be defensible. Cliff refuges, on the other hand, stood for all to see. Their defence lay in their inaccessibility. They were reached either by ladders, which could be single or arranged in a sequence, notched together using natural or man-made ledges, which could then be hauled up; or by finger and toe notch holds, either in a vertical climbing sequence, up or possibly down, or by lateral notch and ledge which were equally easy to defend. A third method was by windlass, rope and basket, recalling Meteora, used also for old people, children, goods and even for rescuing cattle and horses whose stables, stalls, mangers and silos below were normally far more vulnerable.

All these methods were fine for the occupiers – or so they thought – but not for the invader, who was faced with stones, hot or even boiling liquids, pikes, spears and swords and so forth. Such a refuge was found at Cazelles, in Sireuil, in the Dordogne, in a cliff 1200 feet long and 150 feet high, where there was a deep furrow beneath an overhanging cliff, to protect the hamlet below. Behind, further chambers were excavated with, in front, a wooden balcony with beams and props. There were holes cut for hauling up cattle and stores and no trace of a stair; none would have been possible with such an overhang. There were others at La Roche Gageac, also in the Dordogne, and again at Le Peuch St Sour, on the Vézère, where once more it provided a refuge for the inhabitants of the hamlet below. It had once been occupied by the hermit, St Sorus or Sour, before being greatly enlarged to construct the refuge. At the Roc d'Aucor, in the valley of the Vers, in Lot, is a gaping cave high up, heavily overhung and quite inaccessible. However, two stout beams, above and below the opening, revealed the method of entry. This was achieved through a tower built in front of the cave, thus hiding it, with a tiled, lean-to roof propped against the upper, larger and square beam. The lower, smaller and round beam was used for hauling up stores. Inside was a stalagmite, in legend a marble statue of a man keeping guard over a golden calf. There are still others at Boundoulaou, in the Causse de Larzac, Lozère, and the cave of Riou Ferrand, 180 feet up a sheer cliff near Millau. Both these are partly walled up and appear to have been lived in as well as being used as refuges. There are more near Brengues, on the River Célé, and at Les Mées, in the Basses-Alpes; both have poles across their entrances.

There is a dolomitic limestone rock shelter at Fadarelles, in the Tarn Gorges, as well as grottoes at Puy Labrousse, near Brive, and at Soulier-de-Chasteaux on the Couze, a tributary of the Vézère in Correze, with two man-made caverns. All these appear quite inaccessible. Other refuges in the Auvergne region include the Puy de Clierson, Le Grand Sarcoui, and some that were originally quarries at Corent, on the Allier near Veyre-Mouton and Blot-l'Eglise, near Menat. Meschers, a village in Charante Inférieure in a chalk hill above the Gironde, is honeycombed with caves, perhaps once quarries, used as habitations and then by the Huguenots for – what was then illegal and highly dangerous – preaching and singing psalms. But, in turn, the Catholics may have also used them, when the Calvinists were in favour. There are many more in the Ariège, refuges for the Albigenses, and some behind crenellated walls between Tarascon and Cabannes. These refuges were used by just about everybody: during the English occupation, during the Wars of Religion and by the Huguenots.

Britain has some similar refuges. At Mitchelstown in County Tipperary, in Ireland, there is the Old Cave, in which the Earl of Desmond hid after his futile rebellion in the reign of Queen Elizabeth I. There is also the more complex New Cave; both are decorated with cave pearls and stalactites. Cleaves Cove, near Dalry, on Dusk Water in Ayrshire, was a limestone refuge used by the Covenanters. It has a total length of 500 feet and possibly had had prehistoric occupiers. Wallace's Cave, Gorton, is one of several caves in the Esk Valley of Scotland used as refuges and perhaps as habitations. The Cave of Francis, in a rocky bay in the south of the western isle of Eigg, about a mile from Galmisdale jetty, has a narrow entrance, involving a crawl on hands and knees, before it rises up and becomes lofty, stretching for 225 feet into the rock. Many bones were found among the pebbles, belonging to the original inhabitants. These were Clanranalds (sometimes Clan Ranald), a division of the MacDonalds, whose ancestor was Lord of the Isles connected with Castle Tioram in Moidart. Their chieftain was attacked by an invading group of MacLeods of Dunvegan, in Skye. The MacLeods behaved in a very insulting way; for this, and for attacking the chieftain, they were bound hand and foot and turned adrift in their boat. An avenging force of MacLeods followed them in a small fleet of galleys and, having landed, at first found no one; the entire population had hidden in the cave. They were about to leave when they spotted the MacDonald scout and tracked him to the cave by his footprints in the snow. Here they lit a large fire and suffocated all three hundred and ninety-five people. Other refugees in Hebridean caves suffered a similar fate. In the eighteenth century the stronghold of Cluny, chief of the MacPherson clan, was a cave near Newtonmore, southwest of Aviemore, known as Cluny's Cave.

There are many natural caves in Derbyshire, apart from the mines, such as those at Castleton, Bradwell Eyam, Matlock and Buxton. Poole's Cavern, in the country park at Buxton, is named after the outlaw whose haunt it was in about 1440, in the time of Henry IV. He is said to have lived in the inner entrance, together with his loot, protected by the narrow gash-like outer entrance. Behind him, the cave had a smooth floor and ran for some half a mile, although the first sixty feet were a crawl. The cave was later fitted with gas lighting and afterwards with electricity. Reynard's Cave, high up on the Derbyshire side of Dove Dale, is hard to reach, approached through a natural arch in the limestone cliff and up a difficult path. Nearby is the smaller Reynard's Kitchen, which once sheltered persecuted Royalists. High up on the Staffordshire side is the secluded cleft called Cotton's Cave, 40 feet deep, where Isaac Walton's poet friend, Charles Cotton – that careless and impecunious poet – hid in the 1650s from his creditors. The two friends sat smoking their pipes on a sheer precipice known as Lovers' Leap until Cotton's wife lit a watchtower beacon fire to guide him home when the coast was clear of duns.

Thor's Cave, on the Manifold River, near Wetton in Staffordshire, is halfway up a 500-foot limestone cliff, arched at the entrance, and enlarged by its occupiers, who go back to prehistoric times. The name comes from the days when the Norsemen occupied Deira, Derbyshire, as does Jordas Cave in Yorkshire, meaning Earth-Giant. An eighteenth-century mendicant called Pendrill, or Penderel, sought refuge in a cave named after him in the grounds of Weston Park, the home of the Earls of Bradford, near Ironbridge and Newport, in Shropshire. Barely a cave, it was some 7 feet by 7 feet in size, constructed under a cedar tree using blocks of red sandstone and rock rubble, built into Keuper Marl. A Royalist hid in the crevices in Bottor Rock, Hennock, in Devon, and secreted his treasure there also. But bloodhounds found him and he was hanged – and nobody found his treasure. Another

Royalist, old Squire Elford, hid from Cromwell's troops in a granite cave with a very narrow opening, high up on Sheep's Tor, also in Devon, and to pass the time, decorated the walls of the 6 by 5 by 4 foot high space with his paintings. The tor is now part of Plymouth waterworks reservoir.

Caves were built under Druse houses in Syria as safe retreats. The occupants could control the water supply, which was hauled up to the houses from the wells in buckets on ropes. This technique was used to resist the Egyptian soldiers employed by Ibrahim Pasha, Viceroy of Egypt under Ottoman rule, in his campaign against Palestine and Syria. The people went down to their caves, rolled the customary large stones across the entrances, and cut off the water supply; they were then able to withstand the attack. Also in Palestine, the Rabbi Shimon Bar Yohai hid from the Romans in a cave near Peqi'in, in Galilee.

Cliff castles

There were also cliff castles. These seem to have been mainly confined to France and Baring-Gould recognized three main sorts. There were the castles of the *routiers*, or Companies, impious mercenaries frequently recruited to the service of the English during the Hundred Years' War in the fourteenth century. Then there were seigneural strongholds and, lastly, outpost stations guarding fords, the roads into a town and passes leading into a country. Many of these kinds of stronghold were of course common throughout the world but they were only rarely rock-hewn. The Companies built fortified 'nests' in the rocks or else captured castles abandoned by the French, especially in the south from Dordogne to the Lot, between Périgord and Paris, in the Auvergne and around the Loire. One such 'underground' fortress held by the Ribauds (the southern Companies) was the Rock of Tayac, in Périgord, a white cliff streaked with black and containing a network of cliff caves and wooden galleries spread over several storeys. One cave was a stable, reached by a ladder, and there was a well. Later on, the top storey became an hotel, also reached by a ladder, but the stable was damaged and the well had to be filled in. At Corn, in Lot, the routiers occupied caves which they augmented with a wooden gallery. They would sit drinking and gambling at a stone table. The Grotto du Consulat at Corn was used by the villagers to elect their magistrates. Castles literally hanging on to rock cliffs include two at Brengues; there is one at Cabrerets, where the Célé flows into the Lot, known as the Devil's Castle and having one wall of rock; and the Château des Anglais at Autoire. Then there are La Roche du Tailleur at Peyrousse, Rouergue, in Aveyron, inaccessible since the routiers destroyed its only access when they abandoned it, and the lava castle on top of the Roche de Sanadoire, near Mont Dore, which was also held by the routiers.

The seigneurs were about equally as unpleasant as the routiers but they were at least confined to their own little empires. They occupied some rocky tower-castles, like La Roche St Christophe and the Château de Rignac, both on the River Vézère, above the caves at Le Moustier. Much of it consisted of excavated chambers, including bedrooms specially for ladies. La Roche Gageac, below Sarlat, on the Dordogne, was another example in the same region, with two castles and a mass of cave and partly cave habitations as well as houses. Gluges, near Martel, also on the Dordogne, is a fortified cave-castle high up a cliff and hard to reach. Le Trou, Bourou, was a cave-fortress on the River Beaune. La Roche Lambert at Borne, in Haute Loire, is a castle built in a cleft in basalt, through which roars a river, the scene of George Sand's novel, *Jean de la Roche*. Roqueville, in Cantal, has the remains of a castle fortress excavated out of the rock and, also in Cantal, the Roc de Cuze cave castle near Neussargues resembles Puxerloch, which is mentioned below.

A cave castle rather like the cliff villages of Mesa Verde was Kronmetz, nominally held by nobles in fief to the Bishop of Trient but in fact a den of robbers, until it was taken by storm in 1210 and later, in 1480, turned into a hermitage. Between Jung-Bunzlau and Böhm-Leipa, in Bohemia, is the rock castle of Habichstein in a hump of sandstone looking like a Pictish broch. Other cliff castles in Bohemia include the curious sandstone Burgstein, with its many cave chambers, converted into a hermitage in the late seventeenth century. There are more on the frontier of the Wargau and the Hardt in northern Bohemia. The famous Schallaun castle in the Puxerloch, in Styria, was another, built in a 450-foot high cliff. Its top court was in a grotto, 75 feet up, above the lower two courts. The bottom one was entered from a rock-cut path, the middle by a rock stair and the third in the same way. A passage in the rock led to a pool of clear water. Its kitchens were in a smaller cave nearby, reached from the main building by a wooden gallery. This castle was occupied by an old mason and also became a den of thieves until it was dismantled in the last century. There were many rock-top castles-plus-towns, among then Les Baux and San Marino, but since they are built on rather than into the rocks, they are scarcely relevant here.

As an example of outpost guard-castles one can cite the cave-fortress at La Roche Corail, commanding the River Charente, with its many windows and firing slots. Or the Château de Bonnaventure, near Le Gué du Loir. La Rochebrune, below Brantôme, on the River Dronne, has two caves guarding the Bourdeilles-Périgueux road. There is a chamber with six large round holes in the roof receiving light from the chamber above. This upper chamber has eight large round holes in the floor, the six mentioned above and two more which open over the edge of the cliff. One theory maintains that the six holes were for stabbing the enemy and the remaining pair for escaping. Another idea is that the room was a granary or even a malt store and the holes were grain chutes or for hauling up the bags of corn or malt.

A ford at Chauvigny, on the River Vienne, was found to be impassable by Clovis and the Franks, marching to Poitiers in 511 AD. Their plan was to steal back the rich southern provinces of Gaul from the Visigoths, under King Alaric II, to whom the Emperor Honorious had conceded them. Clovis then tried the stony road to Lussac-les-Châteaux, a former Roman highway, where he encountered a mass of stone slabs, said locally to be a fortified cave but looking remarkably like a dolmen. There was another ford further on, at Lussac, and Alaric knew about this; he may therefore well have tried to stop Clovis at the dolmen. However, Clovis pushed on and there was a battle, at which Clovis was successful, marking the end of the Visigoths' empire.

Guarding one of the Pyrenean passes is Urdos, hewn out of the rock in a series of chambers rising in stages from the road up to 500 feet. Similarly, Faron, 1660 feet high, commands Toulon harbour and the Bay of Hyères. The chains of rock forts at Campi delle Alte and Mont Agel, above Monaco, dominate the Corniche. They are all riddled with galleries, batteries and military paraphernalia. Besançon stands on its inaccessible rock. There are the remains of a rock fort, including cave paintings (see p. 83), at Sigiriya, in Sri Lanka. Ehrenbreitstein guards the opening of the Moselle into the Rhine and Frankenfeste guards the Brenner Pass, while Königstein crowns a 748-foot rock above the Elbe and Peterwardein stands over the Danube. Trosky, in Bohemia, is built on two spires of rock, and Covolo, in the Italian Brenta, close to the Austrian Tirol, stands 100 feet above the road and was able to hold a garrison of 500 men. Dover Castle guards the Strait of Dover and Gibraltar the entrance to the Mediterranean.

CHAPTER 13

Burial in stone

From very early times, man has made secondary use of caves as mortuary or burial chambers. The first cave men disposed of their dead crudely, the 'Flower People' of Shanidar, as we have seen, paid them very considerable respect. The caves used for this purpose had often been habitations but since man was afraid to continue to live in a cave in which death had occurred, he would move to a new one. This led to two obvious consequences. There could be a local shortage of caves, a fact which may well have accelerated the move first to build extensions to the cave and then free-standing structures. And the habit of interring the dead in caves led to the move to build what would now be called purpose-built structures: cists and dolmens, cairns and barrows, rock mounds and rock-cut tombs, sepulchres and catacombs. A belt demonstrating this practice extends from Scotland south to the Mediterranean, across Asia to China and Japan and the Americas, where in the southwest USA the modern Navajo and Ute, successors to the pueblo and cliff dwellers, would not enter the old dwellings until led in by white people.

There are some striking examples of underground and semi-subterranean burial structures. Among them are the chambered tomb of Maes Howe and the Dwarfie Stone, a unique Neolithic rock-cut tomb on Hoy, both in Orkney; the passage graves of Clava, Inverness, and New Grange, Ireland; the chambered long barrow of West Kennet in Wiltshire; and the *allées couvertes* of France, especially Brittany, and in the chalk of the Petit Morin. Many of these, however, are totally above ground and therefore beyond the scope of this book. So, too, are the Norse burials; some Norsemen were buried with their chariots and horses and the sea kings in their own piratical ships. When the practice of erecting menhirs and obelisks as tombstones, together with the sacrificial altar-tombs of dolmens, was abandoned, it was back to Shanidar: flowers were placed on graves to perpetuate the mythology of death.

One of the most impressive examples must be the rock-cut tombs of Europe. They were once thought to have been introduced into western Europe by colonists from the eastern Mediterranean, as part of a single 'megalithic complex' which originated there and spread over the whole of western Europe and the Mediterranean. It included megaliths and megalithic tombs, rock-cut tombs and the soul-statue menhirs ('Mother Goddesses') that are found in Corsica.

New carbon-14 dating and tree-ring dendrochronology have now established that this is not so: rock-cut tombs developed independently in the central Mediterranean, having no connection with the megaliths. They are usually in limestone which is so common there. They began in the area around Italy, the most elaborate being in Mallorca, Sardinia and Malta. Further, they were not all used for collective burial, as previously thought: there are many 'singles' and 'doubles'. The megalithic tombs, on the other hand, developed in north and western Europe, but the two groups overlapped geographically and in time and greatly influenced each other.

The first tombs were built in southeast Italy and Malta in the Neolithic (5500 years ago or even earlier) and spread to Sicily; all the others are of the Copper Age (some 5000 to 4500 years ago) and Bronze Age (4500 years ago onwards); in southeast Italy and Sicily they continued into the Iron Age. The earliest – in Italy and Sicily – were all single and double inhumations but singles were also the most common in the Cyclades. In the central Mediterranean, collective burials followed later, the numbers involved varying from less than ten to, rarely, more than a hundred. Malta's enormous Hal Saflieni might have acquired some seven thousand individuals over the many centuries in which it was in use.

Outside the Mediterranean, there are a few rock-cut tombs in the Marne area of central France, cut into the soft chalk and all very similar. There is a large square chamber, often with a small antechamber, both with narrow entrances connected to the surface by a sloping passage. They may well have no connection with the Mediterranean tombs and have developed locally as rock-cut imitations of the megalithic tombs of the same area – the gallery graves of the Paris Basin.

In southeast Italy, the tombs were of the *a forno* type: oven- or bell-shaped chambers, round or oval in shape, with a domed roof. Access to them was by a vertical shaft through a manhole or through a steeply sloping passage; if the tomb was near the edge of a sea or other cliff, there might be a horizontal entrance passage through the cliff face. There were some of this type in Sicily but many were more elaborate, with four-pillared antechambers and facades carved with imitation pillars. Malta had bell-shaped tombs with manholes at the top and include the most spectacular of all: the vast and labyrinthine *hypogeum* of Hal Saflieni. Sardinia had the most: more than eleven hundred, mostly of the Copper Age, and very varied in form and decoration. Entry to these was from a cliff face or by a long sloping passage. They contained many oval or rectangular chambers, decorated, as was commonly the case, in relief or red paint. Here the decoration included bulls' heads and other stylized designs, as well as interesting and unusual wooden beams and lintels.

Greece has some tombs on Crete and on the mainland but they are most common in the Cyclades and Cyprus, where they are mostly Bronze Age single burial tombs of *a forno* design. There are also a few in Palestine and pre-Dynastic Egypt.

In the western Mediterranean tombs are found mostly in the Balearic Islands, southern Spain and Portugal, specially round the River Tagus estuary, dating from the Copper and Bronze Ages; the Iberian tombs were of the *a forno* type. Mallorca had a special shape of its own: long rectangular or sub-rectangular chambers, with some secondary chambers, the whole resembling the megalithic tombs of the islands (*navetas*).

The Minoans of Crete had followed the standard practice of the Mediterranean at the time, around 3000 BC: bodies were placed in natural caves or in circular ossuaries built with dry-stone walls. The Middle Bronze Age marked the introduction of the rock-cut tombs, with short passages, and the practice of cramming human skeletons into storage jars or clay coffins. In the Late Bronze Age the Minoans turned to collective tombs but they also built vaulted chambers, like the round Mycenaean tholoi, into the hillsides, approached by tunnel-like passages.

The Lycians left some magnificent rock tombs at Fethiye, west of Antalya and east of Marmaris, in the southwestern part of Anatolia. According to Herodotus, the Lycians came to Turkey direct from Crete, under their leader Sarpedon, when they were known as the Termilae. The name 'Lycian' comes from the Athenian Lycus, the son of Pandion, although the Hittites record a tribe called Lukka. The Etruscans also had mortuaries and there are many rock tombs and sepulchres in Amasia, Armenia, and in Egypt, as in the Valley of the Kings, on the west bank of the Nile at Luxor. Queen Hatshetsup's 18th-Dynasty funerary temple is built into a cliff at El Deir el Bahari. Some tombs are mixed up with the pyramids near Cairo, and sometimes unfinished. Olivia Manning, in *The Danger Tree*, from *The Levant Trilogy*, described the masons and plasterers following the rock hewers, and themselves followed by the 'decorators', who began their work using the colours red and white. Unlike the Jews, who left no records in their tombs, not believing in an afterlife, the Egyptians built artificial structures, in lieu of caves, to receive the spirits of the dead on their return, as the *ka* returned to the mummy. The Nabataeans, who ruled the northwestern parts of Saudi Arabia from Petra, built more than a hundred rock-cut tombs at Meda'in Salih.

Palestine, too, abounds in rock-hewn tombs and burial caves. There are Bronze-Age burial caves near Khudheirah, on the Plain of Sharon, with clay chests and painted clay caskets shaped like houses and pottery. The chests and caskets were urns used to inter bones after the flesh had decayed. The Hebrew custom of holding cave burials and later coating the bodies of the dead with lime, gave rise to the notion of 'whited sepulchres'. From the Old Testament comes the story of the Cave of Machpelah, at Hebron, where Abraham buried Sarah and is himself said to be interred. The most famous of all rock tombs is, of course, Christ's sepulchre in the Garden of Gethsemane, on the hill at Calvary or, in Greek, *Golgotha*. Over it is the Church of the Holy Sepulchre, built by Helena, the mother of the Emperor Constantine.

Just as impressive in their way as the rock-cut tombs are the catacombs. The many rock tombs in Palestine had absolutely no letters, documents or inscriptions to denote the name of the occupant, probably because the Jews had no belief in an afterlife. Christianity changed this but even before the Christian era, when many Jews from Judea were settled in Rome on the right bank of the Tiber, they built themselves a catacomb, excavated in Monte Verde and discovered in 1602. It was exclusively Jewish, bearing the seven-branched candlestick, but apart from this the later Christian catacombs were precisely similar.

The busy *Via Appia* or Appian Way of Rome, built of huge greenish-grey stones of volcanic *selce* and the most important of the Consular roads, provided the prime choice of burial sites for the rich Romans, who liked to be buried in a public place where passing travellers would read their names and thus bring them fame. The poor Christians also wanted to be buried on the Appia but could not afford it, so they were buried in tiered *loculi* or coffin-like niches carved into the soft rock of the catacombs beneath and resembling *columbaria*, the Roman dovecots and pigeon-holed sepulchral chambers. The catacombs are named after the Hill of Catacomba, west of Rome, its derivation being a mystery since in Greek *cata-kumbas* means 'boats'.

The country around Rome consists of three sorts of stone: the very hard *tufa litoide*, used for building; *tufa granolare*, good for excavating and maintaining its shape but useless for building; and *pozzuolana*, used for making cement. The building-stone quarries were never excavated for catacombs, only the granular tufa, which was probably originally quarried as sand, the quarry tunnels later being re-excavated as cemeteries, mainly between 70 and 410 AD. The multi-stage *piani* stretch for miles in total length, but never extend far from the Eternal City. There were thirteen catacombs in Rome, where an area in the western outskirts of the city has been totally undermined and even now is not built on solely for this reason. There are no easily available maps, although five catacombs, now empty, are open to the public and there is a simplified plan showing how some of the entrances are interconnected.

ABOVE LEFT: St Sebastian catacombs, Rome, Italy. (The Reverend J.C. Allen) ABOVE RIGHT: Graves and burial effigies, Sulawesi, Indonesia. (Martin Coleman/Planet Earth Pictures) ABOVE: Queen Hatshetsup's 18th-Dynasty funerary temple at El Deir el Bahari, Luxor, Egypt. (The J. Allan Cash Photolibrary)

The most famous are the St Sebastian and the St Calixtus, where six Popes are buried, with ten miles of corridor between them. The best preserved, however, are the catacombs of St Agnes. The decorated galleries are from two to four feet wide and eight to twenty feet high, built on several levels. The thousands of graves are arranged on both sides in two tiers, like the bunks in a cabin, cut into the walls and sealed with bricks and stones set in mortar. There are a few small side chambers, also with graves, all originally closed with slabs of marble or *terra cotta*, or tiles: for the rich and the poor, respectively. Otherwise, there was little distinction. Some had their names scratched or engraved on their tombs. Martyrs had a more elaborate grave, in a sarcophagus or *arcosolium*, used as an altar to celebrate their anniversaries. Wealthy families would sometimes have their own chamber or *cubiculum*. Many chapels were added from time to time.

The Crypt of the Popes, rediscovered in May 1854, contains nine third-century popes and three bishops; seven more popes from between 199 and 384 AD lie buried in the vicinity. Also nearby is the Crypt of St Cecilia, martyred by having her throat cut; her body was removed in 821 AD and reburied in a basilica. The catacombs, frequently plundered and centres of pilgrimage, are remarkable for their murals, biblical pictures, inscriptions, poetry, memorials and other works of art, many in near perfect condition.

Catacombs were also built in Naples, where there are five sets, and many other towns, such as Aquila and Venisa, this last possibly being Jewish. Those in Syracuse in Sicily are vast, very like those in Rome, but lofty and wider and originally quarries. There is a large circular hall, lit from above, with niches for use as sepulchres around the sides and early Christian paintings, as at Rome, depicting men and women at prayer, the peacock and the sacred monogram. In Palermo the artistocrats liked to be buried in the catacombs or cave-tombs of the Cappuchin Zita Church. There are catacombs in Malta and at three towns in Spain. In France there is a hypogeum opening out of the early church of St Victor at Marseilles, a catacomb at Carcassonne, and others at Trèves in Germany, Fünfkirchen in Hungary, and Nottingham in England. There are catacombs on the Greek island of Melos and at Salamis in Cyprus, and also at Alexandria and Cyrene in Egypt. In Cairo, half a million people live in the tombs and vaults of the ancient cemetery known as the City of the Dead.

The catacombs of Paris were also not originally built as catacombs but, like those of Syracuse, were the seventeenth-century *calcaire grossier* building-stone quarries. They underlie about a tenth of the area of Paris, all on the left bank of the Seine. At the end of Louis XVI's reign, the main necropolis of Paris, Le Cimetière des Innocentes, became so crowded and surrounded by buildings that it was decided to move the bones, with great ceremony, to the catacombs, solemnly consecrated for their reception on 7 April 1787 by the Archbishop of Paris. The famous fruit and vegetable market of Les Halles was then set up on the former site of the cemetery, although the pavilions were not built until 1854–66. Other cemeteries were similarly cleared until the total of the remains in the catacomb quarries was estimated at three million people, including some Revolutionary victims. The grave style of the martyrs had led the kings, princes and the rich to follow suit and adopt mausoleums but nevetheless, during the Revolution, the royal tombs were profanely destroyed. There they remained, in heaps, until 1812, when they were gradually arranged in a deliberately fantastic manner as an exhibition for the curious. Access to the catacombs is by sixty-three staircases, but no visitors are allowed now: only surveyors and workmen on their biannual tours of inspection.

Akin, perhaps, to the catacombs are the *puticoli*, the sad communal graves of the slaves and the very poor. These were bottle- or funnel-shaped refuse pits, employed also as mass graves; when they were full a tree was planted on top. They were still in use in Naples in the early part of this century, where the bodies were shot into the pit from a cart, carrying a lantern, and the winding sheets were left behind and retained for further use. In Monte Carlo they were known as *les spelunges* and they were common in the chalk of northern France and southern England. The pits of Nottingham and the slave pits of South Africa were similar. More recently, the Guanche of the Canary Islands used some of their caves for burial and ceremonial purposes.

Asia has a long history of cave and rock-tomb burials. Caves at Baghaikhor and Lekhahiya, near Mirzapur in the Benares district of Bihar, India, were both inhabited and used for burials, in which two ritual postures, already described, were adopted. Japan had dog burial rites, and in Sulawesi the Toradja people of Tana Toradja buried their dead in limestone caverns. Nowadays their descendents usually chisel narrow crypts out of the solid rock. The skulls are more visible but the complete skeleton is also present; clothing is buried with the dead and carved hardwood effigies called *tau-tan* are placed to stand sentinel over them.

Finally, in the Americas, there is an Aleut burial cave on Kanaga Island, in the Aleutian group, containing the bones of six people, bits of boat and other artefacts. The Mayas of Guatemala had burial caves near Oxkutzcab, at Zopo, Tabasco, near Coban. Bones were left either open or buried, some partly cremated. This practice may be related to the pagan cult of Nagualism, in which flowers and copal incense are taken to the grave caves: Nagual was the animal double or guardian spirit of the individual. Among the Nahua people, the *naualli* was the sorcerer, diviner and soothsayer in pre-Columbian Mexico, and the cult continued after the conquest. Cave burial was also practised further south by the Incas of Peru. There are burial caves in the limestone of Puerto Rico, close to the villages but never lived in at the same time. Many bones have been found in Antonio's Cave, which is near to a *juego de bola* or ball court. There are no mortuary offerings but shards and pebble tools have been found, together with a single quartz porphyry hammerstone.

CHAPTER 14

Religious life underground

As we have seen, the early cave dwellers buried their dead in caves and themselves moved to new ones. The burial caves became shrines, and eventually chapels, churches and temples. Holy men and hermits settled in some of the caves; thus, as well as places of worship, they became hermitages and monasteries, or in many cases a mixture of all three. As with dwelling caves, the burgeoning move to build outwards, the beginning of free-standing structures, spread especially to temples. This is superbly demonstrated on the River Nile in Egypt, with the temple at Abu Simbel, the statues of King Rameses II in front, extending 180 feet into the sandstone behind, as well as the temples of Luxor and Karnac. Another prime example is Petra, of which more later. Some of the temples of Mithras were rock-cut; there are examples at Angera and Spoleto, facing east in order that the first rays of sun should hit the image of the bull-slaying god. The Nubian rock-temples of Beit el-Wali, Derr, Wadi es-Sebua and Gerf Husein are famous for their beautiful decorative narrative frescoes.

Much of the religious life of Palestine was dominated by caves, as was beautifully illustrated by the discovery of the Dead Sea Scrolls. Near the religious centre of Khirbat (or Khirbet) Qumran, in Judea, on the northwest coast of the Dead Sea, which was built by the Essenes in about 100 BC and destroyed by the Romans, are eleven caves in the Wadi Qumran. The members of this society probably lived not in the centre but in tents and nearby caves. Then in 1947, a young Bedouin goatherd looking for a missing goat chanced upon some of the scrolls, wrapped in linen in an earthenware jar, in one of the caves. There turned out to be hundreds of them, four hundred in one batch, plus tens of thousands of fragments, coming originally from the Essenes' library. They cover every part of the Old Testament (the Hebrew Bible), except the Book of Esther which never mentions God, and are some 1000 years older than the oldest copy of the Bible then known. There were also works which talk about the Teacher of Righteousness, now known definitely not to have been Christ. However, Christ probably knew about the Essenes, as did John the Baptist, who baptised Christ as well as many common

Temple of Rameses II at Abu Simbel, Egypt. (Egyptian Tourist Office)

people. Could John have been an Essene? He ate the same food as them – honey and locusts – and was finally imprisoned in Machaerus, one of King Herod's forts, on the northeast coast of the Dead Sea, where he was later beheaded. Further south and inland is Masada, perched high on a butte overlooking the Dead Sea, another of Herod's multi-storied forts. This was the scene of the mass suicide of 960 Zealot Jews in 73 AD, who committed this act rather than submit to the rule of Rome. Like Qumran, it too was razed by the Romans.

When the persecution of the early Christians ended, and they were able to worship in peace and security, two types of Church battled for supremacy. One, the Basilican, was based on the halls of the wealthy and powerful, made over into churches or *basilica* and the model for the cathedrals and parish churches of the future. The other, the Catacumbal, was based on the subterranean chapels in the catacombs and was preferred by the poorer members of the community, the serfs and slaves, where, out of sight of their masters, they had no need to feel unequal and could enjoy a greater sense of security. Further, they became used to visiting the catacombs to commemorate anniversaries at the tombs of the martyrs buried there. There is no doubt that the

Caves in the Wadi Qumran, Israel, where the Dead Sea Scrolls were found. (BIPAC)

mass of people *liked* an underground religious life; they considered a rock tomb a suitable place for burial and they liked the idea of chapels springing up underground as well – as they had in the catacombs. And they approved the chapels containing tombs: the birth of the monolithic church, the crypt and also the *hypogeum*, sunk perhaps nine feet into the ground, with the roof showing above ground. This word, from the Greek *hypogeios* or ground, can mean a subterranean tomb or an underground chamber: it occurs here again in a different context. So the Popes and the Bishops had to agree that every basilica should also be a mausoleum, containing bones, while the altar sometimes became a sepulchre, containing not the whole body but a box bearing the relics of a saint.

In Rome the relics of the martyrs were eventually transferred to the basilicas to save them from profanity at the hands of the invading Lombards, and the catacombs fell into disuse. But in Gaul, where the people relished the blood of the martyrs watering their soil, there were numerous *hypogean* chapels and when the remains of the hermits and other anchorites were added to those of the martyrs, one can see why the number of underground tombs proliferated, encouraging the spread of crypts beneath all the parish and monastic churches as well as cathedrals. In contrast, Britain had few early martyrs and Germany and the other northern Europe countries hardly any; hence the church in these countries was Basilican from the start.

Rock-cut churches

The Levant has many cave churches, those of Cappadocia in Turkey being perhaps the best known and the subject of chapter 8. The chapel of Agios Niketos in Crete is now just a smoky grotto under a huge rock mass on the mountain side, but was once elaborately decorated with murals of the Gospel story and St Nicholas. So, too, was the rock-hewn church of Dayn Aboo Hannes near Antinoe, in Egypt, thought to date back to the Emperor Constantine. The chapel at Gethsemane over the Virgin Mary's tomb is mostly underground, reached by three steps down with only the porch visible above ground. But forty-seven marble steps follow and the place becomes two natural caves turned into the 93-by-21-foot church, with many sacred sites, and the 54 foot long, 27 foot wide and 12 foot high Cavern of the Agony at Gethsemane. There were caves associated with the Old Testament prophets Samson, David and Elijah, and holy grottoes abounded likewise in the minds of the early Christians. The Grotto of Bethlehem was thought in the second century to be the scene of the Nativity; there is the Grotto of the Ascension on Mount Olivet; the sacred Cave of the Sepulchre; and the Dome of the Rock surmounting a cave. Then followed the Cave of the Invention of the Cross; the Cave of the Annunciation to the Virgin by the Angel Gabriel of Nazareth; the Cave of the Baptism in the Wilderness of St John; and the Cave of the Birth of Christ and the Shepherds at Bethlehem. There were the caves of the hermits: St Pelagia on Mount Olivet; those of St Jerome, St Paula and St Eustochium at Bethlehem; St Saba in the ravine of Kedron; and the remarkable cells hewn out of the precipices of the Quarrantania or Mount of the Temptation above Jericho. Mohammed received his first inspired messages in a cave. Finally, there were the crypts possessed with miraculous springs, such as St Peter's in the Vatican.

France, more than any other country, seems from the days of the Neanderthal and Cro-Magnon people to have taken to an underground life with enthusiasm. Although there are no spectacular examples of a troglodytic life style to challenge those of Cappadocia and Matmata, the sheer numbers of inhabited caves, right up to the present, and the wealth of other ways in which rock-cut chambers and buildings have been used, can be matched nowhere else. Monolithic churches are no exception. The famous church at St Emilion, on the border of Bordeaux and the Dordogne, is based on the cave of the Benedictine hermit, St Emilion who, with the other monks of the order, enlarged the natural caves of the area. The monastery church was founded on his death in 767 AD and the monolithic church carved out of solid rock at the end of the eleventh or beginning of the twelfth centuries. Its base measures 120 by 60 feet and it is in two parts. An anterior vestibule, 21 feet high, with richly flamboyant windows and a sculptured principal doorway, leads at right angles into a nave 60 feet high and 95 feet long, lit by three flamboyant and three plain windows, all excavated out of the rock. Above the church is the Château du Roi, built by Louis VIII, whose thirteenth-century rectangular keep stands on a rocky pedestal, hewn out of a huge underground hall.

Another monolithic church is St John's, some 50 feet high, under the castle at Aubeterre, Charente, on the River Dronne, where it is let into the chalk hill on which the town is built. The door, at street level, gives onto one of two charnel houses, humpy with graves, measuring 70 by 16 feet, followed by a door cut into the rock leading into the nave, side aisle with its monolithic piers, monolithic tomb, gallery and seigneural pew high up over the entrance. There are also: Rocamadour, Lot, where a group of chapels partly clings to, and is partly cut out of, the rock; La Sainte Baume, Lirac, Gard, where a small chapel 60 feet long, 45 feet wide and 30 feet high is hewn out of the rock; Our Lady of the Angels at Mimet, Bouches-du-Rhône, cut out of limestone with stalactites hanging from the roof; St Christophe, Peyre, near Millau, Tarn, scooped out of rock, with its old bell tower; and the excavated monolithic parish church of Caudon, Domme, on the Dordogne. Several natural caves in France have been employed as chapels or churches, such as the Grotte des Fées, near Nîmes, used by the Calvinists before 1567; the Grotte de Jouclas, La Cave, near Rocamadour; the tenth-century St George, Gurat, in Charente, which is hollowed out of the rock; and a cave chapel near Souillac, Lot, in the Borrèze Valley, containing the bones of bears. Lanmeur, Brittany, has a very early Christian crypt, dating from about 544 AD. It is 25 by 15.5 feet in size, divided by two rows of four-foot columns and three-and-a-half-foot arches into a nave and side aisles. The dolmen chapel near Plouaret, Brittany, lies under a tumulus and has two huge granite capstones supported on four or five upright stones. The little tenth- or eleventh-century church at Cangas-de-Ones, near Oviedo, northwest Spain, sits on top of a dolmen which acts as its crypt, and there are other dolmen chapels, as well as a rock-hewn church at Avila.

One of the most remarkable groups of rock-hewn churches are those of the Tegre and Wallo provinces of northwest Ethiopia. Here there are hundreds of Orthodox Christian shrines and churches, carved in the Middle Ages out of the pink tuff mesas, called *ambas*, especially around Lalibela, and famous for their Byzantine frescoes. They were founded by the Syrian, Frumentius, who was sold as a slave but later became a saint, known as the Abba Salama or Father of Peace, and founded the monastery bearing his name. He converted the ruler of the Ethiopian Kingdom of Aksum to Christianity in 330 AD and their sect became similar to the Egyptian Coptic Church. Aksum was the

ABOVE LEFT: Rock-cut church at Lalibela, Ethiopia (N. Vincent/C. M. Dixon) ABOVE RIGHT: A view through the *siq* to the Treasury of the Pharaoh, Petra, Jordan. (Jordanian Tourist Office)

cradle of Ethiopian civilization: Haile Selassie claimed descendency from its ruler. At Lalibela the Abba Salama Monastery is supposed to have the Abba's bones contained in a nearby niche more than 500 feet above, a terrifying climb up a rock chimney and a 60-foot chain. The most famous of all the religious buildings are the eleven churches here, including Emmanuel, St Mary and St George's, while in the north there are more, such as Guh and Qorqor. How the huge stone blocks were quarried, carted and raised up to build the monasteries and churches – the highest, now in ruins, was 110 feet tall – is not known.

Even more remarkable is Petra, 'half as old as time': the rose-red city of pink Nubian sandstone in south Jordan, which can in certain lights also appear yellow, tan and ivory, lying near Wadi Musa halfway between the Dead Sea and the Gulf of Aqaba. It is reached through a deep rock cleft: a sik or *siq*, more than a mile long and only 20 feet at its narrowest, widening to 60 feet, and entered by a gateway, the *Bab es Siq*, which means Gate by a Cleft. The *siq* had a water-tunnel cut through the mountain to drain off flood water northwards to the Wadi Musa, and cavities cut into it just before it opens into the valley may have been shops and store rooms for the trade goods that may have been unloaded in Petra for reloading onto a new caravan. There is a sort of suburb of tombs: pylon-type tombs, cut from the rock but unlike the facade monuments which were blocked out to stand apart as buildings. There are also white sandstone hummocks, rock domes with small chambers, like those on inaccessible mountain tops, that were the troglodytic homes of ancient people who lived on Mount Seir before it became Edom.

Nearly one thousand temples are cut in these stupendous rock cliffs, showing the influence of Babylonians, Egyptians, Greeks and Romans; Petra was occupied in turn by Edomites, Phoenicians, Egyptians and Romans. There are high places, courts, libation basins, temples, altars and tombs. Nearby, flints of Palaeolithic age have been found, but its first history is found in the Bible.

From the time of Saul – 1095 – until 740 BC, the house of Judah more or less dominated the region. But when they declined the Edomites, a proud and arrogant Semitic speaking people, descendents of Esau, discussed by Obadiah, gained power and moved into the territory, naming it Edom. They had settled the Petra basin before 1200 BC, as well as the top of the Umm il-Biyara mountain (the mother of cisterns), but they then migrated to better lands west of the River Jordan. Their place was taken by the strange semi-nomadic and presumably pastoral Nabatu, a tribe descended from Ishmael, who may have helped to drive out the Edomites. Renamed the Nabataeans, they had, by the fourth century BC, made Petra famous as their capital city and a crossroads of the caravan trade. They built most of the monuments.

But first they built defensive walls across the valley, ridge to ridge. They built water runnels along the cliff faces, dammed wadis, built circles of stone to trap run-off water and terraces to guard against soil erosion. They plastered cisterns and laid miles of carefully fitted ceramic pipes to supply Petra and its outposts with water. Then they started on their city. Around 800 BC they built tombs, temples, houses, tiers of streets and stairways. It was during the Hellenistic period and their monumental and stone-carving work made them famous.

Of the nearly one thousand monuments, the majority are Nabataean and thus very interesting. About twenty-five are classical, in the Greek or Roman style, and thus the largest and most imposing, although not necessarily the most interesting. The only free-standing building still extant is a large Roman temple called Qasr el Bint Faroun (Palace of the Maiden). Its timbered roof is gone but all the masonry is still sound, apart from four great columns that formed part of the pronaos. Zibb Atuf has the largest of the Nabataean tombs and there are two interesting altars at its base; the top is reached by rock-cut stairs. Rock steps lead to the *ras* or small rock hill, with the Great High Place of Sacrifice. Sunk into the rock is a large court surrounded by low benches, with two altars. The Nabataeans worshipped the sun god Dushara, whose symbol was an uncut black stone; the Ka'aba stone in Mecca is one such Dushara stone. A large water cistern at the Great High Place of Sacrifice shows that it was a pilgrimage centre.

Past the vast Roman-style theatre, an amphitheatre with a floor 120 feet in diameter and thirty-three rows of seats, thought to hold between three and five thousand people, is El Khubdha. Here are the highest rock faces and the most impressive temples, carved on its west facade, such as the Urn Temple – this has an inscription mentioning a Christian Bishop of 447 AD. There are two marvellous Roman-style tombs also on the west facade: the Palace and the Corinthian. The top storey of the three original storeys is now in ruins. There is El Habis, the Acropolis Hill, and the subterranean Temple of the Winged Lions, which still has plaster on its ashlar blocks, its arch supporting the roof up against the cliff. But the most famous cliff-cut tomb facade is the Corinthian so-called Treasury of the Pharaoh (Ptolemy) or Khaznah Faroun (or Khazneh Far'on), probably a Nabataean king's tomb or a shrine to the Mother Goddess Allat. The second most famous is the Byzantine church, the Ed-Deir or Monastery, a great space cleared in front of the cliff in which it is carved, possibly intended to be a temple to the god Dushara or a royal tomb but never completed.

The Nabataeans produced copper and iron work, painting and sculpture, carving and pottery, all of which are outstanding: Diodorus described them. They traded frankincense and myrrh, gold and gems, aloes, cinnamon and other spices from India and Arabia, and silk from China; they had caravans and their own port and their goods were transhipped at Alexandria. They copied the Egyptians, Syrians and others; built superb tombs and temples, a theatre with far too many seats, and a city with a main street. Then, in 106 AD, the Emperor Trajan took over Petra for the Romans. It remained a very important centre until Rome fell, when it was abandoned, although desert tribesmen continued to live miserably in caves nearby. It was then rediscovered by a Swiss traveller, Jean Louis Burckhardt, disguised as a Bedouin sheikh, in 1812. He returned to tell of its mysteries; it was sacred ground to the Arabs and any infidel who approached it was in danger. Burckhardt sacrificed a goat to the only Dushara stone still in use in that area and this, it was thought, led to his discovery.

India and the surrounding lands have abundant cave temples and caves of architectural interest. Those of Afghanistan, vast in size and dedicated to Buddha, as at Bamian, are carved out of sandstone; so too are the reddish-yellow Jain temples at Aihole, in southern India. There are Hindu cliff-temples carved out of limestone at Elephanta Island, Bombay, and Billa Soorgum, and there are several rock-cut Buddhist temples at Kala – 2000 years old – and in Sri Lanka.

Of the thousand or so architecturally important caves in India, the temples of Ellora and Ajanta, hewn from the Deccan Trap basalt lava of Maharashtra, are often regarded as the culmination of Brahminic cave architecture. Ajanta came first, where Buddhists carved some thirty temples and dwelling halls in the seventh century AD; they then abandoned the complex and it was lost, to be rediscovered in 1819 by soldiers of the British Raj. The Buddhists had moved to Ellora, which was never lost – it was described by Captain John B. Seely, who visited it in 1810 – where they were joined by Hindus and Jains; over the next 200 or 300 years, they carved altogether another thirty-four temples, in a 250-foot basalt cliff. The Hindu temples are dedicated to Siva, and to his wife Parvati, also known as Kali. One of the temples, to Kailasa the Proud, is 96 feet high.

In India there are also the *chaitya*, underground temples of which the earliest known is Nigope Cave near Bihar, built about 200 BC. It has two halls: one rectangular, 33 by 19 feet, and the inner circular, 19 feet in diameter. Later *chaitya* were more like Christian basilicas: one at Poona, cut 126 feet into the rock, has a forecourt followed by a nave and two aisles with columns. The older *viharas* or monasteries were also rock-cut and, like their European counterparts, have cells and chambers. Amarnath Cave, 25 miles above Pahlgam, Kashmir, at a height of over 12,000 feet, is a famous Hindu holy cave, the goal of many pilgrims. It is a grotto, at the back of which is a huge greyish-white pillar of ice, somewhat above man-size, created by seeping water which then freezes, waxing and waning in size with the moon. It is largest at full moon and known as a *linga*; the story is that on a night of the full moon Siva revealed to his wife, Parvati, the secret of immortality.

Tiered temple caves, known as the Caves of Yun-Kang, were dug around 400 to 500 AD by the Toba Tatars in the sandstone cliffs of the Mienshan Mountains, in a loop in the Great Wall just southwest of Peking, in the northern Shanxi Province of China (see illustrations on pp. 172–3). They were filled with Buddhist images and in the distance look rather like Matmata. The people themselves lived nearby in mud huts and little houses, but some were so close that the lower caves could only be reached through the walled yards of the houses; understandably, these caves came to be used as stables and as stores for farm carts and implements, hay, coffins and so on. The most important of the Yun-Kang caves is Shih Chia Fo, meaning Sakya Buddha;

OPPOSITE: Kailasa Temple, Ellora, India. Carved during the 8th and early 9th centuries AD, it is probably the world's biggest monolithic structure. (The J. Allan Cash Photolibrary)

another large cave is O Mi To Fo, or Buddha of Boundless Light. Further south, in Henan, are the Lung Men Caves. The provinces of Shanxi and Henan lie on the great loess belt of China, which is reputed to contain caves at one time housing a total of some ten million people. Far away to the west is Gansu and, near the Silk Route, Xi'an, capital of the fourth province, Shaanxi, so graphically described in 1936 by Peter Fleming in *News from Tartary*. West of Xi'an is the walled city of Tunhwang, and twelve miles out of the town are the five hundred Caves of Tunhwang, honeycombing the 200-foot sandstone cliffs and filled with paintings, frescoes and stuccos of Buddha and his associates. They were assembled over a thousand years and led to the name the 'Caves of the Thousand Buddhas'.

Rock monasteries

When in 336 AD the Bishop Athanasius was at Trèves, in exile from the Upper Nile, he was said to have occupied a cave above the River Moselle. He seems to have inspired many important people, including Bishop Maximinus and several nobles, to reproduce in Europe the monastic life conducted by the third-century fathers in the Egyptian desert. One of these, named Martin, settled in one of the grottoes along the right bank of a broad valley of the River Clain, five miles from Poitiers, and founded Ligugé, the first Gaulish monastery. Then he was made Bishop of Tours and set about founding another monastery, St Martin's, at Marmoutier, in the chalk cliffs along the River Loire, on ground which had already been sanctified. Later, these would be replaced by the great abbey of the same name. But meanwhile, Martin and his disciples – such as Gatianus – began enlarging the caves, to add a chapel and a baptistry. The Abbey of Brantôme, on the River Dronne in the Dordogne, was another cavern monastery, with a beautiful Romanesque tower, sitting on the cliff-side which was honeycombed with the monks' cells. The church consists only of a nave, which had to be built on a curve because of the limited space between river and cliffs. One splendid sculpture, the huge sixteenth-century Triumph of Christ over Death, was never completed. Nearby is a grotto called La Babayou, dedicated to the statue of that name. Another cave monastery was at Moustier-Ste-Marie, on the River Verdon, founded by St Maximus in 434 and famous for its faience. Once again, France's predilection for underground living is demonstrated.

Rock monasteries are also found elsewhere. In Cappadocia possibly as many as 50,000 of the early monk settlers fled, in the eighth century, from the threat of Islam brought by marauding Arabs, as well as from other pressures, and set up settlements underground in southern Italy. There were examples at Massafra, in Calabria, and Matera, in Puglia. The *viharas* of India have already been mentioned and in Egypt there are examples at Der el Adra and also at the Pully, on the top of Gebel el Ferr, 200 feet above the River Nile and reached only by a cave or fissure the size of a chimney. In Israel, between Jerusalem and Jericho and before the monasteries of St George, 'Ein Fara and Deir el Banat were built, the monks lived, in the fifth and sixth centuries, in hermit caves in the Wadi el Qilt. The Mar Saba monastery, south-southwest of Jerusalem also is rock-hewn. In the Caucasus Mountains, Greek priests lived in caves, building walls around them of stone, reed and bamboo.

On the west side of the Black Sea, Bulgaria has cliff monasteries, occupied by peripatetic monks and consisting of cells and a small chapel; Aladja is one example near Varna. On the north side, the Crimea, now the Krymskiy region of Russia, has rock-cut monasteries of which Chekerman, measuring 37 by 21 feet, is the oldest. Others include the monastery near Bakhtci-Sarai, the crypts of Katchikalen, and the 'Valley of Jehoshaphat', where there is a precipitous promontory, with cliff faces several hundred feet high, covered with massive ancient ruins and passages leading down to excavated chambers, their windows opening out on to the side of the promontory. In the Inkermann Valley, near Sevastopol, the monastery and Byzantine church, with its Greek Orthodox cross, are reached by a 50-foot passage.

The church is said to resemble the chapel of St Mary of the Rock or St Mary de la Roche, a quarter of a mile west of the Castle Rock at Nottingham, close to the River Leen, on Castle Boulevard. Also known as one of the Nottingham 'Popish Holes', it belonged to Lenton Priory and had a pigeonry similar to that at Brantôme. It was destroyed as a papists' hole by the Puritans in the Civil War and later became known as Park Hermitage; it is now behind a car and van saleroom. Although these caves may have been originally Romano-British, they certainly became monastical in use. There is another hermitage on the other, east, side of Nottingham, at Sneinton, known since 1518 and later equipped with casement windows. This was the last cave in Nottingham to be occupied and was only vacated in about 1920.

The term rock monastery will conjure up for many the name Meteora, above all others. The custom of seeking peace and religious isolation in the Trikala Mountains region of Thessaly, in central Greece, began in the eleventh century when hermits and ascetics took up their abode in caves and rock crevasses, and monks gathered on Sundays to pray in the tiny chapels and shrines. At first they came under the jurisdiction of the cloisters of Stagi, while their administrative and spiritual centre was the Kyriakon, a communal church at Doúpiani, near Kastraki, where the monastery and church of the Virgin Mary were later built. By the troubled times under Turkish domination

LEFT: Monastery of Agios Stephanos, Meteora, Greece. (National Tourist Organisation of Greece) RIGHT: Map of Meteora showing the location of the major monasteries.

before 1336, when the hermits of the 'Thebaid of Stagoi' were settled at Doúpiani, the monastic community had become the sanctuary for the persecuted and the devout and a major centre of Byzantine art. Legend has it, although it may be history, that there was once a monarch in Constantinople who disliked his brother and so founded this remote brotherhood, building an almost inaccessible monastery called Meteora, 'domicile of the sky', whence he banished his brother. This was the first of the rock-top monasteries, perched on ledges or on top of twenty-four needle-like pinnacles or columns, the highest rising perpendicularly to 1822 feet, the average being 985 feet, above the point there the Pinios River emerges at the foot of the Pindus Mountains and begins to flow downstream through the Thessalian plain. Meteora itself, near the little towns of Kalambaka and Kastraki, derives from the Greek word for 'high in the air'. Overlooking the most splendid scenery, building of the other twenty-three monasteries continued by Byzantine monks under the Emperor Simeon, half hollowed out, half built out in front of the rock. By the fifteenth century they were all complete.

Between 1356 and 1372 the monk Athanasius founded what became the largest and most important, the Great Meteoron or Monastery of the Transfiguration, at Platis Lithos, 1752 feet high. The church of the Transfiguration, built in 1545, has fine frescoes and an intricate twelve-sided dome. Athanasius imposed very strict rules, including the exclusion of women. In 1388 John Uresis, a disciple of Athanasius and a grandson of the Serbian prince Stephen, retired to the monastery as the monk Joasaph and endowed it with many riches and special privileges. The Great Meteoron soon became autonomous and supreme over all the communes and hermitages in the area. It acquired many valuable historical, artistic and ecclesiastical treasures, with a fine refectory and a library with many rare books and manuscripts. However, the development of some of the others, and the wealth they acquired, soon led to bitter disputes which came to a head in the sixteenth century. Thus started their decline and although the monasteries were in more or less full use until the last century, today only four – the Great Meteoron, Varlaam, Agia Trias and Agios Stephanos – still have monks.

Of the other monasteries, Nikolaos t'Anapafsa (St Nikolaos) was built on a low rock around 1388 and expanded, with an annex, in 1628. It has sixteenth-century frescoes by Theophanes the Cretan. Agia Moni, built on a needle of rock in about 1315, is now in ruins. Rousanou, built in 1388 as a hermitage and reached across bridges, was turned into a monastery in 1545. To the south is Agia Trias (Holy Trinity), built in 1476 on a very beautiful pinnacle by the monk Dometius and reached by its circular flight of stairs of some hundred and forty steps. Agios Stephanos (St Stephen), with its museum, was another hermitage, built on a pinnacle connected to the main cliff by a drawbridge and turned into a monastery by Emperor Andronicus II Paleologus (1328–1341). The head of the saint is still preserved in the monastery's cathedral, Agios Haralambos. There are beautiful gold-leaved wood carvings, wall paintings, old icons and iconostasia in the old church of Agios Stephanos.

Further north is Varlaam (St Barlaam), built late, in 1517, by two rich brothers from a Janena family on the site of the old hermit Varlaam's hermitage. The frescoes in the chapel of All Saints are by Franco Catellano of Thebes, painted in 1565 and restored in 1870; there is also a superb Byzantine icon of the Virgin Mary by Emmanuel Tzanes. The monasteries were built with corniced roof tops and wooden galleries and were reached, almost incredibly, by a system of ropes, hooks, pulleys, and windlasses which were used to haul up bags, nets and baskets, as a protection against marauding Turks. St Barlaam and the Great Meteoron had arrangements of successive jointed or removable ladders; Holy Trinity had nets but also 140 steps, as a concession to women and visitors. Down below the monks cultivated fields in the valley: they must have been exceptionally fit and healthy!

Now there are ramps and stairs cut into the rock face for tourists, who love the buildings, the splendid frescoes – some of which depict roving Saracen bands hunting the monks – and the magnificent scenery and views of the valley.

Hermitages

As the Reverend Sabine Baring-Gould reminded us, an *anchorite*, properly, is a recluse who is walled into his cell; a *monk* or *coenobite* is a solitary; and a *hermit* or *eremite* is a dweller in the desert. These terms are used rather more loosely now. The unpleasant custom of immuring prisoners into caves, followed also in the case of the child monks of the Tibetan Buddhist monasteries of Nyen-de-kyl-Buk and Sumde-pu-pe, spread through Judaism to the Therapeutae and the Essenes and thence to the Christians in Egypt. Unlike the Buddhist, however, whose self-torture might be construed as largely selfish, designed to ensure that he reached Nirvana and achieved reincarnation as something less lowly than a bug or a louse, the Christian's belief in hermitage, derived from Manichaeism, was based on the belief that the flesh, like all matter, is evil and ungodly and must be subdued. Anchorites devised many forms of Indian fakir-type masochism. They had themselves walled up in caves, cells, huts and hovels; some settled on the top of a rock or even a pole. Only slightly less stringent were the roofless huts, with only slits for windows, or huts with roofs too low to stand up under. Some encased themselves in leather or horse hair, chain mail or sheet-lead, or in a coffin. They were weighted down with chains or iron bars, or suspended for seven years on iron sickles under the arm pits. In general, the Christians were less addicted to this type of treatment than the Buddhists, although the Irish had something of a predilection for self torment.

Britain has a number of underground hermitages and the north is an excellent place to start. After St Aidan had travelled from Iona and brought Christianity to Britain, founding the monastery on Holy Island, he recruited a monk from Melrose Abbey named Cuthbert, who lived for a while in a retreat on Inner Farne, before becoming Bishop of Lindisfarne in 685 AD. The retreat was a cell in a tiny church, half in and half out of the ground, and St Cuthbert returned there before he died. His body was carried from Lindisfarne to Durham and on its way is said to have rested at St Cuthbert's Cave and Cuddy's Cove, both near Wooler in northern Northumberland.

St Cuthbert's Cave, near Wooler, Northumberland, England.

The first Christian church in Scotland was founded at Whithorn, in the Wigtown Peninsula – where its foundations are currently being excavated – by St Ninian, sometimes called St Ringan, early in the fifth century. His retreat was the nearby St Ninian's Cave, in the yellow muddy limestone outcropping along the coast. Excavated in 1884 and again in 1950, it showed signs of long occupation and pilgrimage, including pilgrim crosses cut on its walls, going back at least to the eighth century. St Ringan also had a hermitage at Billies, near Kirkcormack, in Kirkcudbrightshire. Also in Northumberland, Warkworth Hermitage, on the north bank of the River Coquet, is half a mile upstream from the Castle and only accessible by boat. It was founded in about 1340 and made famous by Bishop Percy's ballad: the hermit in love with Lady Percy of the Castle who was rejected and lived out his life in the hermitage. But this was legend. It was a carefully planned and well-executed hermitage and chapel, occupied by a chaplain until 1567. In some ways it is unique in Britain although it resembles rock chapels in southern Italy. Perhaps it was modelled on one noted there by a Percy off to, or returning from, the Crusades. A later theory is that it might have been the Percy family's private chapel, with its resident priest. The chapel measures 20.5 feet by 7.5 feet; it has an altar, recesses, niches for relics and some interesting carvings. The outer gallery, arched like a cloister and measuring 28 feet long by 5 feet wide, including the lobby at the west end, is the Sacristy. There are three small living rooms – hall, measuring 18 by 15 feet, with fireplace and a window

ABOVE: A view of Warkworth Hermitage, Northumberland in 1835. BELOW: Interior view of Warkworth Hermitage in 1815.

overlooking the river; kitchen, some 15 feet square, with an oven; and solar or sitting room, with fireplace and garderobe. All are hollowed out of the Millstone Grit, overlooking the river.

St Giles's Chapel, by the River Nidd at Knaresborough, is a cave 10 feet long, 9 feet wide and 7 feet high, scooped out of the rock. A knight lived briefly here, until he had had enough, when he handed it over to Robert Thorne – but he too stayed less than a year. There is Roche Hermitage in Cornwall, a spire of schorl rock 100 feet above the moor, variously occupied down to the Reformation. Tong Castle, east Shropshire, in the Old Manor of Tong, had underground chambers and tunnels, but probably no proper cave. The so-called 'hermitage' was a bare little house where Charles Evans lived, a miserable half-wit with a long white beard, dressed in coarse cloth, and said to have been 'employed' as a tame hermit by the Castle's then owner, G. Durant. He was succeeded in 1825 for one month by James Guidney or Jimmy the Tickman, an old army pensioner, until the Earl of Bradford bought the estate and the hermitage and its three poles of land were let to a wheelwright. Thereafter it fell into ruins until little remained and it is now virtually obscured by a new motorway.

The hermitage in Hermitage Bank, Bridgnorth, in Staffordshire, is one of several in the soft red Triassic Bunter Sandstone of the area. It is a series of part natural, part man-made caves on two levels: a lower group of eight or more small caves and an upper group, overhung by pebble beds, containing two or three large caves with rock-cut arches and many niches and recesses. It is known to have been there in 1328 and is possibly of Saxon age, said to have been occupied by Athelstan, brother of the first King of all England. As we have seen, it was lived in again much later. Another hermitage, possibly once a pagan temple, is Blackstone Rock, also known as the Devil's Spittleful or Spadeful. It is a large conical mass of sandstone, 40 feet high and honey-combed with rock cells, on a big farm on the Stourport road near Bewdley, in Worcestershire. During World War II the Steatite and Porcelain Products of Stourport Company hid valuable dies there; it has been decorated with murals, used as a bar, strengthened with a brick wall and is now often occupied by Mr Mills' cows. A third of the several other hermit caves and chapels in the area is Redstone Hermitage, on the River Severn near Stourport and Areley Kings. It is the largest in the area and consists of two groups of caves, the larger having two 'storeys', with many doors and windows, and structural supports in the form of wooden timbers and a metal grid. Bishop Latimer said in 1538 that the Areley Kings caves could 'lodge 500 men, as ready for thieves and traitors as true men'.

When the hermitage at Dale Abbey, in Derbyshire, was being excavated, one of the older workmen said that he had been born and bred in it. 'Robin

LEFT: Bridgnorth Hermitage, Staffordshire, England. RIGHT: The Anchor Church, Repton, England.

Hood's Stable' at Papplewick, in Nottinghamshire, was probably a hermitage: 'an old cell or anchorite's cave' of the same age as the neighbouring abbey. Southstone Rock, Stanford-on-Teme, has a rock-cut chapel dedicated to St John. There is an old hermitage called the Anchor Church two miles from Repton, in a rocky bank upstream of the hamlet of Ingleby on the River Trent. It is a series of chambers, with pillars, excavated in the Bunter Pebble Bed and resembling a Gothic ruin.

There were the hermit caves of St Kieran, Kilkerran, in Ireland; St Moloe on Holy Island in the River Clyde; and Caplawchy Cave in Fife, which housed St Adrian and his band of monks. On Davaar Island, south of Tarbert, Strathclyde, the nineteenth-century artist Archibald Mackinnon painted a Crucifixion scene in a cave lit only by a shaft of light shining through a hole in the rock. There were hermit chapels at Dover and Greenhithe, and hermitages at Evesham, in Worcestershire; Dunfermline; and Pontefract in Yorkshire.

There is a cave at Royston, in Hertfordshire, which is almost certainly of religious significance. Beyond that, however, opinions on its function still vary widely and no conclusion appears imminent. The cave is under the Mercat House, built in 1610, in Melbourn Street. It was discovered in 1742 by workmen improving the shelter for women working in the Butter Market and is a man-made chamber, bell-shaped and hollowed out of the chalk, with a maximum height of 30 feet and a diameter of 20 feet. It was found under a millstone, half of which forms the bottom step of the sloping entrance passage, the other half being on display. The passage was a later addition and runs under the road; the entrance is on the north and the cave under the south side, where its crown can be seen through a small grille in the pavement. Originally, entry was by two vertical shafts, one of which was probably used for working whilst the cave was being dug, and the other for the removal of the debris. There is evidence, based on niches halfway up, of there once being an upper storey; there are other niches throughout for holding lights. There are four post holes in the floor, and a shallow raised bench all round, of unknown purpose unless it was a seat, although such steps were common in churches of the Templar period. Some of the chalk near one shaft has been painted red to represent bricks. The cave now belongs to the Town Council and is a listed building. It has a high humidity and a constant temperature of 50°F (10°C).

The cave is situated near the Cross, perhaps once the Holy Cross, now gone apart from its base, a glacial erratic stone known as the Royse Stone and possibly connected with Lady Roisia de Vere, who may also have been connected with the cave. It is unique in Britain, although caves in Warwick, Burgstein, and Cesca Lípa, in Czechoslovakia, have been compared with it. However, there are others like it in Palestine, visited by the Roman Emperor Severus before he came to Britain. So Royston Cave may have been Romano-British, built over a pre-Roman pit described in 1852 by Joseph Beldam, who

Religious carvings on the wall of Royston Cave, Hertfordshire, England. (Anthony Weir/Janet and Colin Bord)

found it to contain fragments of bone, oak, iron, leather and decorative stones. This older part was previously thought to be the grave of the hermit whose hermitage the chamber had once been. It is covered in medieval, primitive bas-relief religious carvings, dating perhaps from the mid twelfth century but more probably from the thirteenth. They were once coloured but all that remains of the pigment is one patch of grey. They include the Saints Laurence and Katherine, undergoing martyrdom, and St Christopher with staff in hand and the child Jesus on his shoulder. There are Crucifixion groups, each with, probably, John and Mary at its base. There is a multiple group of the twelve Apostles and others representing armies. The largest of the many niches may be the Holy Sepulchre, and on the west, there is an altar. The above passage contains many of the clues to the various theories on the cave's origin. Dr William Stukeley, in the eighteenth century, was the first theorist, claiming it as Lady Roisia's oratory. Many adhere to the hermitage theory and others connect the cave with the Crusaders, with their west-sited altars, and the Knights Templar, known to meet in Royston and whose chapel it might have been. There are even more prosaic suggestions, such as a refuge, a quarry or a granary. It could certainly have been a sepulchre. The carvings could have been done by Lady Roisia; or the hermit, whose patroness she might have been; or a returning crusader; or a Knight Templar. Recently, however, Sylvia Beamon has put forward the evidence for its being a deliberate copy — one of several such known – of the Holy Sepulchre, based on its shape and decoration, including the resemblance between some of the cult symbols on its walls and those depicted among the graffiti in the Château of Chinon, in the Loire. She calls for further and thorough investigation.

In Germany, the Externsteine, a massive rock near Detmold in Westphalia, has a small *sacellum* or chapel with an altar and a curious circular window, perhaps associated with a pre-Christian solar cult. Along the Rhine, at the Wild Kirchlein in Appenzell, in a huge limestone cliff above the Bodmenalp, rich in wild flowers, is a tiny chapel with an altar in a cavern 170 feet up. It was found by some shepherds and in 1621 a Capuchin monk climbed up and consecrated it, declaring it a place of pilgrimage. In Switzerland there are pilgrim hermitages at St Verena, near Soleure, on a Jura spur valley; Verena was a follower of the Thebans. The hermitage of St Mary Magdalen near Freiburg, on the right bank of the River Saane, was enlarged by the hermit John Baptiste Duprés over twenty years in the late seventeenth century. It consisted of a house and a church 63 feet long, 30 feet wide and 22 feet high, dug out of the sandstone, the house with a 90-foot chimney to avoid smoke, and the church equipped with a tower. The town of Oberstein, on the River Nahe, which flows into the Rhine, was known for its agate and sardonyx polishing trade; it has two ruined castles: the Older and the Newer Oberstein on top of the cliffs and a tiny church halfway up. A knight living in the old castle killed his brother for jealousy over a maiden – daughter of the knight of Lichtenberg – and to atone, carved himself a cave. When a spring appeared, he believed it to be his pardon and asked that the little church he had built at the mouth of his cave should be consecrated. But when the bishop came to do so, the knight was found dead. St Beatus, a missionary, settled into a cave – said by the locals to be the abode of a dragon – above Lake Thun, Berne.

Up to the early years of the century, there were many hermits in Languedoc, in southern France, living in remote chapels on mountain tops, caves or ravines. They dressed as Franciscan friars but probably had no right to do so, disreputable as they were. They frequented the taverns on market and feast days, before rolling home to their hermitages chanting ribald cum ecclesiastical songs. St Cybard, who had been Eparchius and died in 581 AD, lived in a cave below the heights on which is built the town of Angoulême, near Limoges, Charente. Hermits installed themselves in the Vallais, and beside the main road from Brive to Cahors, Lot, in a mass of red Permian sandstone, are a number of caves in one of which St Anthony of Padua lived in 1226. The Franciscans erected a convent above it and later the grottoes were converted into four chapels. La Sainte Beaume in Var is said to be the cave in Cretaceous limestone where Mary Magdalen ended her days, with many other anchorites around her. St Amadou's Chapel, 45 by 15 feet, is at Sougé, on the River Loir, just below the troglodyte town of Trôo. At Villiers, near Vendôme, also on the Loir, is St Andrew's Chapel, once a hermitage, with a chapel and a dwelling cave. When it was enlarged, near the turn of the century, to turn it into a 'commodious private dwelling', the work uncovered a number of skeletons interred in rock graves.

In Spain at Montserrat, in Catalonia, famous for its magnificent saw-ridged mountains, with an old monastery and numerous hermitages such as Santa Anna, San Benito and La Roca Estrecha, the hermits, like the monks, were hunted out by the French in 1811. In Andalusia, too, there are many hermitages in the Sierra, above Cordova. And in Italy there are Subiaco, where St Benedict fled at the age of fourteen, and La Vernia, a favourite retreat of St Francis. The island of Ischia is capped by the volcano, Mont Epameo. Its highest vent is plugged by pumice, riddled with caves and tunnels which were once the cells of monks and hermits. Now they have been converted into a small, terraced hotel.

CHAPTER 15

Oracle, legend and fiction

Considering how important caves have been in the development of man, as homes, burial grounds and religious buildings, it is hardly surprising that they figure large in his panoply of myth and legend.

In myths of the Classical period the foremost figure was Zeus, Father of the Gods. He was born to Kronos and his sister-wife Rhea, in the Cave of Psychro on Mount Dicte (Mount Ida), in Crete. Kronos had received the Kingdom of the World, but it was conditional on his rearing no male children. Accordingly, when he gave birth to a son, he swallowed it. But on the next occasion, when another male child was born, Rhea presented him with a stone and he swallowed that instead. The baby Zeus was hidden in the cave and reared by the Curetes (often confused with Rhea's Corybantes), who clattered their weapons, sounding drums and cymbols, and danced around him to drown his cries. The Cretans were told that Zeus was dead and buried.

Zeus's became the most famous of the cave shrines of the Nymphs, from the time of Homer onwards. Porphyry, in *On the Cave of the Nymphs*, tells how the old tribes of Hellas, before they built temples to the gods, consecrated caverns and grottoes to Zeus and also to Artemis and Pan in Arcadia, and to Dionysus on Naxos.

Some Greek cave sanctuaries were probably older, pre-Hellenic or based on oriental importations, such as the Cave of Trophonius at Lebadea, which belonged to a cult of unknown date. In Italy one of the best-known holy caves was the Lupercal on the Palatine, one of the seven hills of Rome, where the Luperci met for their ancient ritual. In both Greece and Italy, these eastern importations involving caves or underground vaults were connected with Mithraism. Rome was the abode of the sibyls and nymphs. Greece was where Pan, Bacchus, Pluto and the Moon were worshipped, and the oracles were delivered. But the source of Mithras worship was Persia, since Mithras, an Aryan or Indo-Iranian, slew the mystic bull 'beneath the Persian cave'; the temples of Mithras were therefore always artificial caves.

The Greek oracles were delivered at Delphi as well as Corinth; Delos, where spoke Apollo, the god of prophecy, and where there is also the prophetic

The Temple of Apollo, Delphi, Greece, site of the Delphic Oracle. (The J. Allan Cash Photolibrary)

grotto, Manteion, where the wind produced suitable moans and pipings; and Mount Cythaeron (Citheron), where the Nymphs had a cave from which they were said to foretell the future.

Incubation was the custom of sleeping in temples to receive oracles concerned with healing, often involving dreams induced by gases emanating from fissures in the temple floors. There was a Charonion at Hierapolis, a deep orifice exuding dense and poisonous vapours to which the priests who

231

ministered to the oracle were supposed to be immune. In fact, says Strabo, they held their breath, while the questioners had to risk standing on a platform over the vent. Perhaps the strangest prophetic grotto was that of Trophonios in Boetia, where gaseous exhalations appear to have induced hallucinations or visions. There is another cave at Acharaca near Nysa, on the Tralles road, which emitted healing gases.

There was the Grotto of the Cumæan Sybil; the Cimmerians at the Grotto of the Oracle of the Dead at Baiae; and the cavern of Cybele at Hierapolis in Phrygia. There were the pilgrimage temples and caves of Aesculapius, Isis, Serapis, Lebedes in Lydia, Sardinia, in Laconia and in the Cheronese. The Emperor Constantine consecrated two churches near Byzantium to the archangel Michael, and there was the Cave of Ramahavaly at Andringitra in Madagascar. German stories tell of the mountains of Venus and the Unterberg and there is said to be a prophetic cave at Toledo, in Spain, with a tower dedicated to Hercules. The columnar mass of Polignac, north of Le Puy, has a castle on top, which was sacred in Roman times. It had a well 260 feet deep called l'Albime, with a huge stone mask of the solar god arranged so that it closed the well, from whose mouth issued oracles. In fact, the questioner was answered by an accomplice in a side chamber at the bottom: the acoustics of the well did the rest.

An Icelandic saga tells of a shepherd who saw the burial cairn of the dead poet Thorleif open and the dead man emerge, promising the shepherd that he would possess poetic genius if his first lyric poem was to be a eulogy of Thorleif himself. A cavern by Lough Derg, in Ireland, represented the cave of Trophonios in the Middle Ages, producing hallucinatory visions. There was a pool in an abandoned mine on Dartmoor where lived a wailing spirit, and the story of Macbeth descending into the cave of Hecate.

Historical legends concerning caves are not uncommon, of which King Arthur has a fair proportion. The story of Kulhwch and Olwen probably relates to Wookey Hole, in the Mendip Hills of Somerset, an area rich in Arthurian lore. On his way back to Wales after hunting a great boar in Devon and Cornwall, Arthur asks Kulhwch how stands the long list of virtually impossible tasks required of him if he is to marry the desirable Olwen. The reply is that all have been completed bar one: he must bring back the blood of the black witch, Pen-palach, daughter of the white witch who lived in the cave called Awarnach's Hall at the headwaters of the Stream of Sorrow, on the confines of Hell. He had sent out two of his men, who had found her but had been overcome by her artfulness and driven out, with kicks and curses. Two more then tried and suffered a similar fate. So, Arthur had a try, using his dagger, Carnwennan. He was successful, slewing the witch and cutting her into two parts for Kaw to collect her blood. The hill at the entrance to the Wookey Hole valley is known locally as Arthur's Point; the River Axe is the 'Stream of Sorrow'; and the approach to the first Great Cave is 'Hell's Ladder'.

All of which suggests that the story is the same as that recounted by H. E. Balch concerning the Witch of Wookey. According to legend, a wicked old woman lived in the Great Cave and was turned to stone. Now she is a stalagmite, with a socket below her left breast, representing a post hammered in when she was killed by the hero-king, Arthur. There is also the Witch's Dog, with its little dish. Harrington's poem of 1748 describes her as a haggard, leering old woman. In fact, an old goatherd lived there alone, with two goats tied to a stake and a black earthenware milking pot. When she died, the goats starved and their bones were partially disturbed by passing animals. Nearby were found some of her possessions: Roman coins, a large, coarse five-toothed comb, a strange polished stalagmite ball and a little brooch; there was also a pit containing human bones, supposed to be hers, as well as implements, a large sacrificial knife, a bill hook and a curiously rounded iron sickle.

Other Mendip legends include the stories of the dogs which ran miles beneath the hills. One such, entering Goatchurch Cavern at Burrington Combe, emerged many days later, minus its hair, at Wookey. Another dog, put down at Cheddar, also reappeared at Wookey while one which entered the caves at Wookey reached daylight at Cheddar. A fiddler from Priddy fell down a shaft at Rookham and would reappear from time to time, as well as trying to lure others to destruction on stormy nights. Similar stories to these are known from Wales, Ireland, France and Germany. Wookey has a reputation for being haunted by ghosts: it was the place to which the parson with his bell and book condemned all the wandering ghosts from the neighbourhood. One of the caves at Burrington Combe was dug out in 1854 by a local peasant because it was thought to contain gold. Ancients who dug for chert in pits in the Mendips were said to have lived in pit dwellings deep in the rock, with only the roof showing above the ground, in the 'metropolis of Caer Penselcoit'. Similar stories relate to the diggers of iron ore in the Yorkshire Wolds. To end the Wookey Hole stories is a letter, quoted by Balch, and written in 1921 to the *Bristol Times and Mirror*:

'Sir – MUHAMMAD AND WOOKEY HOLE – Did the Prophet Muhammad know of the existence of Wookey Hole? This interesting question arises from Muslim comment of Sura xviii of the Koran, called "The Cave". According to Muslim divines, the "dwellers in the cave" are early Christians, and the eminent Muslim Maulvi Muhammad Ali considers that the reference is to Joseph of Arimathea and his followers at Glastonbury. It is suggested that they may have lived in Wookey Hole while seaching for a suitable site upon which to build the church which afterwards became Glastonbury Abbey.

I believe that this legend, in its Muslim aspect, is not generally known.

E. J. Holmyard, Clifton College.'

One of the next English kings, Alfred, is said to have burned the cakes in a cave when he was left in charge of them by someone who did not know of his regal status. This story, recently requoted by Paul Johnson in his *The Oxford Book of Political Anecdotes*, is regarded by him as probably containing some 'charred crumb of historic truth'. Half a millennium or more later, in the fourteenth century, the Scottish King Robert the Bruce really did encounter a spider in a cave. In 1866, seceders from the Reform Party were labelled the Adullamites: the allusion was John Bright's, referring to David who, in his flight from Saul, escaped to the cave of Adullam where everyone in distress, in debt or merely discontented 'gathered themselves to him'.

Worldwide, cave myths and legends abound. France and Germany had what were often termed Fairy, Dragons' or Devils' Caves. In the Middle Ages, northern Germany had dwarf holes: in the Harz Mountains, couples at their weddings used to go to the caves and ask the dwarfs for copper, brass, pewter and other kitchen utensils; they then retired and, coming back a little later, found that all was ready for them at the mouth of the cave. Later, they returned what they had borrowed and offered some meat as thanks. This story derives from the view of the tall Scandinavian people that the Lapps and Finns were dwarfs, endowed with magic powers. In Palestine, interestingly, the converse obtained: the people regarded their tall enemies as giants. Bauman's Hole, in the Blankenbourg district, also in the Harz, was a cave said to be haunted and to contain a treasure guarded by black mastiffs. The fascinating 'bear cult' was observed by people at Wildkirchli (Wilderness Chapel); Drachenloch (Dragon's Den), above Vattis; and Wildenmannlisloch, all in Switzerland; and also at Petershöhle, near Velden, Bavaria, in Germany. All these places are at some 7000 to 8000 feet above sea-level. Cave-bear skulls and long bones were set up along the cave walls or in crude stone cabinets as part of the cult. Moorish children in the hills of Granada, Spain, think the hills contain Boabdil and his sleeping host, who will awake when 'an adventurous mortal invades their repose, who will issue forth to restore the glory of the Moorish kings'. This story is perhaps partly due to the unknown length of the caves.

In Yugoslavia, people used to think that the baby salamanders that were occasionally washed out of caves were baby dragons. As late as 1936, a spelaeologist and his friends, asking for information about a cave near Rodna, in Romania, were told by the villagers how to find it but advised not to enter. This was the birthplace of the vampire legend: blood-sucking ghosts in human form. The group paid no attention but entered the cave and explored it. When they returned, the villagers had encircled the entrance bearing murderous looking clubs; since they had escaped the vampires, the visitors themselves must be vampires. They had to turn tail and were lucky to escape. A story told in 200 AD by Aelianus, who was known as Aelian, relates how the eastern Indians of Areia drove more than three thousand assorted farm animals annually into their abyss and caves which were sacred to Pluto, in order to keep things quiet and avert the evil omen. The beasts needed no urging: they just wandered in of their own accord. The Roman Catholic Church turned such beliefs to their own advantage; for example, in the late Middle Ages, during the time of the Reformation, they maintained that a cave at Bishofferode would cause the death of a person each year unless a priest came, on the right day, to the chapel on the hill opposite, proceeded to the cave, and lowered – and then pulled up again – a crucifix, to remind everyone of Hell and to enable them to avoid the punishment due for their sins. The natural Gothic beauty of the caves, with their minarets and spires, would have encouraged all of this. In a rather different vein, the Aborigines of North Kimberley, northern Australia, believed in All-Mother lore in which Wallanganda, the Milky Way, 'dreamed a spiritual force' which was then projected as red, black and white images on the caves of the Unumbal.

The countries which have produced the greatest number of cave myths and legends seem to be Iceland, Ireland, Germany and India, although many more have contributed. They concern the 'occupants' of caves, among them giants, monsters, demons, ogres, dwarfs, gnomes and princesses. They describe 'the cave' as a refuge or else as a trap or prison, and its entrance as the gateway to the underworld: Hell in Ireland and the lower world in England.

The paradoxes with which they abound can easily be illustrated. Giants live in caves in Iceland; in one such cave, a magic object is found, stolen from the giant who seems to be both friendly and an ogre; in Sweden giants are 'enchanted in caverns'. In India a giantess is frightened to leave her cave because of a hero's statue standing in the entrance. Again in India, an ogress has twenty captive princesses in her cave; but, also in India, an ogre is himself imprisoned in a cave. In Iceland a princess is rescued from a giant's cave where she has been tied to a chair by her hair. And in Hawaii an ogress catches travellers from a cave and devours them one by one.

There were thought to be even more exotic occupants of caves. Originally, the winds were confined to caves and, in Ireland, the wind continually blew from a cave. In India the sun hides in a cave and in Haiti the sun and the moon first came from a cave, while in South America a race of Amazons controlled a river which issued from a cave. In the Marquesas caves are the repository of fire, and the home of gods; in Mono-Alu or Mono Island, in the Treasury Islands, northwest Solomon Islands, spirits live in a cave, while the Chinese describe animal rescues from a cave. There are plenty of treasures secreted in underground chambers and caverns and 'open sesame' seems always to be the password. In Tahiti, the chiefs may be buried in a hidden cave, for religious reasons, but in Iceland a lion is buried in a 'stone cave with gold letters'!

The concept of the cave as a refuge, in Ireland, sees it opening for fugitives, a rock at the entrance falling on the pursuer. In India, the enchanted deer touches the rock with her muzzle and it bursts open to reveal a cave entrance. Caves are an escape from the deluge. But, in India again, the victim is lured into following a deer, sent by a demon, into the cave. And in Hawaii a falling rock or branch kills travellers who have been lured into the cave. Or the cave can be a place of captivity, while in Tuamotu people are abandoned in caves. In Ireland the Celts had a cave where, after death, you achieved a year and a day in paradise, but a cave was also a place to spend a lonely night in penance. Dwarfs live in caves in Germany, and also flee there for protection. The dwarf cave is closed by iron doors; it consists of a large square room with little doors leading off on all sides. It has a ceiling as white as snow; it has a chandelier of gems and crystals. In Iceland, the dwarf's cave has a rock door.

There are some strange legendary stories; this one has various sources. The cave call, 'Hullo, house', is used by an animal suspecting the presence of an enemy in his cave (house). He receives no answer so he says 'Don't you know, oh cave, that we have agreed that when I return from being away, I must call you and you must answer me?' Whereupon the hiding animal does answer and the first one flees. And this one from India: a boy teaches some giants how to lay a carpet of dried grass and naptha on the hard floor of their cave. He then sets fire to it and suffocates them. In Ireland and elsewhere, adventures can happen after following an animal into a cave, the lower world; and in Africa a hunter accidentally discovers a beautiful girl being secretly reared in a cave. There are many more such fables.

One of the most bizarre cave-related stories concerns the people of the Melanesian backwaters of Malekula, Vao and the other small volcanic and coral islands in the north-central New Hebrides. The inhabitants of these islands have developed a megalithic culture. Although they bury their dead in cemeteries, they erect dolmens, stone platforms and monoliths, and megaliths are used to deduce their ancestry. They have a ceremony called *Maki* which they hold, for example, in the dancing ground of Pete-hul, with the megaliths and wooden slit gongs on the 'Upper Side'.

Maki is a kind of ritual rebirth achieved through a labyrinth. It involves the need to ward off the evil Guardian Ghost who guards the Cave of the Dead, through which all dead men must pass *en route* for the Land of the Dead or the Home of the Dead. These are, respectively, a cave for low-ranking people and a volcano for those of high rank; the cave seems to be imaginary and is perhaps a wave-cut perforation in the coral beach. Each island has one of these, such as the shore cave in South-West Bay on Seniang. The penalty for missing *Maki* is to have to eke out your 'life' in a fine cave (the rich) or a lesser cave (the poor). The dolmen is the chief sacrificial monument found in each Home of the Dead.

There is a Great Cave on Vao. The legend here tells how two women and two twin boys lived in a stone called Burto, which became split. The boys went to live in a cave, they all went to a festival, the two boys married the two women and they all went to live in the cave. A simple tale, but highly significant in Melanesia.

This Melanesian rebirth through a labyrinth can be compared with that of the Tamils of south India. Or with Aeneas seeking to visit his father, Anchises, in Hades, but having first to visit the sibyl guarding the entrance, near which is a painted representation of the Cretan labyrinth. In Europe there are the Celtic stone crosses, and the medieval Gothic churches with their mazes and labyrinths on the floor of the nave or over the west door. A similar motive lies behind the turf mazes around which the boys in the village used to dance, and the 'tangled thried' designs the women of Scotland and northern England drew on their thresholds and hearthstones to keep out witches and evil influences.

Fiction

Nor has fiction ignored the cave and underground chamber or their occupants. They feature in novels and plays, films, music, opera, verse and cartoon, while in *The Inheritors* William Golding had much to say in praise of Neanderthal Man, whom he considered gentle, unfallen and blissfully at one with the world, totally unlike our base Cro-Magnon selves. To quote from Spenser, in *The Faerie Queene*, there is 'That darksome cave they enter, where they find/That cursed man, low sitting on the ground'. In *Two Gentlemen of Verona* the outlaws lived in a cave, and the robbers in *Gil Blas* had their lair in a cavern. *Child Rowland* featured in cave legends and in Sir Walter Scott's *Marmion*, St Rule had a cave at St Andrews. Between Harbottle and Holystone, in north Northumberland, there is a spot on high ground known as 'Rob Roy's Cave', although there is no evidence that the gentleman ever visited those parts. However, in *Rob Roy*, Scott does introduce him into this district. George Sand, in *Jean de la Roche*, used the castle of La Roche Lambert at Borne, in Haute Loire, as a setting: 'I may say without exaggeration that I was reared in a rock. . . . The Château de la Roche is a nest of troglodytes, inasmuch as the whole flank of the rock we occupy is riddled with holes and irregular chambers which tradition points out as the residence of ancient savages, and which antiquaries do not hesitate to attribute to a prehistoric people.'

The giants, two of whom were killed by *The Valiant Little Tailor* in the much-loved story by the Brothers Grimm, lived in a cave, where they sat by the fire, each eating a roasted sheep. And surely, in *The Wind in the Willows*, Kenneth Grahame would agree that Mole and Badger, and even Rat, lived in burrows if not caves. Mention should also be made of *Alice in Wonderland*. J. V. Scheffel set some of the incidents in his tenth-century story, *Ekkehard*, in the *Heidenlöcher* of Goldback, south Germany. In 1897 S. Baring-Gould published his famous romantic novel, *Bladys of the Stewponey*. Inspired by the legend attached to Holy Austin Rock, it told the story of Bladys, daughter of the landlord of the Stewponey, a nearby tavern, who is gambled away in marriage over a game of bowls, carried off, robbed, abducted and held captive, and escapes to the Rock Tavern – another nearby hostelry . . . and so on. The book was filmed on location in Kinver village in 1919 and 'Kine Weekly' said of its scenic camerawork: 'Nothing better has been done on the British screen.' A more recent film is *Quest for Fire*. The chimneys of the 'Never, Never Land' where the Lost Boys lived in Barrie's *Peter Pan* have already been compared with those of the present-day caves of Guadix, near Granada. E. M. Forster set the central episode in *A Passage to India* in the notorious Marabar Caves, in Dravidia. J. R. R. Tolkien's Hobbit lived in burrows, and Laura Ingalls Wilder has 'The house in the ground' in *On the Banks of Plum Creek*. Rather earlier, the stories of *Aladdin* and his treasure-filled cavern, guarded by a genie, and of *Ali Baba and the Forty Thieves*, also hiding treasure in a cave, had already become world classics.

Mendelssohn wrote *Fingal's Cave* for the Hebridean Suite. Based on fact, *The Phantom of the Opera* was set in the Paris Opera House. Underneath was a lake which took a day to drain, and was used to drive the stage machinery. It took twelve years to build, after which the master builder had become so used to his subterranean environment that he asked if he could remain down there. John Masters wrote *The Rock* in two parts, half fact, half fiction. The latter part chronicles the lives of the inhabitants of Gibraltar from cave-dwelling Cro-Magnon days, through Medieval and Middle Ages, to the present.

There have been several modern novels set partly in caves. Eric von

Damnikon's *Chariots of the Gods* was one. Another was Jan Morris's piece of fictional travel writing, *Last Letters from Hav*. Here are the Kretevs, gypsy-like folk living in caves on both sides of the big cleft in the escarpment, behind the port. They tilled their fields and sold their produce in the market, especially the 'famous' strawberries. Less well known, perhaps, but superbly imaginative if rather unpleasant in its theme, was Patrick Süskind's recent *Perfume: the Story of a Murderer*. The author has his anti-hero, the odourless Jean-Baptiste Grenouille, living hidden in a cave for seven years as he journeys towards the perfect perfume which will make the whole world love and worship him. In his 100-foot, tunnel-like cave, with many twists and turns, blocked at the end by a rock slide, at the top of the 6000-foot Plomb du Cantal in the Massif Central of the Auvergne, Grenouille lived on ring snakes and salamanders, dry lichen, grass and mossberries. When it was freezing he ate dead bats, even a dead raven. He did no cooking: he had no fire. His cave had never been occupied, by man or beast; its air was cool, moist and salty.

Carleton S. Coon, author of *Seven Caves*, describes how, in 1939, on half-sabbatical leave in the Azores and rather bored, he wrote a play, *The Cave*. Set in southern France, the audience sat inside the cave and watched the action taking place at and outside its mouth. Outside is a hilly landscape, built on a revolve, representing a series of seasonal changes. The first is glacial, all snow and ice. It then becomes temperate, with straw huts in the distance, smoke curling from their roofs. Then there is a hill fort from the Gallic period, or possibly Iron Age, before a late nineteenth-century factory town and, finally, we are back to snow and ice.

The first actors are bears, complaining about the arrival of man, a new animal with the unfair and invincible weapon of fire. The bears know they cannot withstand this and have no hope of winning the inevitable battle but they resolve to fight to the death. This they do and finally, in the last scene, they are depicted after their return to the cave, grumbling about the troublesome although ephemeral intervention that was man and expressing relief that he is by now only an unpleasant memory. In between, the scenes depict Cro-Magnon Man painting his superb pictures on the cave walls; Neolithic farmers bringing in a body for burial in the cave floor; and finally, modern times, when more of the action takes place outside, generally of irrelevance to the cave-dwellers. Coon then lost the script, which must be regarded as a pity.

Finally, there is a rather endearing American animated cartoon, shown on television, called *The Flintstones*. It tells the story of the people of Bedrock, living twentieth-century lives in Neanderthal caves. A fitting epilogue, perhaps!

CHAPTER 16

Tunnels

This last chapter, on man-made tunnels, is necessarily brief. Tunnels have rarely been constructed as dwellings; when they have been lived in, it has usually been as a refuge, for safety, nearly always on a relatively large scale in time of war. Their main functions have been concerned with communication and supply, including the passage of water; with mining and quarrying; and with military purposes.

Tunnels were invented early. The Hezekiah Tunnel, Kidron Valley, in Israel, was built in 700 BC by Hezekiah, King of Jerusalem, to protect his water supply from the Assyrians. This S-shaped tunnel, 600 yards long, was then used by King David to lead the capture of the Jebusite city. The value of tunnels was known also to the Greeks, Romans (who also favoured aqueducts) and the Babylonians. The latter built a passage under the River Euphrates. Another good example, this time prehistoric, is the tunnel in Syracuse, Sicily. A tunnel has, apparently, been depicted in the Bayeux Tapestry. In more recent times, the Chalk of southern England and northern France has been locally honeycombed with tunnels, as have Gibraltar, Taiwan and the Khyber Pass in Pakistan.

But even having attempted to limit the functions of a tunnel, it is not always easy to define one. As we have seen, some of the 'burrows' we have discussed come perilously close to being tunnels, the distinction between them and caves, such as Chislehurst and St Clements' at Hastings, and also with mines and quarries, again being at times very blurred and unclear.

The best-known tunnels are almost certainly those built for roads and railways, including the underground and metro systems. The network through the Alps is probably the most impressive, whether just long 'bridges' or the major tunnels carrying railway and motorway through the heart of the mountains. However, communication tunnels are everywhere: as well as in North and South America, through the Rockies, Appalachians and Andes, and the Urals and the Himalayas, there are road tunnels in Iceland and the Faroes. Water is usually carried by open conduits or canals, but some of these pass underground including irrigation canals and hydro-electric channels, common, for example, in the Alps and Scotland. Drainage and sewerage tunnels, like the Roman sewer under York, are a subject on their own, and can sometimes become mixed up with catacombs. The water conduits built during the Middle Ages in the sandstone seventeen feet below Exeter have recently been opened to the public. There are tunnels under Langton Priory in Guildford, together with an ice house. The Greenwich conduits, a network to which many myths and legends have become attached, were supposed to supply water to an undiscovered Roman city. But they were also said to have been Henry VIII's escape tunnels, with sharp corners to guard against flying arrows sent after his departing person, and even to connect with the Chislehurst caves. Prinny, later King George IV, suffered from gout. To help to conceal this, he had a tunnel dug between his Pavilion in Brighton and the stables, now the Dome, so that he could reach his carriage unnoticed.

There are plenty of examples of short, specially built escape tunnels, but not many long tunnels have been built as escape routes or refuges although many have been used for these purposes. Tunnels have been used, like caves, for cultivating mushrooms and rhubarb and for storing wine. The latest and perhaps one of the most pleasing secondary uses is to provide habitats for bats. In southern England, the disused Greywell canal tunnel near Basingstoke, close to Hook and the M 3, is a hibernaculum for a hundred and fifty Natterer's bats; a problem that has since developed is that boating people now want to open the canal up for boats. In Kent, a long, sandstone mining tunnel has also become a bat hibernation spot; it now has grilles to keep people out and let plenty of air in. Also in Kent, near Ramsgate, concrete pipes measuring some six feet in diameter have been filled with rubble pillars and laid in a disused chalk quarry; the bats have taken readily to their artificial caves.

London is well endowed with tunnels. The first modern tunnel was built under the River Thames at Rotherhithe in 1825–43. Between then and the turn of the century came main drainage; the Tower Hill to Hays Wharf subway; pneumatic railways, such as those at the Crystal Palace, Whitehall to Waterloo and High Holborn to Tottenham Court Road; the first tube railway between Stockwell and Monument, passing under King William Street (the City & London Railway); the Metropolitan Railway, at Snow Hill; and many subways. The Kingsway tram tunnel and the Post Office Railway followed soon after. There are many other tunnels in Great Britain: at Old Sarum, near Salisbury; at Tonbridge, Kent; at Decker Hill, formerly Drayton, near Shifnal; the Leeds and Liverpool Canal in Yorkshire; and the Blists Hill tar tunnel, Coalport, near Ironbridge, in Shropshire, used to drain off the natural bitumen impregnating the local sandstone. There are tunnels at Maastricht, in Holland; a Channel tunnel is under construction. The Guinness

Book of Records gives the world's longest tunnel as the West Delamere water tunnel, in New York: 104.9 miles in length. The longest railway tunnel is in Oshimizu, Japan, at 13.8 miles and the longest road tunnel is at Gotthard, Switzerland, at 10.1 miles. The longest water tunnel in Great Britain is at Kielder, Northumberland, measuring a mere 20 miles in length.

The field of mining and quarrying opens up a vast area of tunnelling throughout the world. Many of the countries where gold, metal, salt and coal are mined are familiar names. Some are notorious – salt in Siberia, gold in South Africa – while others are bizarre. At Coober Pedy, in the outback of South Australia, the opal miners move underground with their families for considerable periods. Here they live in remarkable comfort, shielded from the weather, complete with chapels and churches, bars and restaurants. The Neolithic flint mines of Grimes Graves, at Thetford in Norfolk, are a splendid example of early economic technology; the mines are circular pits, some twenty feet across, dug down some tens of feet to the level of the flint bands in the chalk, from which galleries led off whence the flints were extracted and carried to the surface to be knapped into tools and weapons. Saltpetre has been mined underground in America since the days of the Civil War, when it was needed for gunpowder. In Colombia, the Zipaquira salt mines were started four hundred years ago by the Spanish Conquistadores. Their descendents still produce salt and in the early 1950s their Cathedral was carved out of the rock salt, after the site had been blessed in October 1950 by the Papal Nuncio. There are four 330-foot aisles lined by twelve salt columns, and the main altar, made of salt, weighs eight tons.

Bar in an underground dwelling at Coober Pedy, South Australia. (Australian Tourist Commission)

In Britain, although mines are underground, most quarries are above ground. In Caen, Normandy, the famous French building stone, perhaps the equivalent in usage of the English Portland Stone, has been worked extensively in many underground quarries and there were some British exceptions. The Monkton Farleigh underground quarries, near Bradford-on-Avon in Wiltshire (see below) were used to extract the Middle Jurassic Great Oolite, also known as the Bath Stone and the geological equivalent of the French Caen Stone. Another is the Chilmark Stone, also in Wiltshire, the equivalent of the Portland Stone and used for Salisbury Cathedral. A third is the famous creamy white Beer Stone, which comes from the Middle Chalk and is soft to cut, hardening on exposure to the air. It has been quarried for nearly two thousand years and used in Exeter and St Paul's Cathedrals and in Westminster Abbey. In 1984 the Old Quarry, part of the huge underground quarries at Beer, near Seaton, in southeast Devon, which cover a quarter of a square mile, were opened to the public. The rounded arches of the Roman workings are followed by the square, buttressed arches of Saxon and Norman times, but the oldest of the many signatures on the walls dates from the seventeenth century. There is a chapel and, at the doorway, a niche to hold the Cross, put in place when services were being held, with a stoup of holy water beneath. In the nearby village lives a 100-year-old lady whose morning job as a child was to light the candles through the workings to show the miners their way. Legend has it that a passage links the quarries with a cave on the nearby coast, but it has never been found. In the late 1940s and 50s, mushrooms and rhubarb were grown on a large scale in the Old Quarry, until they were killed by a virus. Also in south Devon are the Kitley Caves, half a mile southwest of Yealmpton; these are smallish limestone caves eaten into by quarries. The Jurassic Purbeck Limestone was quarried underground at Durlston in Dorset, near the Tilly Whim caves, and hearthstone – a refractory sandstone – was worked underground in mines and quarries near Godstone in Surrey, such as Marden, Chaldon and Merstham.

The Clearwell Caves, in limestone, some of it dolomitic, one and a half miles south of Coleford, in the Forest of Dean, Gloucestershire, were mined for iron ore since pre-Roman times up to World War I. Now they are only worked for red ochre for use in paint. There are the tin and copper mines of Cornwall and Devon; blue john (fluorspar) and lead mines in Derbyshire; mining caverns at Castleton and elsewhere in Derbyshire; the limestone Stump Cross Caverns six miles east of Grassington, North Yorkshire, which are linked with the lead mines; gold mines at Dolaucothi and many slate mines, all in North Wales; and coal mines in South Wales, the Midlands and Newcastle. Finally, there are the deneholes. These problematic underground chambers were probably early chalk mines, developed for agricultural use,

Operations room in the Cabinet War Rooms, London, during the final stages of World War II. (The Trustees of the Imperial War Museum, London)

and later adapted for a multitude of other purposes. The Anstey Castle cave, said to be the spot where Blind George the Fiddler disappeared and his dog lost its fur, may have been a chalk adit or 'heading' – a denehole, perhaps. They are best known from Durham, Berkshire, Kent, Essex and Suffolk, where there is the Bury St Edmunds chalk-mine tunnel.

The last and most extensive use of tunnels has to do with military activities, especially and understandably in wartime. In Britain, the use of the London Underground tunnel network as air-raid shelters in World War II is probably the best-known example, followed perhaps by Sir Winston Churchill's Cabinet War Rooms and even the many other miles of Whitehall tunnels dating back to the priest holes and escape routes used, among others, by the Royalists in the Civil War. There were also many more deep shelters, the air-defence system at Uxbridge and the Medway underground fortress through the North Downs of Kent and known as the Chatham Lines, linking

244

Fort Amherst with Cave Yard. In America, probably the development of the atom and hydrogen bombs, the space programme and underground nuclear shelters have prompted the most impressive tunnel systems. All over the world, this type of activity, together with ammunition storage, hospitals and so on have resulted in underground networks.

A good example of underground ammunition storage in Britain has recently been opened to the public. Part of the Monkton Farleigh Mine, previously a 200-acre quarry for Oolite building stone, became a vast ammunition store, covering twenty-six acres, built in total secrecy before World War II. It took 7500 men seven years to build it while a further 5000 were involved in the movement of ammunition. The store was bomb-proof, had a vast generating powerhouse to provide 25,000 lights and huge ventilation fans, all hewn out of the limestone 100 feet below the surface. Its own railway and conveyor systems carried the shells and bullets around within the five miles of tunnels and linked it with the main-line railway. It served the Korean War and Suez, and was sold by the War Office in 1975. Planning permission failed for use for mushroom farming and as a bonded warehouse, and it was finally opened as a museum in 1984.

LEFT: Conveyer at Monkton Farleigh Mine. RIGHT: The munitions store in the Maginot Line, February 1940. (BBC Hulton Picture Library)

A concert given by E.N.S.A. in January 1942 to people sheltering in the Aldwych Underground station. The audience is on the track. (BBC Hulton Picture Library)

War has also made front-line use of tunnels; in World War I miners from the coal fields and construction workers from the London Underground were taken to Flanders to dig galleries and tunnels so that explosives could be placed under the German trenches. At Messines alone, nineteen tunnels had been constructed by 1917. After the example of World War I, the French built during the 1930s the Maginot Line as a defence against Germany; it included many underground chambers and tunnels and was garrisoned but was disastrously outflanked in World War II. Tunnels were also used as prisoner-of-war escape routes in both wars. The story of one from World War II has been told in *The Wooden Horse* by Eric Williams, and was made into a film. He also wrote *The Tunnel*, a novel on the same theme. During World War II – and since time immemorial – partisans have hidden and lived in caves and tunnels, for example in France, Greece, Yugoslavia and Afghanistan.

One of the most fascinating 'partisan' stories must be that of the British Resistance, told by David Lampe in his book *The Last Ditch*. Alone among the countries that opposed Germany in World War II, Britain had a complete Resistance organization, armed and trained, waiting for the Germans to invade. It was set up by Colonel Colin Gubbins, under the mantle of MI(R) – Military Intelligence (Research). Of interest here were the hideouts, many of which could be termed 'burrows' whilst others were deneholes or old mines.

The members of the force were, understandably, country folk. They included poachers and gamekeepers, ghillies and New Forest Verderers, tin and coal miners, farmers, market gardeners and fishermen. They understood the type of hideout required. The first training centre was an old farmhouse in Kent, called 'The Garth', and the officer in charge was Captain Peter Fleming, who had travelled across China (see p. 170) and Brazil, sometimes writing for *The Times*. One hideout was dug under a chalk hill above Charing, in Kent; it was typical, a modern denehole, reached via 'rabbit holes', trap doors and ladders, with elaborate 'triggering' devices to obtain an entrance. Others were not new; enlarged badger setts, genuine deneholes, smugglers' caves, the seventeenth-century man-made cave at Manston near Margate and a World-War-I airship landing place near 'The Garth' in Kent provided some of the chalk hideouts in East Anglia, Sussex and Kent. In Devon and Cornwall the smugglers' caves were too well known but the tin and other mines, up to a quarter of mile deep, made excellent hideouts, as did the Welsh, Durham and Northumberland coal mines. From Cornwall to Scotland ice houses and pits were used, as well as Iron-Age Pictish dwellings and then unvisited ruined castles in Scotland. In Berwickshire a cave on the Bowes-Lyons' estates was reached by scaling a sheer cliff overhanging a river and leaping in through a waterfall. There were in all 300 hideouts by the end of 1940 and 534 by the end of 1941 – and the Germans never invaded.

Gibraltar must arguably be the world's best example of tunnelling on the grand scale; much of it was described by John Masters in his book, *The Rock*, half of which was fictional and has already been mentioned. The island, 1370 feet high, is riddled with natural caves, which are still coming to light whenever the local Cave Research Group is active. But there are also the tunnels, which reached their peak in World War II, when their total length was extended from four to more than twenty-eight miles. The largest is the Great North Road, the length of the Rock from northwest to southeast at about 400 feet above sea level. It carries vehicles and has room for a full range of service pipes and cables. There are also many chambers and galleries, fully equipped with all mains services, to house barracks, magazines, stores, offices, headquarters, hospitals, power stations, cinemas, even a football pitch. The hard limestone meant that no roof supports were necessary, even in a vehicle workshop complex measuring 400 by 80 feet. Other major works included the Admiralty Tunnel, the North Face galleries and the water tunnels. In World War II the whole complex housed some seventeen thousand men; some of the installations are still used by NATO, while others are to be opened to tourists. The tunnels were begun by a Cornishman named Ince during the Great Siege of 1780 and the nomenclature used was that of Cornish mining. The work was then completed by miners and artificers, who became the Royal Engineers, and the various projects tended to be named after the engineers who designed them or after historical events associated with the regiment which built them. Also most impressive are the military tunnels and bunkers – and a fine art museum – which honeycomb the mountains of Taiwan and its small associated islands.

To conclude with two examples from the east; the Khyber Pass, on the North-West Frontier of Pakistan with Afghanistan, has a famous road and a perhaps even more famous railway which was opened in 1925. The railway has thirty-four tunnels, which with many others were built by the Indian Army to maintain the King's peace along the Frontier and defend the border against Russia, in the years following Kipling's 'Great Game' of the last century.

Tunnel warfare came right up to date in *The Tunnels of Cu Chi*, described by Tom Mangold and John Penycate in the book of that name. After the conclusion of the trench and air war in Vietnam, the American 'tunnel rats' fought the Vietcong in the 'stinking, claustrophobic and booby-trapped labyrinth' of tunnels which extended from Saigon to the Cambodian border.

CHAPTER 17

The mind of the troglodyte

So, a million or more years after *Australopithecus* first moved into a cave – the obvious thing to do and full of good sense – where have we arrived? The amazing thing is the number and variety of people who have chosen to live in caves or similar dwellings, and to find so many other ways to make use of them.

Some appear bizarre: the cone houses of Cappadocia and the pit dwellings of Matmata, and yet these are some of the most popular of this type of house today. There are even hotels constructed in them, for tourists, evidence of the increasing interest in caves, as more and more are opened or reopened to the public. There are people living quietly in caves in Guadix and perhaps not so quietly in Chinon. It was only in 1974 that the last occupied British 'closed' cave was vacated, and Cyril Taylor still recalls living in perhaps the last English 'open' cave until 1928. Now, many Chinese are returning to cave life.

Generally speaking, caves are no longer used as catacombs or castles or even as refuges; Sawney Beane and his dreadful family have been relegated to the London Dungeon. But, perhaps predictably, the hippies moved into the old leper caves of Crete and elsewhere. Now the bourgeois have discovered the caves of France, as weekend cottages, while others are used for wine evenings and banquets. It is perhaps surprising that English yuppies have not yet caught on to the idea. 'You simply must come down for the weekend, to our country cave.'

The cave man was just being sensible. There was a cave; he was cold, it was raining, who wouldn't move in? More importantly, it would protect his offspring and his whole family – from predators, more than from the climate and the weather. Even so, his average life span is thought to have been less than twenty years. At an early stage he began to use caves for hiding food, weapons, sacred images and ceremonial paraphernalia, as burial places and for performing sacred rites. The idea of a habitation as such may, at this stage, have been secondary.

There can be few, if any, better measures of man's development than his habitation, and the cave was the simplest and by far the most durable of these. Early man soon demonstrated that he appreciated this fact, especially when he developed first the use and then the making of fire, but from Neolithic times, or earlier, he was quite capable of building houses and demonstrated the fact abundantly. Yet some still chose to live in caves, and a few still do, to this very day. What makes a troglodyte?

The development of the widespread secondary use of caves as burial places followed on from man's natural fear of inhabiting a once-occupied cave in which death had occurred. So some caves became mortuary grounds or catacombs. Two natural developments followed: their use as retreats by priests who had withdrawn from the world, and the custom of using and extending caves as tombs, then as shrines and finally as temples. This can be seen across the world, from China to the southwestern states of the USA. An amazing range of names have been used for man's various holes in the ground: souterrains, *erdställe*, *heidenlöcher*, *hypogea*, fogous, weems, Picts' houses, deneholes, earth houses. Now, as we have seen, they have become a minor tourist craze: Cappadocia, Matmata, Dénéze-sous-Doué and Meteora as major attractions, with hotels built out of troglodyte homes in Matmata, Cappadocia and Ischia, bars in Coober Pedy and Minorca, gala nights in Chinon, week-end caves for sale on the Loire. Meanwhile, the Van Nostrand Reinhold and University of Minnesota group in Minneapolis are studying caves – warm in winter, cool in summer – to help build nuclear shelters and energy conserving earth-sheltered housing.

After all, apart from Isaiah's prophecy, the Book of Revelation of St John the Divine did say: 'And the kings of the earth, and the princes, and the chief captains, and the rich, and the strong, and every bondman and freeman, hid themselves in the caves and in the rocks of the mountains.'

Selected Bibliography

To assist people who live in London, or have access to London libraries, the following initials after relatively scarce or out-of-print books and journals indicate libraries where they can be found. The last three are not open to the public but genuine enquirers would probably be allowed to consult the literature they required; also, the list is far from complete:

BM/BL: British Museum/British Library.
BM(NH)-PAM & G: British Museum (Natural History)-Palaeontology, Anthropology & Mineralogy Library and General Library.
IA: Institute of Archaeology, University of London.
MM: Museum of Mankind (Royal Anthropological Institute Library), British Museum's Department of Ethnology, Burlington Gardens, London W1.
RGS: Royal Geographical Society, Kensington Gore.

American Anthropologist, formerly New York, now Washington, vols 1–89 (1888–1987). [MM]
AUBARBIER, J.-L. & BINET, M. *Sites préhistoriques en Périgord*, Rennes 1984.
BALCH, H. E. *Wookey Hole – Its Caves and Cave Dwellers*, Oxford 1914. [BM(NH)-PAM]
BANDI, H.-G. et al. *Art of the World–V: The Stone Age*, London 1961. [BM(NH)-PAM]
BARING-GOULD, S. *Cliff Castles and Cave-Dwellings of Europe*, London 1911. [MM;RGS;IA]
BEDFORD, B. *Underground Britain: A Guide to the Wild Caves and Show Caves of England, Scotland and Wales*, London 1985.
BILLS, D. M., GRIFFITHS, E. & GRIFFITHS, W. R. *Kinver Rock Houses*, Kinver 1978.
BRENNAN, L. A. *No Stone Unturned*, London 1960. [BM(NH)-PAM]

BREUIL, ABBÉ H. *Four Hundred Centuries of Cave Art*, Montignac 1952. [BM(NH)-PAM]
BROWN, B. *The Art of the Cave Dweller*, London 1928. [BM(NH)-PAM]
CAMPBELL, B. G. *Humankind Emerging* (4th edn), Boston 1985.
CLAIBORNE, R. *The Emergence of Man: The First Americans*, Amsterdam 1973.
CLARK, G. *Prehistoric England*, London 1940. [BM(NH)-PAM]
CLARK, G. *World Prehistory in New Perspective* (3rd edn), Cambridge 1977. [BM(NH)-PAM]
COLE, S. *The Prehistory of East Africa*, New York 1963. [BM(NH)-PAM]
COLES, J. M. & HIGG, E. S. *The Archaeology of Early Man*, London 1969. [BM(NH)-PAM]
CONSTABLE, G. *The Emergence of Man: The Neanderthals*, Amsterdam 1973.
COON, C. S. *Seven Caves*, London 1957. [BM(NH)-PAM]
CRAWFORD, H. (ed.) *Subterranean Britain: Aspects of Underground Archaeology*, London 1979. [IA]
CRESPIGNY, X. DE *Peoples of the Earth – 15: Troglodytes of Cappadocia – Turkey*, Europa Verlag 1973. [MM]
DAWKINS, W. B. *Cave Hunting*, London 1874. [BM(NH)-PAM]
FEWKES, J. W. 'The cave dwellings of the old and new worlds', *American Anthropologist*, N.S., vol. 12 (1910), pp. 390–416. [MM]
FOLSOM, F. *Exploring American Caves*, New York 1956. [BM(NH)-PAM]
Geographical Journal, London, vols 1–153 (1879–1987). [RGS;BM(NH)-G]
Geographical Magazine, London, vols 1–59 (1935–1987). [RGS]
JENNINGS, J. D. *Prehistory of North America*, New York 1968. [BM(NH)-PAM]
KOPPER, J. S. 'Troglodytism', *Proceedings of the 6th International Speology*, Prague, Sub-section Ea (1977), pp. 31–7. [MM]
KOSTOF, S. *Caves of God: The Monastic Environment of Byzantine Cappadocia*, Cambridge, Massachusetts 1972. [BM/BL]

LAMING-EMPERAIRE, A. *La Signification de l'Art Rupestre Paleolithique, Methodes et Applications,* Paris 1962. [BM/BL]

LEAKEY, R. E. & LEWIN, R. *Origins,* New York 1977.

LEROI-GOURHAN, A. *The Art of Prehistoric Man – in Western Europe,* London 1968. [BM/BL]

MASTERS, J. *The Rock,* London 1970.

MEGAW, J. V. S., SIMPSON, D. D. A. et al. *Introduction to British Prehistory,* Leicester 1979. [BM(BH)-PAM]

MEGGERS, B. J. *Prehistoric America,* Chicago 1972. [BM(NH)-PAM]

MOORE, G. W. & SULLIVAN, G. N. *Speleology: The Study of Caves,* Teaneck, New Jersey 1978. [BM(NH)-G]

NANCE, J. *The Gentle Tasaday: A Stone Age People in the Philippine Rain Forest,* London 1975. [MM]

National Geographic Magazine, Washington, vols 1– 172 (1899–1987). [RGS;BM(NH)-G]

OAKLEY, K. P. *Man the Tool-Maker* (6th edn), London 1975.

PENNICK, N. *The Subterranean Kingdom: A Survey of Man-Made Structures Beneath the Earth,* Wellingborough 1981. [IA]

PFEIFFER, J. E. *The Emergence of Man: Cro Magnon Man,* New York 1978.

SAMPSON, C. G. *The Stone Age Archaeology of Southern Africa,* London 1974. [BM(NH)-PAM]

STERN, P. V. D. *Prehistoric Europe,* London 1970. [BM(NH)-PAM]

SOLECKI, R. S. *Shanidar: The Humanity of Neanderthal Man,* London 1971. [BM(NH)-PAM]

Subterranea Britannica, Royston, vols 1–23 (1975– 1987). [IA]

UCKO, P. J. & ROSENFELD, A. *Palaeolithic Cave Art,* London 1967. [BM(NH)-PAM]

WHITEHOUSE, D. & WHITEHOUSE, R. *Archaeological Atlas of the World,* London 1975. [BM(NH)-PAM]

World Archaeology, vol. 10 part 3, 'Caves' issue (1979). [IA;BM(NH)-PAM]

WORMINGTON, H. M. *Ancient Man in North America* (4th edn), Denver 1957. [BM(NH)-PAM]

Index